CARP:

Location, Feeding
and Bait

CARP:

Location, Feeding and Bait

JON WOOD

PUBLISHED BY
FishingBookSender

First published by Fishingbooksender, 2012

For ordering information contact:
Fishingbooksender,
Caerbannog,
Sarn,
Powys SY16 4EX
www.fishingbooksender.com
Telephone: 05601 972040

ISBN 978-0-9567297-9-8

Contents

Dedicated to Graham and Jennifer

"And he liked fishing, so I said, 'Why don't you quit? And I'll quit. And we'll just go fishing.'"

Sid Watkins to Ayrton Senna
Imola, 30th April 1994

About the author

Jon Wood is a marine biologist with a master's degree in aquaculture from the University of Stirling, Scotland. He has been a fish farm consultant for more than fifteen years and when he's not studying fish you can often find him trying to catch them. Apart from carp, Jon also has a soft spot for surfcasting and holds the IGFA World Record for small-eyed flounder.
Currently he's completing a PhD at the Universidad de Chile where his research is involved with increasing appetite in fish. Jon has written for several angling magazines and has previously had two other fishing books published.

CARP FISHING SCIENCE

WHY MEN FISH

Introduction

If someone's going to write a book then it must fill a space among the available literature. But at the same time it's not enough to attempt to fill that space if the author can't communicate effectively with the reader.

Over the last four years I've received a great deal of feedback about *Carp Fishing Science*. After considering the comments, both positive and negative, I've decided to redirect the project in the form of this new text.

As a result, this new book has three purposes.

First of all, it's a synthesis of the most relevant aspects of the previous publication with the carp angler in mind. This is in response to the realisation that the carp angler is most interested in the following things: 1) locating the fish, 2) presenting the correct bait, and 3) understanding how the fish reacts to and interacts with that bait. These are the key aspects that have been addressed in this text and by concentrating on these it will hopefully lead to more productive carp fishing, including less time lost and more fish on the bank.

Secondly, I've removed the science from *Carp Fishing Science*, and as a result, what is left is quite simply carp fishing. Gone are the big words and chemical symbols. This is now just a description of what the carp does and how by understanding what that is and how that works, you can become a more successful angler. I've simplified the most important aspects and hope that this new, less complex and more easily understandable text will allow you to better comprehend the fish and its world. Where I've felt a real need to include a scientific word, it has been done so using brackets with an explanation in layman's terms.

You will also find that I refer to carp, because this is a book about carp fishing, but that doesn't mean that the information I present is always specific to the carp. It may equally apply to other species. In many respects, both biologically and behaviourally, carp are the same as other fish, but in others they are not. When something is particularly specific or unique to carp, then I've tried to express that so as to make it clear.

Finally, I've been lucky enough over the last couple of years to be involved in the study of fish at doctorate level where my research has allowed me to increase my own personal understanding of the factors affecting feeding in fish. As you will see further ahead, the principles of fish farming are highly applicable to angling. Carp are the group of fish produced in greatest volumes every year for the table and the amount of scientific information regarding their growth, feeding requirements and behaviour is immense. I'm therefore fortunate to be in an advantageous position; between the worlds of aquaculture and angling and therefore able to understand the principles of each and interact and translate between the two. It's my hope that my knowledge will be beneficial to the angling community and will not simply be lost in the day to day coming and goings of a fish farm or a university and instead can be applied to carp angling and help others to enjoy our great sport even more.

As a result, the information presented here consists in part of the findings of recent research that have become available since the publication of *Carp Fishing Science*. In some cases this is based on personal studies and experiences that my work and bibliographic revision has brought to my attention. And in the same way as the most relevant existing information from *Carp Fishing Science* has been distilled and simplified, the same has been done with these recent additions.

This book therefore breaks these topics down into four sections which make up the new chapters. The first of these is fish location. This time around I've taken the different factors which have been covered previously and singled out those which have greatest relevance. For me, these are wind, currents and temperature. All of these are found to some extent on any water and they all influence the fish and therefore the fishing. Understanding how these three factors change on any water will help an angler to achieve better results. This is not to say that they are the only influences. As you'll see, they are not and for that reason I have mentioned the others too, albeit more briefly and principally regarding their relationship to the wind, currents and temperature. The objective of this chapter is to familiarise anglers with the physical factors that influence our fishing and the ways that they affect the carp, its behaviour and location.

The second chapter is also about location, but this time it is the fish doing the locating and not the angler. Here we'll look at how the carp locates its food. There's a biological component to the chapter since location depends on a mixture of senses that the carp uses to locate a stimulus in the water and then find its source. As we'll see, this depends principally on olfaction followed by taste and visual detection of food items. However, as far as what we are concerned with as anglers, detection is just the beginning. What we are also interested in is that the carp is able to find our bait in amongst the free offerings we use to attract it and sucks it in. After detecting the food or bait, the fish can become stimulated enough to ingest it or simply reject it and move on and it's necessary for us to understand how and why that happens if we are to come out on top when this inevitably occurs while fishing. So, this chapter is particularly relevant to working out what's going on under the water's surface and how the fish reacts to and interacts with our bait. Also covered in chapter 2 is an overview of the food types available to the carp in the waters where we might fish for them and how the supply of natural food items changes throughout the year.

Food availability and competition for it depend to a certain extent on lake and water type so these subjects have been selected to begin chapter 3. This doesn't just refer to competition between different carp for the available food, or even between different species of fish which share the same dietary preferences, but also the two main types of competition which exist for the angler's bait. These are the baits of other anglers and the supply of natural food, with the latter presenting a safer and potentially more nutritional alternative to what an angler is offering. Following that, we will look at the factors affecting feeding, which are both externally and internally regulated by the environment or the fish respectively. These directly affect the intensity of the feeding response and also the times at which feeding occurs. This is variable between different lakes and rivers but it will always be possible to discover tendencies and patterns on and between each location. The chapter continues with a description of the feeding phases which fish experience and finally we return to the biological side of things with a look at appetite in fish and how the feeding mechanism works, from ingestion to separation and swallowing of food items. The contents of the chapter are aimed at providing the angler with an understanding of how the fish physically interacts with the bait and feed and provides information that can help with ideas on rig design.

The fourth and final chapter is concerned with that thing that's talked about by carp anglers more than any other. The section on bait begins by looking at what the nutritional requirements of the carp are and how they vary seasonally. Much of this information is from the field of aquaculture where carp have been farmed for hundreds of years. However, the sources of the material presented are much more recent, in the majority of cases from the last twenty years where, in order to improve the profitability of carp farming, there has been investment in research to find out what the fish needs in order to grow quickly. Although our objective in angling is different from that of aquaculture, there are many things that are shared between the two activities. For example, satisfying all of the nutritional requirements of the fish not only results in faster growth in culture, but also in the wild. As anglers we are interested in bigger and healthier fish, which a nutritionally adequate bait can produce. If the fish can get more of its requirements from one source, then in theory it wouldn't have to look elsewhere and a certain level of dependency on that bait would develop. This is key for us anglers, since it eliminates competition and ensures better results for ourselves.

We then move on to look at attractants. This will elaborate on information provided in chapter 2 regarding stimulation of the carp's senses and how to include those in the bait for optimum results. We will only look at and evaluate those substances for which evidence exists and it's positively been shown that they are worth including in your bait. I've seen and heard bait companies marketing their wares which include every possible substance and, according to them, each one is a proven carp catcher. Obviously, if you say that everything is great, or a bait includes a bit of everything, then sooner or later someone will catch a huge carp on it and it will be put down to a particular ingredient. However, there are very simple rules for bait formulation and in chapter 4 I'll tell you what I think they are, with one of the fundamentals being to only include ingredients if there is a strong and verifiable reason to do so. That chapter concludes with a look at the costs involved in bait production and finally field testing, with ideas on the way it should be carried out and why.

You've probably already got a good idea of the reasons why I'm returning to these topics in the form of this improved text. There are several factors that have motivated me this time around. One of those is my displeasure with how marketing has affected our sport, particularly in the area of bait development and hopefully this will be an honest look at the things that interest and concern us most as carp anglers.

The sport continues to grow. Each year there are more new carp anglers (and for that matter more old ones too). The carp fishing industry continues to supply the new recruits and existing aficionados with the latest and greatest gear to get the job done. Anglers are often lured into buying a particular piece of equipment because of a catchy advert or a quote from an angling celebrity. Some bait companies now offer every flavour and 'attractant' imaginable to the angler, with each one assured to catch the fish of a lifetime. My main motivation for writing this is to show you the substances that have been shown to stimulate feeding in carp and those which have not.

As I understand it, there is very little standardised testing of baits. Here I'm not talking about field testing of baits by a select number of paid anglers. Standardised means replicated and comparative and being able to make objective observations.

13

Bait companies have the potential to take advantage of the unknowing and, at the same time, many anglers simply trust the well-known angler to guide them towards their next personal best fish. But a little understanding and a bit more watercraft will mean that the angler is able to make more informed and more assertive decisions. And I think that even though the sport has become so massive, so commercially orientated and so publicity-based, there's still time to preserve the mentality of anglers who even now prefer to think about their fishing on a more strategic and rational level without believing all the hype.

This text may not make any difference. But for those of you who are interested in my opinion, that trust my impartiality regarding how carp react to and interact with the feed we throw at them, then I thank you and hope that you'll get as much from this book as is humanly possible and that you catch the fish you want based on knowledge and strategy instead of just marketing, coincidence and luck.

Jon Wood

Cumbria, UK
1st of May 2012

Chapter One

Carp Location

A great bait, the latest rig and intimate knowledge of carp behaviour is no use if you're fishing in a place without any carp nearby. This is a more common mistake as the size of the water increases and it becomes more difficult to locate the fish.

Smaller carp are gregarious animals which means that they prefer company. That's why small carp are more often found in shoals. There are several reasons for this. Small fish are more vulnerable to predators. Carp have a number of these including fish-eating birds, predatory fish and otters. There is, as the saying quite correctly states, 'safety in numbers'. If a fish is in a shoal, then the likelihood of it being picked off by one of those predators is much lower than if it were alone. Therefore, as with the majority of animals, the first years of life are spent in groups and then, when feeding and time have led to a larger size that prevents being caught and eaten and a faster swimming speed to enable escape, then it's relatively safe to move off on your own and lead a more solitary existence.

The other important benefit that living in a shoal provides is the search for food often being easier. Once food is located by one of the many individuals that make up the shoal, the others get to know about it fairly quickly. It's therefore easier to get fed, but at the same time, the food that's located has to be shared between a large number of mouths.

So, living in a shoal can have its benefits and its drawbacks and once the carp reaches a larger size, the drawbacks begin to outweigh the benefits. Since hunger is the most important motivating factor for the carp, in order to find the increasing amount of food it requires as it grows, it turns to a solitary lifestyle, or a halfway point where it may be accompanied by a small number of similarly sized individuals. This means that it doesn't have to share too much, and it gets additional help with food location .

As we'll see further ahead, species of fish, carp included, don't feed for every minute of every day. Therefore, it's understandable that if you are consistently looking for the carp where the natural food is, then they might not always be there. This is because the carp has other things to do apart from feeding. For example, it needs to locate favourable environmental conditions which may not be in the same place as its preferred feeding areas. These conditions include temperature and oxygen, which the carp seeks out in order to live more comfortably. Also, the carp, like other animals, engages in social activities during the day. It may need to rest. At other times it may be involved in looking for a mate or spawning .

It's therefore necessary for the carp to move around the lake during the day and night to find those things that it needs to feel comfortable. This includes having food in its stomach, which also provides the fish with a feeling of satisfaction, much in the same way as a correct temperature or oxygen level.

On some lakes, it will be easier to understand carp movements and on shallow, clear waters it will be possible to watch them move around the lake and patterns will probably develop. My understanding is that carp movements are not random. I believe that fish know where they are in a lake at all times and that all movements have purpose. Whether or not the angler is able to decipher any patterns that he discovers is a different matter, but all discoveries should at least boost confidence and better prepare the angler for his fishing.

On other lakes it may be an even more difficult task to locate carp. Water depth is an obvious problem for fish spotting and discovering fish movement patterns. An echo-sounder might be a solution, but on some waters, the diversity of fish that may be present means that the fish you might be tracking could very well not be carp at all.

Fortunately, carp are fish which show themselves in different ways and this might enable the angler to locate them. They often jump and roll, and when they're feeding, they often give their presence away by the bubbles they produce or by the discolouration of the water that occurs. So, the angler can use these to his advantage in order to locate the fish.

And there are other clues. We should record all catches, including time of the day and the location of successful captures. We can also talk to other anglers and learn where they've caught fish, the time that happened and if there were any particular conditions at that time. Which way was the wind blowing? Was the sky clear or overcast? Was it warm or cool? Hopefully this will allow the angler to piece together the puzzle of carp movements, with the ultimate aim being the placing of the bait where it's possible to intercept moving fish.

Unfortunately, two fishing sessions are never the same. They may be several days or even weeks apart. And over that space of time, the lake can have changed considerably. There may have been an algal bloom, reducing visibility even more. There could have been a drastic change in pressure that might have affected water temperatures, wind direction and as a result, the carp have adjusted their movements, making interpretation of the situation difficult. However, the good thing is that the fish are still there somewhere and that's where experience will be useful to relocate the fish.

Fish are often not given enough credit for their intelligence with the rumour of the goldfish's three second memory adding to that injustice. I'm sometimes asked about just that, whether a fish has a memory at all. The truth is that fish are of relatively high intelligence. Maybe not very close to that of humans, but they have a large amount of cognitive processes. This means that they make conscious decisions about things and are not acting on impulse. This means that they consciously choose to do things instead of relying completely on innate or inherent behaviour, meaning that the fish is not depending on something that it was born with such as the urge to eat or to breathe.

Cognitive behaviour is very much based on learning. And in order to have learnt and to make a decision based on that, then it's clear that the fish must have a memory. In fact, many studies have attempted to determine the extent of the fish's memory and it's been shown that fish can be trained to carry out certain behaviour when a particular stimulus is applied. For example, when a tank of fish are shown a light and then are immediately fed, they come to associate the light with being fed (e.g. Nilsson *et al.*, 2008). In the same way, on a fish farm, the appearance of the member of staff who feeds the fish, wearing the same colour sweater every day can be a signal that feed is about to become available in the pond. This is very similar to the famous example by Pavlov, who fed dogs after ringing a bell and then after several days of repetition, dogs were observed to salivate after a bell was rung even in the absence of feeding.

This same memory in fish has been analysed in other ways using the result of catch and release fishing to show both the ability of fish to learn and to change their behaviour. Fish have been shown to form memory in a similar way to us, in that both positive and negative experiences affect our future responses to different stimuli. In fishing, capture can be described as a negative experience since it results in the fish becoming stressed, no matter how much we care about the fish's welfare by gentle playing and unhooking of it and ensuring that it spends as little time as possible out of the water. This stressing leads to the release of cortisol, often referred to as the stress hormone.

Different stressors can cause this release. They may be of natural origin such as the presence and activity of a predator or be due to an unnatural cause such as being hooked by an angler. Whatever the source, the release of cortisol has several implications for the fish. You would imagine that all stress is a problem for fish but, in fact, it can be beneficial. One example is what is described as the 'flight-or-fight' response which, as its name suggests, can help the fish escape predation, which is obviously beneficial. However, prolonged stress can be detrimental or even fatal. It can lower resistance to disease and reduce food intake.

Therefore, as anglers it's counterproductive to stress our carp, since negative experiences have a tendency to mould the behaviour of the carp in the future. As a result, it's easy to understand how a fish which has been caught might stay away from a similar bait or rig in the future and this is why anglers often state that they have 'blown'.

Previous experience is used by carp to optimise survival and success in the future, as far as everything that the fish does, including the places it frequents, what it prefers to eat and which other fish, if any, it prefers to spend time with. Fish will stay away from places that have been responsible for negative experiences and the same goes for foods. If a fish has been caught on a particular bait in a particular area of the lake, it's unlikely for that to be repeated, particularly in the short term. Sooner or later the fish has to return to feeding and if tackle is cunning enough to get the same fish to take or the previous capture was 'low stress' then there may be exceptions to this rule.

It should be remembered however that the fish's memory is probably not as developed as our own, since it's been shown that fish behaviour can be modified by a stimulus, but that when that is taken away, the fish cannot remember indefinitely. In the experiment by Nilsson *et al.*, (2008), which occurred with Atlantic cod, when lights no longer accompanied feeding, the fish gradually began to forget their significance. After three months, the appearance of the light meant nothing at all to the fish.

The information on memory and cognitive behaviour can be very useful for the angler, especially since here we're dealing with aspects that require the carp to make conscious decisions regarding their behaviour, namely location, feeding and bait. In order to optimise our fishing, we should understand why the fish chooses a particular bait over another and when and where it prefers to feed. These things are very much affected by memory. Clearly we cannot read the fish's mind, but based on observation and common sense, we can improve our chances of success.

As we've already mentioned, the fish is constantly looking to be comfortable. It requires food, an adequate water quality and access to shelter. In the absence of shelter it may prefer the company of other fish, which can provide similar benefits regarding predation and access to resources such as food and a mate. This can also be a disadvantage since, as we have already seen, the presence of other fish of the same species can mean increased competition for the same resources. However, the driving force for the fish is satisfying the need for comfort, including having food in its gut. It cannot indefinitely not eat. Sooner or later it has to succumb to the feeling of hunger and as you'll see later on, the reason for feeding is to obtain energy from the food with the lack of energy ultimately leading to death. The fish also requires a large number of different substances, each of which it needs for specific functions and purposes. It has no choice except to locate those in the natural environment and feed on them.

It's the angler's task to intercept the fish in the act of obtaining what it needs. For that, he must have an idea of location. By observation and previous sessions on different parts of the lake and by talking to other anglers, he will have formed a picture of fish movements and the most likely spot to attempt an interception. Then, the rig and bait are placed in that spot, or is more usually the case these days in two or three spots around there.

The fish's memory is based on experience but it's not infallible and irresponsible behaviour such as greed can lead to a fish's downfall. Therefore, using a bait that maximises the feeding response will be more productive. However, carp fishing is not always about catching large numbers of carp. It's often about catching a particular fish, which will obviously take longer and requires a greater amount of background information combined with a similar amount of luck.

The fish's memory is responsible for the behaviours that we can observe in any lake and it shouldn't be underestimated. It has been the cause of why certain anglers have spent, in some cases, thousands of hours of their lives trying to catch one fish. In fact, if we examine the use of fish memory in greater detail, we find that its capacity is even more surprising. This has been studied in greatest detail in the field of feeding, since this is particularly relevant to the commercial production of fish in farms, but also for recreational and industrial fishing.

If a fish has spent its whole life in one lake, we can suppose that it has collected through experience a lot of information about its home.

It should know, for example, where the sources of feed are at any particular time. These areas of better feeding are referred to by scientists as patches. Each patch may be represented by one or more different food types and they vary according to the time of the year. In winter, the carp may feed principally on invertebrates such as bloodworm, but in spring, diet might change towards larger crustaceans and in summer, this may be complemented with plant material. Therefore, the patches of food will be found in different parts of the lake at different times of the year and it's been shown that fish are capable of tracking and monitoring the appearance, disappearance and productivities of these in order to optimise feeding. By optimisation, I'm referring to the greatest net energy gain per day, which can be translated as the greatest energy intake for the least amount of expended energy. In other words, the location of the greatest amount of food per unit of area should be where the fish should naturally be found during their period of feeding. We must consider, though, that the carp will not be feeding all the time and will therefore not always be there and the availability of a preferred source of food, maybe offering a nutrient that the fish requires at that moment, may affect its feeding location.

Carp will often experience conflicting responses and if that happens, then it will need to make a choice. The result will be that which at a particular time is more beneficial to the fish, or at least that which the fish thinks will be more beneficial at that moment. For example, a feeding fish may need to deal with the internal motivating state of hunger, which it does by feeding. But at the same time it may be exposed to an external environmental threat such as a predator. It has to make a choice. Does it prefer to satisfy its hunger with the predator nearby or is it better to find a safer place to eat, even though that place may have a lower availability of food? The predator may take the form of a bird, fish or a mammal, but you could also describe anglers as predators. This is highly relevant to our cause, since if we consider that our presence affects fish behaviour and most importantly feeding, then, by reducing our presence and interference and also the stress that we inflict on the fish, we can have a positive effect on our fishing success.

Whether feeding location is determined solely by the abundance and diversity of food or whether it's important that that location is within the carp's 'comfort zone' is difficult to say. My opinion is that the two are not mutually exclusive and that if a feeding patch is particularly attractive to a fish, then it will venture outside the comfort zone. But in general, it's likely that the fish will exploit those patches that are inside its comfort zone by foraging.

Foraging refers to searching for and exploiting food. It's important for any animal because the way that it goes about foraging can greatly affect the animal's ability to survive and to reproduce. A number of factors affect the foraging behaviour of an animal and several theories have been developed by ecologists to explain why animals forage in a certain way. These theories are collectively known as optimum foraging theory (OFT) and although there are several versions of OFT, foraging theory is usually referred to in terms of optimising a payoff from a foraging decision. In the models of foraging that have been developed, the payoff is the amount of energy an animal receives per unit time or the highest ratio of energetic gain to cost while foraging (Hughes, 1990). And if the decision that the animal makes results in a high payoff, then in the future it will select for it and repeat the same decision more frequently.

Even before we examine OFT in more detail, this initial description would suggest that a carp is interested in obtaining more energy in return through the food that it consumes than the amount of energy expended in locating, consuming, digesting and absorbing that food. This is because net energy gain depends on all these aspects and not just the energy used for movement over and between patches. It also suggests that if a carp finds abundant food energy and uses little energy to do so, then the decisions that the fish made to obtain that result will be repeated. For us, in a practical sense, this means that the fish will frequent the patch more often, increasing the chance of us locating and catching the fish. This may also mean that it will feed repeatedly on the same food items and if this occurs with our loose feed, then we might be onto a winner sooner or later.

However, in the same sense, if the carp makes decisions that result in a low payoff then it will be less likely to repeat those. This means that on a water where patches are poorly defined and which are made up of generalised areas of low densities of food items, then it might be more difficult to locate the fish because the payoff is low but frequent. This is a very different situation to a water with a small number of very well defined patches which allow abundant feeding and consequently high payoffs.

In these two cases, the bait input by the angler will have different results because it is easier to compete with low payoff areas than it is with one or more high payoff areas. However, this will depend on several things, including the size of the water, the distances between the patches, the number and size of fish and the amount and composition of the food that's available.

We can add to this the reverse situation where the payoff is not optimum but minimum. In contrast to what happens when a fish receives a high net energy gain, being caught will produce the opposite effect. Instead of frequenting a location more it will use the same learning process to avoid feeding in a particular area or on a specific food. This will mean that the carp may avoid a bait and since the fish is likely to be accompanied by other individuals, it's likely that the group or shoal will move to a safer patch containing safer food item alternatives.

Learning is an important part of foraging theory. In behavioural ecology, the term is used to describe an adaptive change or the modification of a behaviour based on previous experience. And since the environment of an animal changes over both short and long periods of time, such as daily and seasonally, it's necessary for an animal to be able to adapt its behaviour in order to optimise foraging. This occurs by learning which, as with other animals, a carp can obtain either by experiencing something personally or by observation. Fish have been shown to have a good capacity for learning and clearly, those experiences that result in more intense feelings are those which are remembered more easily. In this sense, at one end of the scale a high payoff will be remembered and so too will a very low payoff or being caught. As a result, the fish will avoid a place where it has been caught and prefer those where it hasn't with a similar effect occurring regarding bait acceptance.

One concept of learning in the context of foraging is referred to as foraging innovation, which has particular relevance for anglers and the baits they use. Although it's possible for angling baits to be considered as a replacement for or an addition to natural food, it will always be the case that new baits are brought out and will therefore appear in waters where they have never been seen before. These will be considered a new food by the fish even if a new bait differs only in colour or smell from those they already know. Foraging innovation refers to an animal consuming a new food or using a new method of foraging in response to environmental change. This is considered learning because the animal, the carp in our case, makes a decision to try the new food item instead of relying completely on any experience that it might have obtained directly or by observation in the past.

The ability to learn has been related to the size of the size of an

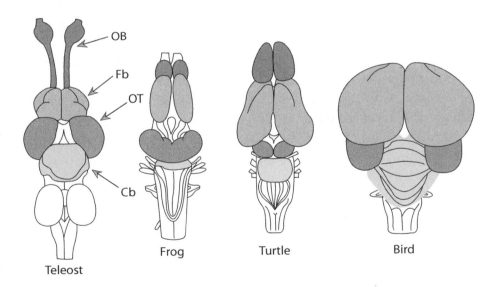

Figure 1: Diagrammatic representation of the main brain divisions in four vertebrate groups. Cb, Cerebellum; OB, Olfactory bulbs; OT, Optic tectum; Fb, Forebrain (redrawn and modified from Broglio *et al.*, 2011)

animal's forebrain. Compared with other vertebrates, the forebrain of ray-finned fish (teleosts) such as the carp is relatively smaller (see figure 1).

Despite this relatively lower capacity for learning, the carp is known in the angling world as a fish that can learn in a range of different ways, including avoidance of rigs and baits especially when these can been associated with a negative experience such as that of being hooked or captured. This has been and can be observed by us when fishing. Similar observations including more innovative methods of feeding have been observed in higher vertebrates such as birds and mammals. And in all animals, foraging innovation has the potential of allowing the individual to improve fitness and survival.

There are two main types of foraging, both of which can be observed in the carp. The first of these is solitary foraging which, as the name suggests, is where animals forage by themselves. The other, group foraging, refers to animals foraging with other animals of the same species. The carp can choose between these two foraging strategies and it may stick with one or alternate between the two as food abundance or environmental conditions change.

Solitary foraging is when the carp finds, captures and consumes food items alone. The fish may choose this strategy when there is higher abundance of food and particularly when the number of other individuals competing for the same food is low. Solitary foraging means that interactions with competitors of the same or other species are fewer and the benefit for the solitary foraging carp will be greater or, in the context of what we've already said, the payoff will be greater. This is particularly true of fish because one of the characteristics of any group of fish, either wild or farmed, is the presence of a hierarchy, which is expressed most clearly at feeding time. This is where the most dominant or simply the biggest member or members of the group receives a disproportionately high amount of the available food compared with smaller, weaker or less dominant individuals. Other well-known examples of this are litters of animals feeding on their mothers' milk. The more dominant individuals receive more of the available milk whereas the runt receives the least.

Those in between receive ration sizes according to their position in the hierarchy. A consequence of this is that ration size is directly proportional to growth and as the more dominant animal grows faster than the runt, the effects of the hierarchy are exaggerated. For this reason and others, it may favour a carp to feed solitarily to avoid interaction with competitors.

Carp with more experience are more likely to make the right decisions regarding foraging. Those that benefit most from foraging activities could be termed optimal foragers and such animals have been used to develop the theories included in OFT. Such an animal has enough knowledge of its environment and has experienced the results of enough correctly and incorrectly made decisions that it could be described as having a near perfect control of what to do to maximise food intake. If this occurs, then it's probable that both energetic and nutritional requirements are satisfied.

However, the vast majority of a natural population of carp or any other animal probably do not feed optimally, although many may get close to it. When these animals are not feeding optimally, it helps scientists understand what kinds of constraints (limitations) affect the behaviour of the animal or its way of thinking and making decisions regarding feeding. OFT has been shown to be very useful for describing the foraging activities of these animals and has been able to identify the lack of random feeding activities. In other words, the way that a carp feeds is not random and even though it may not feed optimally, it's composed of strategies to maximise efficient energy intake, including decision-making and choices that may be constrained for different reasons.

Different versions of OFT are relevant to different foraging situations. All of these involve an objective function, which is generally the optimisation of energy intake per unit time. These versions also include decisions which are the choices that are under the control of the animal (in our case the carp). The other factor they have in common are the constraints that affect the choices in order for optimum foraging to be achieved. These constraints may include genetic, physiological or morphological limitations. For example the carp can only feed on food items that are less than nine percent of its body length which is an example of a physiological and morphological constraint.

Two of the most well known versions of OFT are described here in the context of the carp:

The optimal diet model (1) refers to a carp searching for and locating different food types and having to make a decision regarding which to consume or not based on which items are more profitable. This profitability depends on variables such as the time required to handle the food as far as finding, capturing and consuming it and ultimately the amount of energy that the food item provides compared with that of another. In most cases, the carp will settle for a choice between maximising the rate of food intake and the period of time required for the location of other food items.

Patch selection theory (2) refers to foraging when food items are concentrated in relatively small areas (patches) which are located considerable distances from each other. Here, a carp has to choose between how much time it spends at one patch before moving to the next. The longer the carp stays at one patch, the fewer food items remain in the patch and it must therefore decide when to move. This decision stems from the fact that as it continues to feed on the same patch it becomes gradually more difficult to locate food items and the amount consumed per unit time diminishes. However, the effectiveness of this will depend on the distance of one patch from the next and the time it takes the carp to get from one to another and also how much energy the carp is able to obtain from one patch rather than another.

Carp are generally found not feeding in a solitary manner but with other individuals. This has resulted in a number of other theories and ideas to describe group foraging behaviour. These suggest that the success of foraging depends not only on the animal's own foraging behaviours but also those of the other individuals in the group. There are two situations which can lead to group foraging, the first of which I've already mentioned earlier in this chapter.

The first is when foraging in a group rather than individually is more beneficial to the individual. This is referred to as aggregation economy. The other situation arises when animals forage in a group but it might not be in the organism's best interest to do so, which is referred to as dispersion economy. An example of this is when there is a supply of natural food or bait present that would be energetically advantageous for the carp to consume completely but the presence of other members of the group or shoal reduces the amount that the carp is able to eat because of simultaneous feeding by the other group members. In that case, the amount of food that the carp is able to eat not only depends on the total amount present but also on the amount that the other fish consume.

Foraging in a group results in advantages and disadvantages for the different individuals of a group. The benefits of group foraging for the carp include the reduction of the threat of predation and increased probability of being able to locate patches especially if they are sparsely distributed. On the other hand, the costs associated with group foraging include greater competition for a finite resource. What usually happens is that the individuals that make up the group try to eat as much as the available food as possible (termed scramble competition) or the presence of competition means that the carp is unable to access the food items (called interference completion). By either method, the carp's payoff is reduced compared with what it would be if the carp were to forage solitarily.

If we compare these possible carp foraging behaviours with those of other animals, we can see similarities and some differences. In terrestrial environments a grazing animal such as a cow or a foraging animal such as a pig might be suitable comparisons. Although we know these as farm animals, in the wild they are similar to the carp in that they may adopt either of the main foraging types of solitary or group. These animals may benefit respectively from greater food rations or reduced predation threat or suffer from having to share with other herd or group members in the same way as the carp. However, the carp differs from these animals in that, due to its nature of not taking care of its young, fewer concerns come into its mind while it's feeding apart from the actual feeding.

While they feed, many terrestrial foraging animals of all kinds, including carnivores, omnivores and herbivores have to protect their young and sometimes their territory as well while they feed. Because of this, these animals don't often forage optimally. Instead, they sacrifice a certain quantity of available food energy in order to protect their young and their territory. There are also examples of aquatic animals that have these shared priorities of obtaining energy and protection and among these are several classes of animal including some fish. Carp don't care for their young but the survival of the adult carp by adopting effective foraging strategies obviously has implications for reproduction.

The theory that scientists have used to comprehend group foraging is referred to as ideal free distribution. This is a model that asks the question why animals would choose to form groups rather than feeding individually and how this affects their behaviour. It suggests that animals make an immediate decision about where to forage according to the quality of the available patches, which translates as the abundance and amount of food that they contain. The result will be the choice of the patch which is the most profitable for the group meaning that it's the one that optimises energy intake.

However, this profitability will depend on the original quality of the patch and the number of competitors already feeding there when the group arrives. These competitors might be individuals of the same species or others that share the same diet preferences. In the carp's case, these might be other cyprinids such as tench, bream or roach. Ideal free distribution suggests that where the largest number of food resources can be found then the number of animals that congregate to feed there will also be the highest.

But what does the adoption of these foraging strategies by the carp mean for us anglers? Well, these theories are exactly what they say they are, theories, and the behaviour of carp in real situations may not always be exactly what these theories say we should expect. A lot of the time, anglers make decisions based on their own observations by a water without knowing anything about OFT. However, one of the main points that we should consider is that explained above regarding ideal free distribution. This says that wherever the most profitable patches are, more fish will be found, so it's in our interest to try and locate the best patches since these will lead to us locating more fish.

Carp will forage either solitarily or in a group. If we know which of these is more common in the water we're fishing, this will influence the amount of bait that we need to put in to catch. By observation we are able to both locate carp and get an idea whether fish are feeding alone or with others. If we can obtain both pieces of information, then we can employ a more specific or more generalised baiting strategy in order to optimise our own efforts in the time we have available. As anglers we should consider how different foraging behaviours fit into the context of the fish's life and how this affects the decisions that the fish makes regarding foraging. If we are able to understand these on the waters we fish, then we'll have discovered one of the keys to more successful carp angling.

Another option is provided by loose feeding. If a lake is regularly fished by anglers, and a considerable amount of bait is introduced to the water by loose feeding and groundbaiting then it's reasonable to suggest that the regular appearance of this food in different parts of the lake could be considered by the carp to be additional natural patches in the ecosystem. The appearance of a patch and its ability to be regarded by the fish as a profitable alternative to existing patches will depend on the composition of the bait, its energy content and the amount of bait that's available per fish that's feeding on it. This stresses the need to use bait that is both nutritionally adequate to help increase the intensity and duration of the feeding response .

As I've done previously, it's possible to compare the energy value of natural feed with that of fishing baits, including boilies. I found that the energy per gram is similar, but whereas the energy expended to locate one gram of natural food is high, that to locate one gram of boilies (usually the weight of one boilie on its own exceeds that) is comparatively very low. Therefore the net energy gain for feeding on our loose fed baits is more than a little attractive for the fish. It appears so, since, in the same way as a fish may learn the location and productivity of different natural patches, it's likely that the regular introduction of bait can be seen as simply another patch. These may be less reliable than the natural patches due to the fact that they're appearing and disappearing as anglers frequent different swims on the lake and the amount of food may be much more variable as anglers bait up with less or more.

Our presence on a water is noticeable not just because of the days we spend there each season but also because of the bait that we throw into it. The fish are able to notice our presence by the amount of bankside activity and the appearance of amounts of baits in the lake or river, which they may be able to associate or not as being there due to human doing.

We have already mentioned that fish are often underrated as far as their intelligence and memory capacity. But likewise they are sometimes overrated by anglers. This is common when an angler is 'done' by a carp or he blanks on a session. It's a normal reaction and is easily explained by an excess of intelligence on behalf of the carp rather than a lack of intelligence on behalf of the angler. The truth is that a carp is only as intelligent as any other fish. Fish have been shown to be able to learn by experience which means that it's logical to find fish that have experienced more and have therefore learned more. Behavioural studies in fish are almost as abundant as nutrition and feeding studies and although I'm no expert it's clear that in some aspects a fish is relatively close to a human as far as intelligence but in others it's well behind. I'm sure that anglers would like to consider a carp as a worthy adversary but I think that that depends on the situation and to a certain extent on the fish itself. But I also think that there are things that make a carp very difficult to catch which are not directly related to the intelligence of the fish, such as the size of the lake and the location of the fish within it. For example, if the biggest carp in a lake that measures a kilometre across spends all its time right in the middle of it, out of casting distance from any bank, then it is a difficult carp to catch but it might not be any more intelligent than any other carp.

However, what I've mentioned before is how very well adapted the carp is to its environment. And there is a part of that which is due to learning and experience but the carp is equipped for life in the water particularly well and this has a great deal to do with the senses it possesses. Amongst these, taste (gustation) and smell (olfaction) are the ones that interest us most as anglers since it's those that we are most interested in stimulating. However, apart from these, we should also mention the carp's senses of sight and hearing since they are both relevant to us, but in different ways.

Carp use sight for locomotion, feeding and many other things. They are principally monocular, which means that because the spherical eyes are placed laterally (one on each side of the head) the fish has a very wide field of view. The carp also has a limited area of binocular (using both eyes) vision at the front (see figure 2). The fish also possesses two blind spots. One of these is to the rear where sight is restricted due to

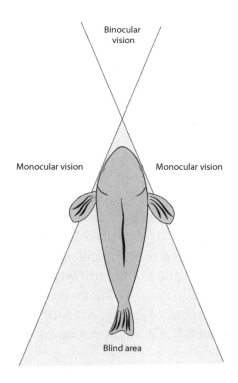

Figure 2: Carp vision in different areas.

the eyes not being able to see past the wide body to the rear of the eyes and the other is right in front of the fish's nose. In the monocular areas the fish is unable to perceive depth as it is in the binocular area. This has implications for feeding because the majority of suction is aimed at items in the binocular area or in the front blind spot as it moves towards them.

The fish's ability to see in dark or turbid water is not a particularly big problem for the carp because it has a great dependence on smell and taste in order to feed. However, carp especially use sight at short range and for feeding in clear water and we are able to observe a different use of the senses during bottom and surface feeding. For the former the fish depends much more on taste and smell particularly in turbid water but at the surface sight is clearly much more important.

Fish see the area above them in what is referred to as a window. This window uses the bending of light to compress the world above the water into a cone of 96 degrees. Outside the cone, the fish sees a reflection of the bottom or the lake of river. These 96 degrees are the same no matter at what depth the fish is positioned in the water column so this means that the deeper the fish, the wider is the window through which it is able to appreciate the world outside. A wider window means that the fish is able to see more although the detail with which it can do this depends on whether the flat surface of the window is disturbed by waves and ripples. When there is a lot of surface movement, the fish may be unable to determine anything such as movement on the bankside. This means that in the same way that we can observe the fish, the carp can observe us too. How well it can do this is affected by water movement, the fish's depth in the water and the fish's experience of humans and other predators.

Carp have relatively small eyes compared with predatory fish because they are relatively less important for most feeding situations. Piscivorous (fish-eating) fish have big eyes with which to see their prey. Traditionally, carp have been thought to be tetrachromatic like many other fish, being able to see red, green and blue light as we are able to do but also ultraviolet. However, recent studies have shown that carp are also sensitive to near infrared (NIR).

Since common carp are nocturnally active, the possession of NIR-sensitive eyes would seem to be evolutionarily beneficial. This would allow them to see better at low light intensities such as dawn and dusk and even at night. Moonlight and starlight are rich in infrared and so carp would theoretically be able to see better on nights with a full moon or starry skies. This would explain why some anglers prefer to fish during these periods and swear that they are more productive than other times of the month with a smaller moon or cloudy skies.

Apart from the eyes, fish have another organ that aids with differentiating different degrees of light and dark. This is the pineal organ and is referred to as the 'third eye'. This organ is located at the top of the brain but can be stimulated by light passing through the translucent layers above, which include skin and cartilage. Since the organ contains cells that are sensitive to light in same way as those on the retina of the fish's eyes, it helps the fish determine changes in light intensity. These changes are responsible for the secretion of a hormone called melatonin. The darker the fish's environment, the more melatonin is produced but as it gets lighter the amount of melatonin secretion is reduced and in the daytime it may stop altogether. The production of this hormone is responsible for other things as well and we'll cover the relationship between light intensity and feeding rhythms in chapter 3. Suffice to say that as well as its eyes, a carp has an alternative way to determine the time of the day and this has relevance for the fish's behaviours including that of feeding.

Fish do not have an external ear as we do. Their hearing structure is buried inside the cranium near the midbrain on either side of their head. In the same way as humans, the fish's ear is made up of the same three semicircular canals which are filled with fluid and contain sensory hairs. The canals are able to detect pitch, roll and yaw and are involved in maintaining balance.

Apart from this hearing apparatus, the carp has a lateral line which is not specifically for hearing but does contain mechanoreceptors in the same way as the canals in the ear which give it a certain capacity for vibration and touch. This consists of a cluster of hair cells embedded in a blob of jelly, combined to form something called a neuromast and which is able to detect vibrations in the water column. Detection of movement in the water surrounding the fish allows it to be in contact with other fish during shoaling behaviour and to sense prey, although this is not the primary sense of food detection in the fish. This may also be useful as an early warning system for the location of predators since the neuromasts are not only able to detect vibration but also sense things that they cannot see.

The swim bladder of the fish also possesses some resonating properties. In the carp this is connected by a chain of small bones to the fish's ear. This connection of bones (Weber bones) form part of what is called the Weberian apparatus. This is a linkage of bones and structures which connect the inner ear to the swim bladder. Fish which possess this have particularly acute hearing since the swim bladder serves as a resonating chamber and the bony connection amplifies sounds and transmits them to the inner ear. This results in a magnification of the sound and allows the fish to hear at much higher frequency than most other fish. The detection of these high frequency sounds allow the fish to sense danger and can result in evasive behaviours such as shoal forming.

To summarise, sight and hearing are two very important senses for the carp. Both are involved to some extent in feeding but the most important of the senses for this in the carp are smell and taste, which will be discussed in much greater detail in the following chapters. Even so, hearing and sight in the carp both include specialisations which have improved the capacity of these two senses. In the case of hearing this is the Weberian apparatus, which, although not found only in cyprinid species is a structure which characterises fish as possessing better auditory capacity. And in the case of vision, although the size of the eye is not especially large, the sensitivity of the carp's eye to additional wavelengths to just the red, green and blue that we are able to sense highlights a specialisation for feeding in low light intensities which are present both at specific times of the day and month and while feeding in turbid water.

Both sight and hearing are also mentioned here in the context of capture effectiveness. Locating the carp is clearly one part of the battle

35

but in this respect I can only tell you so much. Unfortunately I can't tell you which spot to cast to on your next session. I can only explain how the fish lives and where and why it moves around. The senses are important because through them the fish is equipped for life in its environment as well as if not better than we are for ours. The carp may not be as intelligent as we are but it is able to receive and analyse information on its environment, the presence of food and predators and the changing climate, and process that information in order to make decisions.

How the fish perceives us is just as important as how we perceive them in the capture scenario. To them we are just another predator. It's therefore important to keep out of view and not to make excessive noise if we are to maximise our chances of capture.

In fish capture, whether we are talking about rod and line, the assessment of stocks using nets and traps or any other method, the probability of capture is related to the size of the population. Using any effective method, the larger the population, the more fish you expect to catch. However, it's been shown there are a large number of variables that affect the probability of fish capture and as some of these change, feeding motivation can increase or decrease. Since the majority of fish capture methods involve the fish taking a lure or eating a bait or at least getting close to the bait (in the case of trapping) in order to be caught, these changes in feeding motivation can affect capture results either positively or negatively.

In a review by Stoner (2004), he focused on a number of variables that are involved in the environmental control of feeding behaviour and the effects of their variation on capture success. Although these are in general examined with reference to the capture of fish using baited hooks in marine environments for consumption and study, the principles that he discusses are in general applicable to our angling situation and in all cases modifiable. The variables considered were temperature, light level, turbidity, currents and tide, barometric pressure, wind and turbulence, bottom type as well as the availability of prey and competition and social facilitation. Clearly some are these don't involve carp or carp fishing. I have therefore modified one of the figures that he included in the article for our situation (see figure 3).

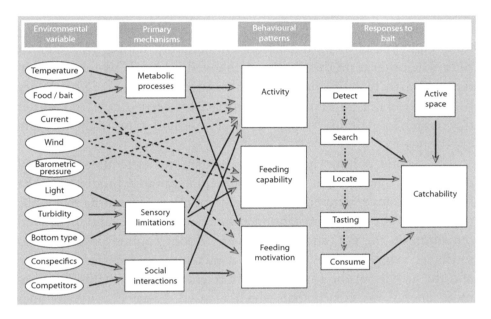

Figure 3: Environmental variables that affect activity, feeding **capabilities and feeding motivations and changes that increase or decrease the probability of fish capture (modified from Stoner, 2004).**

This diagram helps to put into perspective what we have been talking about in this chapter and some of the things that we will cover further ahead. As you can see, on the left hand side are a list of the environmental variables. I have replaced prey with food/bait because the fish's hunger in the fishing situation will depend on the availability of natural food items and also the amount of bait that is present in the water. These two alternatives will determine to some extent how hungry the fish is, a parameter that has been determined to be directly proportional to fish capture. The hungrier the fish, the easier it is to catch. However, if there's an excess of natural food and/or bait in the water then there's a lower probability of the fish accepting the baited hook. So, if you fill a lake in with bait then you may well be reducing your chances of catching, at least initially and as you can see, the availability of food and/or bait will have a direct effect on the fish's motivation.

I have also changed the title of the fourth column to responses to *bait* instead of *baited gear* since this is a reference to long-lining for ocean species in particular rather than carp fishing in a lake or river. The other term that has been changed is 'attack' which has been replaced with 'tasting' due to the former being a reference to predatory fish which is not particularly appropriate for carp which taste rather than attack food items. All the other columns and items of the diagram are the same.

The second column 'primary mechanism' refers to the method of detection of change that the environmental variable produces in the fish. For example, temperature and bait abundance affect the metabolic processes of the fish because hunger is a result of 1) the amount of food remaining in the gut, and 2) the energy /food required by the fish to satisfy its energy needs. As temperature increases, so does metabolic rate and the activity of the fish. It uses more energy and therefore requires more energy to replace that which is used. Since activity includes feeding activity we see an increase in feeding activity as the temperature increases. However, the rate of change in temperature may sometimes be so rapid that feeding is inhibited.

Following those, barometric pressure, currents and wind also have an effect on the activity of the carp (dashed lines mean that there is a direct effect on behaviour as opposed to an indirect one). Although it's difficult to determine how these different variables individually affect behaviour and there's little published information on these to support any theories, their collective change can either increase or decrease feeding activity. Currents and wind can sometimes also affect a fish's ability to feed (feeding capability) although maybe not so much in the carp's case as in that of predatory sea-fish species which use these over larger distances and longer periods of time to locate food.

Light, turbidity and bottom type also influence feeding since light allows fish to see and capture their food whereas increased turbidity, for example when the fish is attempting to feed in silt and visibility is reduced, means feeding effectiveness may decrease since carp feed most effectively when they can use a combination of visual, gustatory and olfactory senses. This leads to sensory limitations. This is expressed in the second column of the figure which is true when light levels are low or turbidity is high. In turn, sensory limitations have an effect on both the fish's capability to feed and its motivation to feed (feeding motivation). Here we refer to feeding motivation for all intents and purposes in the same as we would talk about hunger in humans.

Finally, the influence of other shoal members (I'll refer to them from now on as shoalmates) and competitors for the food that the fish eats are other important environmental variables because they are responsible for social interactions which in turn influence activity and feeding motivation. This is explained for example by the density and size of shoalmates which will influence how much food a particular carp is able to obtain. As we have already seen, being a member of a shoal has its benefits and disadvantages and as a result, interactions with other fish can either provide a fish with more or less food (a larger or smaller payoff).

The primary mechanisms shown in the second column directly influence the behavioural patterns shown in the third column. These are activity, feeding capability and feeding motivation whose influences have already been explained. Therefore the environmental variables, made up of four basic groups, can have either direct or indirect effects on the three behavioural patterns.

Stoner describes how the consumption of the bait involves a sequence of behavioural responses shown in the fourth column. These are influenced by the three behavioural patterns described and result in a sequence of detection followed by a search which leads to location of the source of the stimulus and this is tasted by the fish and then it might finally be consumed. The three behavioural patterns are closely linked to the feeding sequence. For example, changes in the activity of the carp or the speed at which it swims will increase or decrease the probability of it locating or detecting the bait or any chemical signals that the bait gives off. Changes in activity will also affect the intensity of the search for food and the possibility that the bait is located in a certain period of time.

In the same way, changes in hunger and the motivation to feed affect the threshold for the detection of chemical signals. This is to say that a fish that is hungry is more highly motivated and for that reason may more easily detect a chemical signal compared to when it is satiated (full of food). This in turn affects what Stoner refers to as the *active space,* which is the area over which any feeding attractants from the bait are present in concentrations above the level that can cause a positive response in the fish (threshold level). This space is determined by the rate of release and transport of chemical signals through the water and the levels that can be detected by the fish, which interests the fisherman.

In our context, the active space would refer to the distance that any of the substances that we use in our hookbait, glug or loose feed can cause attraction of carp according to the level of each that the fish is able to detect. This can be considered not just in terms of distance but also as volume of water over which it's possible to cause a positive stimulatory effect on the carp.

Some recent studies have confirmed that the active space will increase in size as the hunger level of fish increases and as the threshold for detection of a chemical stimulus decreases. This suggests that a hungry fish is searching more actively for the stimulus and it would be theoretically able to detect a lower concentration because of this behavioural change. In our context, what this means is that an area baited with a level of attractant above the carp's threshold concentration (see chapter 4) would be perceived differently by a hungry carp as opposed to a carp that is already full. Bait detection abilities, swim speeds and general feeding motivation all decrease with satiation and this results in a smaller active space, a reduced probability of a carp locating the bait and overall reduced fish catchability.

Although this is not a bombshell for the experienced angler, it certainly appears that Stoner's theory and his interpretation of these changes in behaviour and evaluation of the effect of environmental variables is perfectly applicable to the carp angling situation.

a. Temperature

As anglers we know that the weather can affect fishing. It's not the same fishing a lake in winter as it is in summer. We are able to observe the behaviour of the fish in summer but in winter this might not be so easy, basically because during the fishing session, we might not see any fish at all. It's therefore important to take advantage of this ability whenever we can because it will improve our understanding of movements and when the fish are feeding and maybe other things as well.

Weather takes all kinds of forms. We enjoy clear weather, but blue skies and no cloud is not the normal type of weather in northern Europe and the usual weather type is a mixture of wind, rain and occasional sunshine. Although we know all too well that the weather plays an important role in our fishing, it's often difficult to predict how the fish will react to long periods of the same or changing climate.

When the water temperature is highest we can expect better sport compared with cold temperatures. Carp are most comfortable at higher temperatures and as the temperature increases so does their metabolism. This increase in metabolism has a number of consequences for the fish. Firstly, its requirement for energy increases because the biological processes in its body are occurring faster and as a result they need more fuel. The fuel comes in the form of food which the carp has to find, ingest, digest and absorb. In order to do those things it requires more oxygen than at lower temperatures when the fish's metabolic rate is similarly lower.

However, hot weather is often not the most productive time of the year to fish. Even though it might be the time of the year when the fish are most active and are feeding the most during some times of the day, at the hottest time of the day, around midday and for some hours after, the fish can become very lethargic and really not take much interest at all in feeding. This is because, even though the carp is considered a warm water fish it has, just like other fish which share a similar optimum temperature range, metabolic limits. This means that when it becomes too hot or too cold for the fish, they will basically shut down. And during those times, it will become very difficult for an angler to catch them. If it's too hot, for example over 32 degrees Celsius, the fish may stop feeding and look for an environment in which they're more comfortable. That more comfortable environment might be an area closer to an inflow with a lower temperature and one that will probably contain a higher concentration of dissolved oxygen. At the opposite end of the scale, in the depths of winter, carp will be found where the water temperature is higher.

In this respect carp are a lot like us. They look for the place which offers them the best of everything at a particular moment. They want to be near to a source of food but will eat it when the conditions allow. Since higher oxygen levels and a temperature between, say, 15 and 32 degrees Celsius allows comfortable feeding they will feed more often between these temperatures.

But why do carp feed less or not at all when they're outside their comfort range of temperature? The answer to that is because of biological processes and the fact that they use enzymes. An enzyme is a substance that speeds up a reaction and allows reactions to work properly at lower temperatures. In a chemical and industrial sense, reactions such as the hardening of a resin use a catalyst. If the temperature is higher, the resin hardens faster because the rate at which the catalyst works is directly proportional to the environmental temperature. At a lower temperature, the hardening process will take relatively longer. The maximum and minimum temperatures of the catalyst's range are respectively the fastest and slowest that that reaction will take place and if you exceed those, you won't see any improvement. The same thing happens in the carp. When the maximum and minimum temperatures are exceeded, what you get is the enzyme becoming useless and for that reason, the fish becomes inactive.

If the temperature were to get to forty degrees Celsius, you don't get the fish eating like madmen. Instead what you get are fish that are ready to pack it in altogether. It's a bit like us really. We go to the beach and might even play a bit of volleyball or go for a run along the shore with the dog, but once the sun gets to its highest and hottest, all we want to do is lie there, look for shade and try and survive until the sun starts going down again.

Fish activity is dependent on temperature and it's the range of enzymes that a fish has in its body that determines the optimum temperature for the fish to live at and the top and bottom limits of temperature for that fish. If we compare carp to trout, the trout's preferred temperature is much lower, maybe 10 to 15 degrees and once the temperature gets over that, a trout is a harder fish to catch than a carp is.

Not all lakes react in the same way to temperature. This is mainly because they are different sizes and depths. But a shallow lake can change very quickly in a short space of time because it's much more sensitive to temperature than a deep lake is, which accordingly needs to be exposed to a longer period of heat or more intense temperature for it to be altered in the same way.

Since fish are cold-blooded and unable to regulate their own body temperature as we are, temperature has an important effect on them and affects not just the rate of enzyme function but also metabolism in general, the amount of energy required and therefore the amount of food consumed up to a certain level. Temperature is therefore critically important to our sport as it affects success and the probability of capture as it does in many other branches of angling, from Inuit ice fishing to sword fishing in the tropics.

The original source of heating of water bodies is the sun and both heating and cooling of our lakes and rivers is due to the amount of light that reaches them. When this light reaches the water's surface, there are two possibilities: it can either be reflected or it can enter the water. The amount of light that is absorbed is that which is available to change the temperature of the water body. Under some circumstances, such as wave action or the surface being covered by ice, reflection can be more important than absorption. However, when light is able to pass into the water itself, the effect is for it to be converted to heat. This amount of absorbed and converted light depends on the angle of the sun, cloud cover, the concentration of algae and other things which are able to absorb or reflect the light.

The transmission of light to greater depths in a lake also depends on the amount of suspended material in the water. If there is little suspended matter such as phytoplankton, the light can reach greater depths. The depth of the water can also affect the light frequencies (colours) and therefore the perception of those colours by aquatic organisms, including fish. However, with depth, the heating of the water similarly decreases as the intensity is reduced and the normal situation is for the surface to become heated more than the deeper water. This will depend on the amount of mixing that occurs in the water body.

In a fast flowing river, there is a great amount of mixing and even if it's quite deep, any heating of the water by sunlight will be evenly mixed throughout the water column and the width of the body of water. In a deep lake the situation is very different because there's very little water movement either horizontally or vertically and as a result the heating of the water is more intense at the surface and decreases with depth in the water column.

In temperate climates such as northern Europe, what we get as a result of this gradient of heating of the water column is something called stratification. This is the name given to the formation of layers in the water column due to the unequal heating of each one. Stratification can also occur when different salinities are present but that doesn't apply in stillwaters or in non-tidal rivers. Stratification as a result of heating is particularly common in summer when the light intensity and hours of daylight are greatest.

Stratification occurs because as water is heated it becomes less dense. Water is at its most dense at four degrees Celsius. Above and below that temperature water expands, either to form ice at lower temperatures or to form less dense water at higher temperatures. The higher the temperature, the lower the density. So in summer, as a result of higher temperatures and little vertical water movement, the surface of the water becomes heated and stratification occurs. What commonly occurs is that two layers form. The surface layer is warmer and less dense and the lower layer is cooler and denser. You can see these in the following diagram (figure 4). This shows that with depth the temperature decreases. Between the two layers there's an area where the temperature changes rapidly with only a small change in depth. This is referred to as the thermocline.

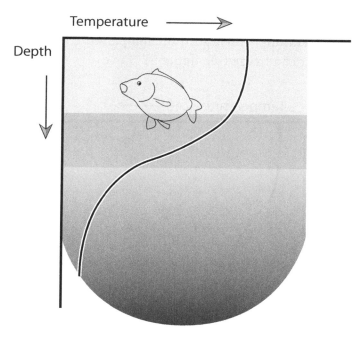

Figure 4:   Stratification in summer as a result of the heating
of the water surface and presence of the thermocline.

As summer progresses, the temperature and density of the water column becomes more distinct and it's possible for three layers to form which are an upper warmer and less dense layer, followed by a narrow band (thermocline) which is colder than the upper layer but warmer than the lower layer and a third layer, the bottom layer, containing colder water.

When autumn arrives and light intensity and duration are reduced, surface waters cool until they become as cool and dense as the bottom waters. Wind action causes the mixing of the lake which eventually results in the disappearance of the thermocline and a fully mixed water column between the surface of the lake and the bottom.

In winter, stratification returns. At this time of the year it is the surface layer that is again the least dense but in this case it's the coldest layer because of contact with cold air and winds. With depth, the temperature increases and during the colder months it is often the bottom of the lake where the temperature is highest. If the temperature drops enough, the low density layer can freeze (see figure 5).

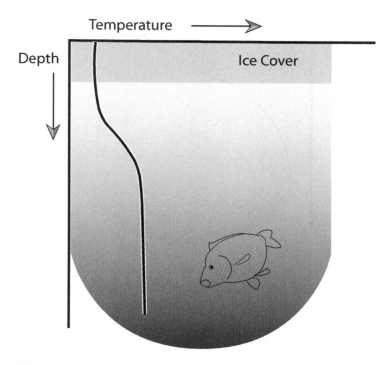

Figure 5: Stratification in winter as a result of the cooling of the water surface and formation of ice.

In winter, carp are usually found on the bottom in a state of low activity. They often shoal up at this time of the year. The stratification is more noticeable in colder countries since those with very mild winters do not stratify in winter.

As winter progresses and spring approaches, the temperature begins to slowly rise and as a result, the density of the surface layer increases and begins to sink. This causes a similar vertical mixing to that which occurs in autumn and eventually the water column again becomes totally mixed.

It's easy to see how lakes can become more or less stratified according to their depths. It's less common for shallow lakes to become stratified because the heating of the surface of the lake is the same as heating the total depth. The same is not true for deep lakes where it's more difficult for light to cause heating of the lower parts of the lake. That's why a thermocline is particularly evident in summer and winter and as the amount of heating decreases or increases, the depth of the thermocline in the water column changes accordingly.

Temperature is a particularly important parameter to consider, not only because of its direct effect on fish as a result of the warming or cooling of the water with changes in the climate and the time of the year, but also because of the effect that temperature has on other parameters. In fact it influences almost all of the other constituents of both fresh and seawater in one way or another. These effects are obviously less marked when the heating or cooling of the water is reduced by cloud cover because under those conditions the amount of light that is able to cause heating of the water is less. Temperature is also responsible for variations in the toxicity of some substances but in the vast majority of natural situations where we fish, this is of little or no importance.

One of the variables that is particularly worthy of mention is that of oxygen. In water, oxygen is present as dissolved oxygen. This is in the water due to the air becoming mixed with the water when water is in movement or agitated because of the diffusion from the air into the water or because of the photosynthesis of aquatic plants which release oxygen into the water column. Water has a specific capacity for oxygen to be dissolved in it. If you notice when a kettle boils it bubbles. That is air being forced out of the water as the temperature increases. As the temperature goes up the capacity for gases being dissolved in it goes down. The same thing happens in lakes and rivers as the temperature increases or decreases and the oxygen is forced out of or absorbed from the surrounding air. So, as the temperature of the water increases on a hot summer's day the amount of oxygen in the water goes down. It's therefore understandable that carp, while searching for comfort, will stay away from the warmest parts of the lake at the hottest time of the day or year because those not only put their metabolism to the test but will also contain relatively lower oxygen concentrations than cooler areas. High temperatures not only mean that the carp's metabolism increases but also that more oxygen is needed. So it's easy to see why it's energetically preferable to find locations and depths that offer a comfortable but not excessive temperature since they provide higher oxygen levels than those of the warmer areas.

It's relevant to add that the carp is a fish that requires much lower oxygen concentrations than others. For example, a trout has a preference for oxygen levels to be above six or seven milligrams per litre (mg/L) and those need to be even higher for very small fish and eggs to hatch healthily, but a carp is not particularly demanding when it comes to oxygen and it can survive in environments with as low as one mg/L. However, that doesn't mean that its preference is anything over one mg/L. In fact I'm sure that its preference would be for the same levels as the trout. It's just that the environments that the carp is usually found in, by which I mean still and shallow with large amounts of organic matter decomposing in them, are not the types of water that characteristically have abundant oxygen in them. As it decomposes, organic matter made up of things such as dead leaves, plants and invertebrates requires bacteria to break it down and that requires oxygen. It's for that reason that the typical stillwaters where carp are found are low in oxygen, particularly near or on the bottom.

So, even though carp might not need it, they will still prefer an oxygen richer environment as long as that doesn't compromise another of the fish's comforts such as temperature or food abundance. The fish is looking for 'the best of both worlds' although there are several factors that it will weigh up when making a choice as to location , and oxygen and temperature are just two of these.

We should remember that water temperature changes very slowly compared with air temperature and it's easy to think that once the sun comes out and the land has warmed up a bit, that the same thing has happened to the temperature of the lake. But unfortunately cold water requires much more energy than cold air in order to warm it up and so it takes a lot longer.

It's the cold weather that's more problematic than the hot weather for the carp angler. It's much more agreeable to be fishing at the side of a lake in summer than in winter. Cold weather, apart from making you uncomfortable is responsible for much slower fishing. Even on the hottest day in summer when catching fish can be difficult, there are opportunities in the evening, at night or early morning when the water temperature is lower and the carp more active. Cold weather can be unpleasant and it makes the carp so inactive that tempting them is sometimes impossible and very unpredictable and catching carp at that time of year can be extremely difficult.

It has been shown that carp are able to overcome particularly warm or cold conditions by moving away from them. It's for that reason that it's important to consider the possibilities available when you set up to fish. If you know a lake well enough and are familiar with the water depths in different parts of the lake (bathymetry), then this will help you to find the fish when the lake is warm or cold. If the lake is shallow, the changes in temperature during every 24 hour period will be more severe than those in a deeper lake.

If I had to pick a spot on a shallow lake in winter then it would be where I have access to the deepest parts where I would expect the fish to be in greater numbers, to take advantage of the slightly warmer water that is there even if that's only a fraction of a degree higher than the more superficial water. Likewise, in summer, the surface is more productive but so would be the bottom of the shallower parts of the lake and features with parts that extend closer to the surface.

If the lake is deeper and lacks any features then locating carp can be more difficult, even in summer. In that case, temperature doesn't give you as many clues and it's important to combine your experience of past sessions on the lake (if you have fished there before) with your knowledge of how temperature affects the water. Also, observations of fish crashing, basking or cruising will give their location away and may indicate something of their willingness to feed.

In both cases you should take notice of the parts of the lake that warm up more quickly. Although this might be a very small change in temperature, it can still make a difference during the day. When the sun rises, it will often fall first on the opposite side of the lake with greatest intensity and it's likely that the fish are used to that and as a result are found in greater numbers in the part of the lake that receives sunlight first.

Temperature is responsible for affecting the behaviour of the fish and determining how comfortable that fish is in a particular location. From an angler's perspective, the best kind of fish to find or to find you is one that has everything it needs with the exception of food. This means that it will be environmentally comfortable but hungry.

Although the temperature can vary greatly throughout the year, if you fish the same waters frequently, you'll observe the changes in such things as the natural food that's present and the movement of the fish during the day and with changes in the seasons you'll experience the changes in temperature that we've been discussing. Hopefully you'll be able to join the dots and understand how temperature change affects the carp in your lake. Whether or not you are able to do that quickly or it takes you longer depends on how often you fish there, but whatever is happening you can be sure that the fish are in there somewhere. They are adapting, hourly, weekly or monthly to the changing conditions in order to survive and develop normally and it's the angler that's able to adjust in the same way to changes in feeding and location as a result of changes in temperature that will come out on top.

b. Wind and currents

Temperature is not the only physical variable that affects our fishing. The other two important physical influences are winds and currents. The availability of food and comfort are both affected by these and as a result they influence the movement and location of the carp in a lake.

Hopefully, the angler is able to read the signs on a water and this will mean that he has more chance of finding the fish and putting a bait in a spot that increases the probability of capture.

The main source of water currents in shallow lakes is the wind. This blows across the surface of the lake and causes waves with their height depending on the distance over which the wind blows and the strength of the same. Of the total amount of energy that wind possesses, only a very small part results in the creation of waves and most of it is responsible for forming water currents below the water's surface.

When these horizontal water currents reach the shore of the lake, they have to return. This can occur at the lake's surface but is more common by what are termed 'return flows' which occur deeper in the water column. Figure 6 shows surface movement caused by the wind in a stratified lake and the return flows that are produced.

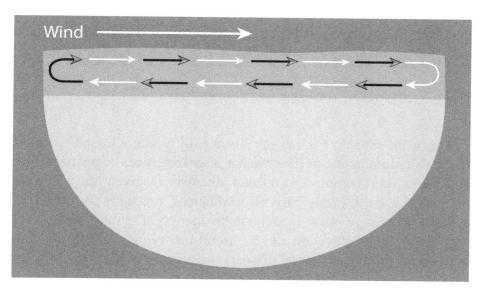

Figure 6: Return flow caused by wind in a stratified lake.

If the lake is unstratified, either because of the season (spring or autumn) in a deep lake or because the lake is completely shallow or shallow in the area of interest, then a similar situation can develop. However, instead of the horizontal water current reaching the shore and returning across the top of the denser lower layer, in the unstratified lake what it does is return across the bottom of the lake. This is depicted in figure 7.

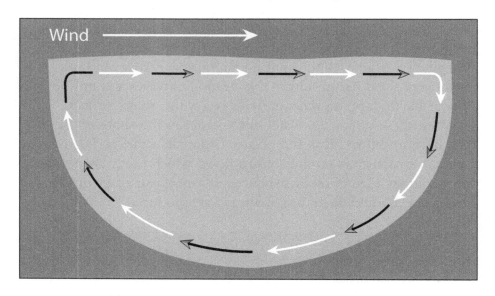

Figure 7: Return flow caused by wind in an unstratified lake.

The wind direction is never constant on a lake although there is often a predominant direction. What also sometimes happens is that different wind directions can affect a lake over relatively short periods of time. These will create currents in different directions and therefore a principal current may be difficult to identify. Defining a principal wind and current direction can be useful for trying to determine fish movements and location and this can also indicate where surface food items are being moved to and concentrated, which may become a source of food for the carp. Even if this isn't true, the principal direction may help you understand the movements of individual fish and shoals.

Apart from the presence, absence or direction of the wind, another consideration is that of wind temperature. Air movement over the land in summer will result in a warm wind and the heat energy which this contains is transferred to the surface of the lake resulting in warmer surface temperatures as well as any direct heating of the lake's surface by sunlight. And as we have just seen, the wind pushing water against the shore is able to produce return flows. If the water is heated by warm winds before reaching the shore, then this will increase not only the horizontal movement of water in the opposite direction but also the temperature of the water lower in the water column or on the lake bottom depending on the depth and the degree of stratification. If the wind is cold, then it will have a cooling effect on the surface and wherever that water ends up as a result of the return flows or additional surface movement.

The movement of water in a vertical direction is caused by the heating of water layers. Since water expands on heating, it becomes less dense and migrates towards the surface of the water body. Similarly, when water cools down it becomes denser and therefore sinks. This means that in summer the cooler water is found on the bottom because the warmer, less dense water is found at the surface and in winter the densest water is found on the bottom and the less dense, coldest water is found at the surface where, if cooling is great enough it forms ice. This is because, as we have already seen, water is at its densest at four degrees Celsius but below and above that temperature the density of water decreases.

These changing densities result in layers of water rising and falling in the water column. It's therefore possible to create vertical water movement due to changes in the vertical location of these water masses. The combined effect of wind and currents means that it's possible for the lake to become totally mixed because of a mixture of rising and falling masses, surface movement and reverse flows.

Maybe the vertical movement of water is of less importance than horizontal movement and it's probably much less obvious to the angler. It's something that happens below the water surface and is unobservable compared with horizontal water movement, which can, at least in the case of surface movement, be observed by the angler. Vertical movement is also something that usually happens more slowly and over a longer time period compared with horizontal movement and in some waters the only vertical movement might be seasonal. This is referred to as spring and autumn turnover and happens as masses of water are warmed or cooled and which rise or sink as the seasons change. However, both types of water movement potentially lead to changes in the movement of carp but in the short term it's the horizontal movement that will influence carp movement more and is therefore relevant to locating carp.

In the same way, both water movement types are able to influence the dispersion of attractants used by the angler (e.g. a glug). On rivers, the angler can use the current to draw fish upstream towards his bait but in lakes, there are few situations where such strong currents may be found. One possibility is near the inflow of the lake or near the outflow. By positioning the bait in those areas and using an effective attractant, the angler can potentially create a trail of the attractant from his bait in the direction that the current is heading. With distance from the bait the concentration of the attractant becomes gradually reduced although over a short distance it's possible to go from a high dose that is easily detectable by the fish to a hardly perceptible or imperceptible amount with a correspondingly reduced stimulus for the carp. With even greater distance the carp is no longer able to detect the substance and no attraction can be expected. There's further discussion of this in chapter 4.

It's important to use exceptionally high doses of attractants in a glug for just that reason. You don't have to move far from the bait for the dilution to be so high and the resulting concentration to be so low as to have no effect whatsoever on the fish. However, depending on your opinion, the use of attractants can be more effective in lakes because of the very low amount of current present compared with rivers. This is particular true for baits that are used on the bottom since with depth in the water column, the strength and frequency of currents decreases. This is to say that the strongest currents are usually at the surface of the lake because it's here that we have the effect of wind and the horizontal surface currents that it causes and reverse flows in the case of stratified lakes.

In lakes, the use of an attractant in the absence of water current leads to dispersion in the immediate area to the source of the attractant. This is usually applied to a PVA bag or a hookbait. Where there's no current it will diffuse into the surrounding water but will not go very far. This will therefore help to maintain high concentrations in the near vicinity. On the one hand this is advantageous but on the other it means that there'll be little influence of the attractant over carp that may be further away.

The movement of water masses either horizontally or vertically gives rise to changes in temperature and oxygen concentration in the water column. As we have already seen, oxygen can be added to the water by photosynthesis, diffusion from the atmosphere into the water at the surface and by movement and agitation. It can be removed by several processes too. These include its use in respiration by aquatic organisms including bacteria and diffusion back into the atmosphere as the temperature rises. The movement of water can therefore speed up these processes or decrease or increase the temperature or oxygen levels of different parts of the lake or river.

A good example of this is at the inflow point of water into a lake. Here, the water usually comes into the lake as a stream which is faster moving and has maybe been highly oxygenated on its journey from the hills. Streams are also usually lower in temperature because they are often formed from groundwater that joins the stream at different points of its catchment. The inflow of cooler, more highly oxygenated water into a lake particularly during summer can make it a preferred location, and although carp are more active during the warmer months, this will not be at all cost. And since they will seek more comfortable conditions, this must be accompanied by a food supply which meets their energy requirements and preferred environmental conditions including the oxygen level.

Water currents are important in lakes for another reason. They are the source of nutrient transport around the lake. Those nutrients are absorbed by phytoplankton which are in turn eaten by invertebrates. These are the food for many species of fish including carp.

Changes in atmospheric pressure also affect both fish and anglers.

Some anglers prefer to fish when the pressure is changing as opposed to times when it's permanently high or low. It's been suggested that fish with swimbladders are able to detect changes in atmospheric pressure and that this may have an effect of feeding motivation (Stoner, 2004). There are a number of other factors that affect the fish's motivation to feed but these will be covered in greater detail in chapter 3.

Chapter Two

Food Location by Carp

Fish are the largest group of organisms in the animal kingdom, represented by more than 22 thousand species. Among these, a tremendous amount of diversity exists.

If you are anything like me, as an angler, then you think about fish for 90 percent of each day. As a carp angler, 90 percent of that is taken up thinking about carp, with the remainder left for different species. But such a diverse range of fish enter into that remainder, and in just a space of a few minutes it's possible to conjure up images of anything from the strangest to the most common and normal species.

The diversity which you can imagine is expressed in all shapes and sizes, from fish that start their lives a few inches long to those which may never reach more than an inch in length as long as they live. There are differences in diet, from those which filter microscopic plants and animals from the water column to those that can swallow other large fish whole. Some have evolved to prefer certain habitats, from clear mountain streams to the filthiest sewage outfall. You can find species from the purest freshwater source at high altitude to the deepest depths of the salty. And each of them comes with its own particular adaptations to deal with diet, habitat and ensuring the survival of the next generation.

All animals must feed. And for that purpose, every one of the species of fish has evolved physically and behaviourally in order to both locate and deal with its food. Some fish exclusively eat a particular food. This can occur when that food is plentiful all year round and is locally and permanently available. Other fish do not eat one particular food but a mixture of animal and plant material, which may be daily or seasonally available and sporadically distributed. This is the case of the carp.

The carp, as we will see in this chapter, is a fish which has developed a preference for omnivory. An omnivore is an animal that, according to its Latin roots, 'devours everything' and basically means that its diet consists of a mixture of plant and animal material which may be dead or alive upon consumption. However, this denomination doesn't mean that the fish lacks preferences and just eats everything that it can find. On the contrary, if it were, then carp fishing would be much easier than it sometimes is. An omnivore is able to digest a wider range of items than a carnivore and this means that several structures are different in a carp than in carnivorous fish.

If we compare a carp with a trout, then we see that they are both freshwater fishes and they both have the typical fishy characteristics like scales, fins and gills. The two fish prefer different environments. However, there are physical differences that are less easy to detect unless we look closely both inside and on the exterior of each fish. The trout has teeth and the carp doesn't and whereas the trout has limited protrusion of the jaws, the carp has very extensible mouthparts. The predatory trout's teeth are required to catch and disable live food, ranging from crustaceans and insects to fish. These are often difficult to trap and immobilise without teeth and for that reason the carnivorous trout is armed with them. The carp, on the other hand, possesses a different feeding system which is based on extrusion and changes in water pressure and movement in order for feeding to take place. In the case of the carp, food is a mixture of living or dead plant and animal material which in general is relatively slow moving, with some exceptions. Therefore it's not necessary for the carp to grasp the food and it benefits from a larger oral volume and processing of food by the palatal organ within the mouth.

Another important physical difference is the construction of the gut in these two fish. The trout has something called a true stomach, which, as the name suggests, has the form of what we would expect from a stomach; it has a tube going in with a sphincter at the entrance, a wider, rubbery part where the food collects and the process of being broken down occurs and then there's another sphincter at the exit which leads to another tube which is where the intestine begins. It sounds very similar to our own stomach, which in fact it is, with the only real difference being a collection of other tubes called caecae which are attached to the trout's stomach wall, increasing the surface area of the stomach and its efficiency. As with our own stomach, this is where acid is added to the food and where proteins in particular are reduced to smaller molecules.

The carp, on the other hand, does not have a true stomach. If you were to see the gut of a carp, then you would be surprised to observe that it has no real additional structures attached to it. There's no bulge where the stomach should be or anything that would make you think that the animal was even distantly related to us. It's basically just a tube and one that receives food at one end and what it can't utilise is pushed out at the other. Unlike the carnivorous trout, the gut is not designed to deal with large amounts of protein. Instead, it's designed to cope with a bit of everything. It's the stomach of an omnivore.

The final difference that I'd like to mention, and the one that is the reason for pointing out the major differences between the two fish, are the eyes. This is easier to spot on a large fish. The eyes of a trout are larger in relation to the body size than are those of a carp. The reason for this is related to the feeding behaviours of the two fish, which are very different. The trout is primarily a visual feeder and therefore it needs good eyesight, something that can be achieved by having evolved a larger eye size. The same is true for other predatory animals which depend on their sight for hunting. Good examples include owls and cats. On the other hand, those which use alternative methods of detecting their food, be it live or otherwise, have other specialisations, but their eyes are often small or non-existent.

There are a number of specialisations which all animals can have to detect food. Visual detection is one of these and predatory fish tend to use this more frequently and preferentially. This is not to say that it's the only method of detection that they use. It isn't. It's advantageous that a fish be able to use more than one sense. Their senses of taste and smell are not as highly developed as those of a carp or a catfish, but they do use them for certain situations, and even more so at night, when visual capacity is greatly reduced, or when water is coloured and it's impossible to see very far.

In the same way that a trout uses a combination of different methods of food detection, the carp does the same. However, the carp's preference is gustation (taste), which has evolved over millions of years to be particularly acute. This is followed by smell and visual detection. Other fish use other combinations which may include electro-detection, using electrical pulses to determine the presence of objects in the water, including their size, shape and quality, or mechanoreception whereby stimuli such as sound and vibration are used to locate potential food. Predatory fish such as bass and salmonids use mechanoreception using an abundance of receptors present along the lateral line of the fish.

a. Food types and seasonal variation

The carp requires a range of different substances in order to develop normally. These are found in different food items that are present in the lake or river where the fish lives. The availability of each of these may differ from water to water but they can usually be found in one way or another in each one.

Also, different amounts of each substance are needed according to the life stage of the fish. For example, a carp fry requires different quantities and qualities of each substance compared with an adult fish. Different life stages have different requirements and efficiencies to digest and absorb the food that the carp ingests.

In several ways, carp are very similar to us. They require many of the same substances but not in the same proportions. In chapter 4 we will look at these requirements but in general these are the macro-nutrients protein, fat and carbohydrate and the micro-nutrients vitamins and minerals. However, one way in which the carp is different from us is in the way it goes about finding its food and satisfying the requirement for each of the nutrients. The carp can't just pop down to the supermarket and fill a trolley with what it wants for the week. What is does is swim around and search until it finds the food items that it needs. The fish cannot be too choosy because its natural environment is full of competitors who would be only too pleased to come across an abundant patch of food in some part of the lake and get it down their throats as fast as possible. Therefore they have to ensure that they don't lose out on food but that they don't feed at any cost.

It's important for the fish to obtain what it needs. Sometimes it will be a struggle for the carp to find any food at all which may be more frequently the case in nutrient poor (oligotrophic) waters that have a low amount of primary production and therefore low numbers of invertebrates and other food. At other times the fish will have to choose between 1) simply filling its gut with one food, or 2) continuing the search and obtaining what we would refer to as a balanced diet.

The second strategy is preferable if the fish finds food but if it doesn't, then the former would have been better. It's the experienced fish however that's able to feed more effectively because if you know where to find the different types of food, then you're not risking anything by leaving the first or eating just a small amount before moving on to find other, more energetically favourable foods.

We have seen and will see in other sections how hunger is provoked by two different stimuli. The first is the absence of food in the gut which motivates the fish to feed and the other is the lack of energy that the fish feels that motivates it towards the same. If I were to choose between feeling hunger and feeling overly full, then I would always choose feeling ready to burst. They are both quite unpleasant but the thing is about feeling full is that with time you feel better whereas if you're hungry, as time goes on you only feel worse.

Carp and other fish are able to go for extended periods of time without any real negative effects of not ingesting food. This is not the same for us. Even if you aren't starving, most people experience a change of mood once the stomach is pretty much empty. In fish, as time goes on, the motivation to feed increases and this is caused by the production of a variety of hormones that let the fish know that the gut is emptying and energy levels are dropping.

So the fish is in a constant state of decision-making regarding whether to feed and what to feed on and whether to not consume one thing in preference of another. It's here that we're involved in this process because among the selection of items that the carp is offered is our bait. And it's obviously in our favour that the bait that we offer is able to compete with other items. We will see how to do that further on.

For now we'll look at the selection of foods on offer to the carp and where they come from. This will only be a superficial look at the main groups of plants and animals in order not to repeat what I've published previously and we'll discuss a little of what each contains in the way of nutrients.

Food items that the carp can benefit from can enter the fish's aquatic environment in a number of different ways. Firstly, and the most common way, is for the item to be similarly aquatic and to share the fish's space. This is the case for both aquatic plants and animals which live and die in the water. The aquatic animals include a range of invertebrates and fish which are consumed by the carp either alive or dead although chasing fish in order to consume them in the same way as predatory fish is not their preferred method of feeding or their favourite food. However, this may be an option at some times of the year or when alternative food items are scarce or competition is high.

Aquatic invertebrates can be divided into those which spend their entire lives in the water and those which pass through several life stages before hatching into adults and spending part of their lives, albeit a short part in many cases, as terrestrial insects. Those groups of animals which form part of the carp's diet and which spend their whole lives in the water include flatworms and rotifers, nematodes and nematomorphs, annelids, molluscs, arachnids and crustaceans. On the other hand, those that are initially waterborne and undergo transformation into airborne organisms include principally those of the subgroup Insecta which includes mayflies, dragonflies, stoneflies, caddisflies, midges, beetles and some moths.

Many of these animals are familiar to anglers because they are large enough to be seen in the water, emerging from it or flying around us while we're fishing. Basically any of these can become food for the carp since it often feeds without any particular preference and even when we think that they are feeding on a particular source of food of a specific food item such as a bloodworm bed, it's more than likely that some proportion of the food that is ingested is made up of other organisms.

This is because the carp is specialised to feed on suspended or benthic organism but is to some extent limited in its differentiation between animal types or species. What often happens is that it all gets sucked into the mouth, the non-food is separated from the food and the food is then chewed and swallowed. This is true for when the carp is feeding on planktonic animals just as much as when it's bottom-feeding. Its vacuum-like feeding apparatus is highly effective and food can be sucked up from distance at a speed of up to 60 centimetres per second. It is also a precise system that can be finely modified regarding the direction and force of suction. For that reason, many types of aquatic organism suffer the same fate almost indiscriminately. However, the appearance of food items in concentrations in the lakes (patches) is usually the motivation for the carp to focus its feeding on a specific area.

It may also sometimes appear as if the carp are feeding on nothing at all. However, we should remember that many of the carp's foods are extremely small and in some cases microscopic. This means that the fish will carry out the two forms of food intake, (gulping and particulate intake for suspended and particulate feeding respectively) and it will not be obvious what they are feeding on, only that whatever it is it's very small. These small organisms include phytoplankton and zooplankton which are suspended in masses in the water column as well as bacteria which may be suspended or attached to the bottom substrate as mats.

Additionally, the carp is a detritus feeder which is made up of a mixture or living and dead material of different origins. This might include invertebrates, small vertebrates, plant material or bacteria and again, feeding is indiscriminate, with the fish's objective being that of consuming the food part of the food/non-food mixture. Detritus has been shown to make up an important proportion of the food ingested by the carp (21.6%) and have a high occurrence among the carp population that was sampled (56%) (Adámek *et al.*, 2003).

The other way that food items can get into the carp's environment is by falling from bankside vegetation or out of the air. Adult insects die or simply collide with the water and this happens more frequently during or after rain. Also, bankside vegetation, grasses, bushes or trees can release their seeds or fruit directly into the water or they can be blown into the water from a short distance or further in the case of some seeds. Terrestrial plants also decompose and pieces of leaves can end up in the lake or river. In some cases, the roots of bankside vegetation, although terrestrial, can emerge through the soil underwater and provide a source of food for fish including carp.

Carp are omnivorous and therefore have evolved to deal with a large range of food items. The situation when the fish is feeding on natural food items is reflected somewhat in the diverse number of baits that can be used to catch carp. We are able to use anything from artificial flies and lures to cereals and seeds which contain high levels of carbohydrate to different meats, which are higher in protein and fat and synthetic baits that are nothing more than bits of foam or rubber. Then there are more elaborated baits such as the boilies and pellets, which contain a bit of everything and are aimed at providing a balanced diet.

Even if they aren't all equally successful when it comes to catching carp on the same day or at the same water, the sheer variety shows us that carp are willing to try different foods and recognise the nutritional value of those baits. It is also clear that even though the baits are not a natural part of the carp's environment that the carp is able to accept them as such. We are able to increase the probability of their acceptance by the carp by prebaiting and adding bait in the right amount while we're fishing. This acceptance is likely to be easier if the fish has seen the bait before or at least something similar or if the amount of competition for food with other carp or other fish populations is high or there's a lack of natural food in the place where we're fishing. Acceptance and preference will both depend on the fish's normal level of hunger. If the natural food levels are high and the amount of fish in the water are low, then it can be assumed that capture by anglers will be more difficult, mainly because the fish will be relatively full for much of the time and can continue to feed on safer alternatives.

As we'll see later, carp are able to effectively digest carbohydrate. The main source of carbohydrate in the aquatic environment is aquatic plants with the fish ingesting parts of plants such as leaves and roots either on purpose or accidentally while feeding on other food items. However, the carp is limited somewhat when it comes to dealing with plant material and the crushing and grinding that they use to break it up for easier mixing and swallowing is not particularly effective for large flat pieces of leaves. Processing is much better for harder, rounder particles such as seeds which can be broken up by compression as opposed to plant material which may be flattened slightly but is little affected by the feeding mechanism . Additionally, carp don't possess teeth at the front of the mouth which could theoretically be used to tear smaller parts from submerged plants.

It's likely that some proportion of the carp's diet must contain plants for the carbohydrate or the micro-nutrients they contain. In the same study by Adámek et al. (2003), plant debris was found to make up 16.4 percent of the amount of food ingested with an occurrence in 88 percent of the carp population sampled.

The plant material consumed by carp, with the exception of phytoplankton which are microscopic plants, includes macrophytes which may be aquatic or of terrestrial origin. In a few cases whole plants may be consumed but according to studies on plants eaten by carp these are usually parts that have broken off the plant and are therefore dead as well as the soft roots of some species (e.g. Miller, 2004). It has also been found that carp prefer to consume parts of plants that they are able to handle since, as we'll see, the feeding mechanism used by the fish is not particularly specialised for whole or large portions of macrophytes because of high tissue toughness and fibre content.

Plants serve several purposes in the carp's environment apart from food. They provide protection such as in the case of lily pads and silkweed and are also indirectly responsible for carp feeding since the roots and leaves shelter a wide range of invertebrates that constitute an important proportion of the carp's diet. They are found in many parts of lakes and rivers and their distribution depends on the characteristics of the plant in question. For example, some are unattached to the bottom and float and others are attached but have parts that float on the surface (e.g. the lily pad). Others are completely submerged apart from when they are flowering and others are referred to as emergent plants, which have roots in the lake or river bottom but a large part of the plant may be above the water surface (e.g. the bulrush).

Plant growth and cover change spatially (in space) and temporally (in time). Anglers who frequent the same water year round will be able to recognise the particular changes that occur. But in general terms, the amount of plant cover both below and above the surface of the water increases as the temperature increases, which corresponds with increased light intensities allowing photosynthesis and plant growth to occur. This has a number of implications for the carp and the carp angler alike. For example, from late spring to early autumn plant growth is greater and this provides more cover for fish. Also, during this period the colour of the water may change as algae also prosper as a result of longer days and higher light intensities.

But plants are not the only organisms that vary in space and time. Animals such as invertebrates change in both numbers and diversities as the year progresses. For example, Sukop & Adámek (1995) assessed the similarity of food eaten by tench and carp that were between one and three years old. They discovered that the similarity of the food eaten was between 23 and 62 percent and that as fish got older, the similarity of what they ate increased. Also, from May to September, the similarities in what the fish ate decreased. This is because as spring turns into summer the diversity of invertebrates increases and therefore the probability of two fish species eating the same amount and the same combinations of different food items decreases.

Some species of invertebrate are found in shallow water whereas others prefer deeper parts of lakes or rivers. The populations are constantly changing. Effective feeding by carp and other fish means that some species and areas become depleted of some organisms although the majority of these are highly reproductive. This means that even if a very few individuals remain, they are able to reproduce fast enough to replenish the population. And if one patch becomes depleted, another can appear to enable the fish to continue feeding.

Seasonal changes in temperature and nutrient levels have important effects on both the number and diversity of plants and animals in a water. Aquatic plants, in the same way as terrestrials, require a mixture of sunlight, water and nutrients containing elements such as nitrogen, phosphorus and potassium in order to grow. In the aquatic environment there's no problem with obtaining water. Water currents supply the plants with a source of the nutrients they need and light is available during the hours that sunlight falls on the water. When there are high and continued light levels, aquatic plants from the microscopic algae that make up the phytoplankton population to massive macrophytes such as water lilies prosper. Phytoplankton is particularly important because it's the source of food for the zooplankton, which is consumed directly by the carp but this in turn also provides the larger invertebrates with food and these are also eaten directly by the carp.

Throughout the year, an observant angler will notice the changes in the numbers and varieties of plants and animals in and around the water. He will see the macrophytes flourish and flower and the pondweed multiply in summer. These will recede as winter approaches. And an examination of the landing net after a fish has been caught can reveal a wealth of organisms that frequent the margins, particularly in summer. As the seasons change, some will disappear by a system of natural progression or because pupae have hatched leaving other species to dominate different areas of the water.

Carp can also be interested in small vertebrates that can be found in the same environment. These include small fish and amphibians such as frogs, newts and tadpoles. Feeding on these organisms is not usually preferred by the carp since it's not well equipped for dealing with slippery, fast-moving creatures due to an absence of teeth. Some may be eaten dead which obviously makes them easier to deal with and others may simply be ingested as a consequence of generalised bottom feeding. However, the amount of alternatives such as these that are ingested by the carp is likely to increase when other foods that may be preferred are unavailable or in short supply or when there is increased competition from shoalmates or other species and populations of fish. The same preferences are often shared between the carp and other species, especially other species of cyprinids such as roach, bream and tench which feed in a similar way to the carp, have similar feeding specialisations and share preferences for food items.

Seasonal differences in natural food item preferences have been determined previously. Uribe-Zamora (1975) showed that the diet of the carp varies according to the time of year. Differences in diet were shown to occur between different seasons and also from lake to lake according to the food organisms present in each one. Despite these differences, the general scheme is that in winter carp feed little as a result of the lack of available food and the temperature which reduces the feeding activity of the fish. However, chironomid larvae (bloodworm) and tubificids form an important part of the fish's reduced diet at this time. Then in spring the carp begin to feed predominantly on larger invertebrates such as daphnia and cyclops, which is triggered by the proliferation of zooplankton as the water warms up and there is increased growth of phytoplankton which is food for the zooplankton. In summer, the appearance of fish larvae causes reduced availability of plankton and adult carp exploit the expansion of areas of aquatic plants in the margins which shelter large numbers of invertebrates including snails, caddis and worms. Then, with the onset of autumn the fish may return to deeper water as the size of margin invertebrate populations decreases and a larger proportion of their diet is composed of small invertebrates again including midge larvae and oligochaete worms.

There have been relatively few studies carried out in order to determine the composition of the invertebrates that form an important proportion of the carp's diet at any time of the year. However, Giles *et al.* (1990) showed that a diet overlap exists between several species of fish including carp in the sites that they sampled, which included gravel pits. Also, Driver (1981) estimated the calorific content (energy content) of 23 species of aquatic insects with the range running from 3682 to 6270 calories per gram (15.4 to 26.2 kilojoules) with an average of 5525 calories per gram (23.1 kilojoules). In all cases, the researcher found that the water content of all the animals studied made up more than 50 percent of wet weight with the highest water content of 93.6 percent belonging to a species of fairy shrimp.

In an earlier study, the same author evaluated the protein content of some common invertebrates and this ranged from 31 to 80 percent dry weight (Driver *et al.*, 1974). Amino acid content of the same invertebrates was analysed in the same study. This was shown to vary considerably from species to species. This supports the theory that in order to satisfy its nutritional requirements for essential amino acids it's beneficial for a carp to consume amounts of a variety of species rather than feeding on one alone. It has also been shown that the protein and fat proportions of invertebrates change throughout the year and that as they increase in age, protein levels decrease as a result of partial replacement of protein by fat (Stockner, 1971).

It's interesting to wonder how the addition of our bait mainly in the form of loose feed and groundbait affects the aquatic environment and in particular whether it forms an important part of the food that carp ingest during their lives. It's only possible to speculate because the studies that have analysed this are few and far between (e.g. Niesar *et al.*, 2004; Arlinghaus & Niesar, 2005) and in those cases they have examined particularly the environmental impact of bait use in specific regions rather than determining what proportion of total food ingested by cyprinids is made up of bait as opposed to natural food.

However, it's safe to say that this proportion will vary greatly depending on the amount of bait that we use each year, the proportion of that which is consumed by the fish, the abundance and type of natural food the number of anglers and the frequency that they fish a particular water. As we know, there is a wide variety of waters and some of those are always busy whereas others receive very little angling pressure. And not only the waters but anglers are very different too. Some throw in five kilos of bait as soon as they get to the water and others can make a bag of boilies last all day.

So it's a difficult thing to calculate due to such a large amount of variability. Therefore I'd expect the proportion of bait in the total amount of food consumed by carp specifically to be anywhere between almost nothing and almost 100 percent. I'm sure there are waters where elaborated baits such as pellet and boilies have still never been seen by the fish and anyone fishing may choose more 'natural' baits such as maggots over those. On the other hand there may be some commercial waters where there is little natural food and the carp now consider a boilie to be a natural food item because they are so used to seeing it and maybe nobody is using more natural alternatives.

However, this is something to bear in mind when we fish a water and especially when we embark on a new venue. Carp will almost certainly try to consume a selection of food items because it's nutritionally beneficial for the fish to do so. Eating a bit of everything is more likely to provide them with everything they need even though they might not consciously realise it. Hunger is another factor that motivates fish to feed but how a fish reacts and interacts with a bait is something that will vary from water to water depending on how much bait goes in, what kind of bait that is and how much natural food is present and of course what that is. Even though the amount and types of bait and natural food might be extensive, even excessive, carp will exercise preference when they eat and it's also important to understand that apart from considering the availability of these two main alternatives, we have to consider how we can improve our bait to make it more attractive to the carp. With regards to natural food items we are, after all, trying to compete with something that may not be as nutritionally beneficial for the fish in terms of energy and macro- and micro-nutrients of a single natural food item but it's definitely a safer option for the fish.

b. Taste versus smell

It's currently thought that chemoreception, the detection of chemical signals in the water, is the principal method of food location utilised by the carp. However, since chemoreception can be employed by either the olfactory system (what we would call smell) or the gustatory system (what we would call taste), as anglers it's important to know which of these is used and how we can stimulate either one of them or both with our bait.

Fish can pick up on chemical signals in the water, in some cases over great distances, such is the sensitivity of the chemosensory system. In carp it's particularly well-developed, something that has been shown by a number of studies into its capacity and function. The results of these have shown that smell is used in social behaviour, such as finding a mate and testing water quality. Carp olfaction is also able to distinguish certain chemicals in the water and allows the fish to determine the direction from which the stimulus is coming. As the fish nears the source of the stimulus, it is taste which replaces it as the primary sensory system as far as finally locating and testing the potential food item.

While I was writing *Carp Fishing Science*, in a communication with Nand Sibbing, someone whose studies in this field of research are continually cited even today after several decades, he told me that vision is very important to the carp during the daytime and even in low light intensities. Also, that taste is important during the day and night and even more so when the fish is probing and feeding on the bottom. Through personal observations while fishing and also during the tank trials that I've carried out with carp, I tend to agree with him on all counts.

When the water clarity allows it, surface fishing for carp using baits which have little or no chemically attractive properties over very much distance, can be very effective. In that situation, the carp can be very actively interested in something that has caught their eye much more than it has their sense of smell or taste. It is then that visual detection is clearly more important than taste or smell regarding feeding. The same thing can be seen in a tank or aquarium, since the arrival of food is met with a change in behaviour by the fish in the way of opening and closing of the mouth (referred to as snapping), tail flicking and more agitated swimming. It's clear in that case that it's the visual stimulus that has provoked that reaction as opposed to the smell or taste of the food.

This shows how variable the use of different senses by the carp is depending on the situation. The captive environment is one in which food is brought to the fish rather than the fish having to seek out its source. The fish may have been conditioned to feeding at a certain time and the food may be constantly of the same type. For these reasons and others, senses of smell and taste may be used little or hardly at all. The opposite is true at the bottom or a turbid lake where visibility is very low and the principal detection methods available to the carp are smell and taste, which under difficult conditions such as these would be the most effective.

In general, the primary use of visual detection is probably the exception to the rule. At least in Europe, carp spend most of their time on or close to the bottom as opposed to the surface looking for zig rigs and artificial dog biscuits. We should therefore focus on the chemosensory aspect of carp as the best way to catch them, due to the fact that this is what they depend on most in order to keep themselves fed. However, we should bear in mind that the carp uses a combination of senses at all times and as anglers, we should not forget that a bait that is attractive, or interesting to more than one sense may be more productive than a bait that appeals to just one.

Debate has raged among anglers for several years regarding the importance of smell and taste in the location and ingestion of food. A lot has been written about the subject, but there has been a great deal of supposition regarding this topic, as there has a great deal of other things that are carp fishing related. Some people in the carp angling world have been able to bridge a gap between the biological and chemical and the practicality of the modern carp angler. However, it's not surprising that others have had the opposite effect and they've either kept you in the dark on purpose or have explained things which were the opposite of the truth, otherwise referred to as lies.

A good example is the way that bait companies push flavourings on the carp fishing public as if they were working in an ice-cream shop. I wouldn't be surprised if someone had brought out a mint choc chip flavoured boilie. It often seems to be too much about stimulating the angler and his wallet than it is about stimulating the carp's senses.

However, whereas this concept is erroneous, that of considering the perception of the taste and smell of the bait by a carp the same as it is by our own senses, there have, even among the aquaculture bunch, been similar misconceptions regarding how to stimulate feeding in carp. In fact it's very easy to think of carp in the same way as we do ourselves. When we consider how a carp would behave to danger, we think about how we would respond. When we wonder where the carp might be in the lake, we think about where we would be at a particular time of the day or season. This is often why we fail as anglers, but what is true, is that by constantly comparing carp to human, or vice versa, we are able to make some progress regarding improving tactics, tackle and bait, even though we might only get it right some of the time. This comparison does help us to understand though and that's why I'll do it several times here as a means of better explaining some things. However, where in some cases the similarity between fish and humans is undeniable, in this particular topic of reception of stimuli in the water by the carp's olfactory and gustatory systems, jointly referred to as chemoreception, we have to reconsider.

The main difference between the perception of a smell by a human and by a carp is that with humans we're dealing with the transfer of molecules from one point to another through the air which is a gaseous medium. In other words, the thing that makes the smell, the object, is releasing part of itself and is moving through the air until it gets to receptors inside our nose which tell our brain what the object smells like. We can't smell things underwater and it's likely that a carp can't do the same in air meaning that the carp has evolved to sense smell in water and the human likewise in air. We can therefore say that both the perception of the smell in a carp is totally different from that in a human due to the different medium, the structure used to do the sensing and, most importantly, the properties of the substance being smelled, which can change greatly between being present in the air or in the water. These properties include the solubility of the same substance in water and that a smell is usually made up of a mixture of substances. Only some of these may be able to be detected by fish and, as a result, what

73

a carp is able to perceive in the water may be very different to what we perceive in the air.

In chapter 4 we'll discuss why each ingredient that we put into a bait has implications for our fishing and ultimately our angling success. As you'll see, very few substances have been shown to effectively influence the feeding response and the amount of feed or bait ingested. Therefore, it's important to understand what negative effects the inclusion of something that has no demonstrable benefit for carp attraction or nutrition might have apart for creating an appealing smell so that the angler buys the bait.

The human nose has a capacity to distinguish a very large range of different smells and to determine between similar odours of different intensities but not as many as some other land animals that have an even more acute sense of smell . It is clear that the carp's sense of smell is able to determine a 'scent' over a greater distance than a human nose and that it's able to differentiate between as many if not more types of 'odour'. If the sense of taste that the carp possesses is to be used as a reference, it's possible that the sense of smell in fish is hundreds of times more acute than that of a human. It's also likely that the types of smell which each are able to detect are probably those which are most valuable to recognise. In the carp's case, these are those which have relevance for social behaviour, for example the detection of pheromones released by other fish at mating time, the smell of a predator, as well as those associated with the location of food.

Within the nares of the fish, which are the equivalent of our nostrils, there are sensors that can detect different substances. Among the different sensors that have been identified in the carp olfactory system are receptors which are involved with feeding. These are diverse and respond to a wide range of different substances. In the same way as many of those which have an effect on the taste buds and are processed by the gustatory system, it's been found that amino acids are particularly active and the majority are able to bind with receptors in the olfactory organ. Wherever there is life and death, you can find amino acids and that means that fish associate them with food, be it living or dead.

This capacity to identify a wide range of amino acids as well as other substances is an evolutionary advantage because it allows the fish to sense the location of not only a diversity of food which will produce amino acids in various combinations but also other signals that might allow the fish to stay out of danger or locate companions.

Threshold level is the term given to the concentration of a substance that is possible to detect. In the case of carp, the olfactory organ is able to locate concentrations of between 10^{-7} to 10^{-9} M which would be equivalent for some amino acids of one litre of the substance in ten million litres of water, or in other words a teaspoon of the substance in a swimming pool that measured ten metres by five metres by one metre deep. The threshold level for taste is higher, meaning that for stimulation of the gustatory system to occur, the carp would have to experience a higher concentration than that of a particular stimulant. It makes sense then that olfaction is something that a carp uses for initial sensing of 'smell', allowing the fish to determine the direction from which the stimulus is coming and to act on it and then as it nears the source, gustation takes over or is used in conjunction with olfaction. The mistake that many researchers made when they began to look at the taste preference in fish was very similar to the mistake that anglers make when they sniff a boilie, or add to it a substance that stimulates the angler's sense of smell without knowing what kind of effect, whether acceptance or rejection, it might have on the carp. Researchers began by testing the classic taste substances on fish, which, as you might guess, were the same substances that were used for testing taste preference of humans.

When you're at school, you're told that the tongue is able to sense sweet, sour, salty and bitter on different parts of it. So, when researchers began testing on fish, they used the corresponding substances in an attempt to provoke similar reactions which were measured. For this they use inert pellets containing test substances and then they count the number of times the pellets are accepted or rejected by the fish during a set period of time. This is an indicator of taste preference or palatability of the taste substance.

With time, they began to look at other substances and found that amino acids had a much more intense effect on fish. Also, they discovered a number of other things about this diverse group of substances that are relevant for the angler and the bait manufacturer, whether that be at home or industrially. They found, for example, that there were very different reactions of each fish to each amino acid and that even closely related fish, such as two species of trout or two different species of cyprinid often reacted very differently to different aminos. They also discovered that there were different reactions to acid, basic and neutral amino acids and that there were also very different reactions to different isomers of each amino acid. An isomer is a version of molecule which has the same components but a different structure. This means that a substance can have the same molecular formula but different structural formulas and this can give each isomer different properties. In the case of amino acids, they can have L-isomers or D-isomers. And with respect to the stimulation of both the gustatory and olfactory systems, it's the L-isomers that were shown to be particularly effective.

So, as anglers, what important information have we found out so far about these systems? Firstly, that both smell and taste are important. Secondly, that amino acids provoke a much more intense response than the classic taste substances and thirdly, that only certain amino acids are stimulatory and this depends on their chemical and structural properties. At this point, I imagine that you just want me to tell you the ones to put in your bait and which ones to leave out. Don't worry, I'll get to that very soon.

Most of the talk about amino acids is about their inclusion in the bait mix and not in a dip or soak. Anglers talk about which amino acid might be missing from a carp's diet and how much it might need and it's all about making sure that none of them are lacking because of what you put in the bait. Now, I might not have made as much bait as some or caught as many thirties as others, but I can tell you that the potential of amino acids in a bait is as chemosensory stimulants and not in the bait itself. As I see it, once you have satisfied the protein requirement of the fish and ensured that the essential amino acids in the protein source

76

satisfy the requirements that I've included in the appendix (table 2), and you make the relevant adjustment for digestibility, then there's nothing much left to be said for amino acids in the mix itself. The baits that are sold to the public probably have little if any individual amino acids added in order to boost amino levels to requirement level. This is not a complaint. In the aquaculture industry, the same thing happens because it's often just too expensive. Instead, protein sources are mixed in order to provide the right amino acid profile We'll have a look at this in greater detail in chapter 4.

The information regarding the stimulatory effects of some of the amino acids is so overwhelming that it's impossible to deny or ignore. It's for that reason that there's such great potential in carp fishing for amino acids that has until now been underexploited. In five or ten years from now, those of us who are still around will look back and laugh at the things we're using now and the concoctions that we're launching out into the water, in the same way as some of us smile at the thought of the monkey climbers or Dacron hooklinks we used to use.

Before we look at stimulation and rejection, it's important for me to add that fish have been classified into two groups regarding their olfactory and gustatory reaction to amino acids, although this could similarly be applied to other substances on a case by case basis. The classification is simple: the first is 'broadly tuned' and responds to a wide range of substances and the second is 'narrowly tuned', responding to a small number of amino acids. The carp belongs to the latter group, since only a small number of amino acids have been found to be stimulatory to the fish.

It's for this reason that I feel that many bait producers are missing the mark, for whatever reason. They are including substances which boost aminos and in doing so may be including amino acids that do nothing at all, or even worse, provoke rejection by the carp. Commonly used mixtures include minamino, liquid fish extracts and others. There is no reason for these substances to be stimulatory if they do not include only the positively stimulatory aminos or amino acids that in conjunction with the former can increase the response by what is called synergism, where the effect of one enhances or magnifies the effect of the other, and exclude those aminos that cause rejection.

c. Stimulation and rejection

As you get older, you tend to forget certain things. I have trouble remembering the names of people I knew fifteen years ago at university and many of those from my childhood are already forgotten. What I don't have trouble remembering though, are those experiences which resulted in very strong positive or negative feelings.

I'm pretty sure that other animals experience something similar, and events which mark them deeply, such as a near escape from a predator or even capture by an angler, are more difficult to forget than day to day banality. As we saw in chapter 1, memories from negative experiences are particularly important for learning and developing and helping to avoid mistakes in the future and preserve the fish from harm. In the same way there are memories associated with feeding that remind the fish what is worth eating and what is not. And at the same time, there's an innate (inborn) signal from each of the potential food items in the lake which influences the fish when it has to choose whether to accept or reject what's on offer.

A very wide range of substances have been tested as possible attractants for fish of many different species and it's been possible to differentiate those which result in acceptance (positive stimulation) from those that produce the opposite reaction of rejection (negative stimulation). And if we compare the amount of research carried out in this area, we find that almost all of it has been directed at those species of importance in fish farming. Luckily for us, our carp, *Cyprinus carpio*, is one of those farmed in greatest numbers and for that reason we have a large amount of information at our disposal that we can apply to our fishing.

For me, of all the things that I've read on carp in both the mainstream press and scientific papers, the topics that really get me excited are those about attractants and appetite. This is because these two subjects are crucial to our sport. If the fish hasn't any appetite, then it isn't hungry, so it won't feed and that makes catching it impossible. But if we use an attractant or stimulant, is it possible that the lack of appetite could be reversed and that we could intervene and turn an inappetant fish into one that feeds? That desire is what I like about these two themes. They are very much related to each other, intriguing and highly relevant to us as anglers.

In the aquaculture industry, this greater amount of research has led to a number of advancements in these two areas. For example, in appetite, the industry is looking at ways to modify the production of hormones that the fish secretes in order to increase feed intake. As a result, the fish could grow faster and more efficiently. Also, increasing the amount of food that a fish ingests can also reduce the amount of wasted feed and the environmental impact that this can produce. Then, in the field of stimulants, a large number of substances have been tested, but up until now, no 'Substance X', a magical miraculous ingredient, which would be the answer to every carp angler's prayers has appeared. Therefore, although I've never worked on the inside of a bait company, where they apply a much lower research budget compared to the aquaculture industry, I can hazard a guess that they have not found 'Substance X' either, even though they might make out that they have.

The other thing to bear in mind is that of those substances for which some kind of positive stimulatory effect has been identified, this has more often than not been shown to exist in other species apart from carp. If we look only at carp, then the number of substances that can cause an undoubtable increase in the intensity of the feeding response in our carp as a result of chemoreceptive stimulation can be counted on two hands.

Also, the fact that a substance appeals to just a few species shows us that taste preference is highly diverse and we should therefore not generalise about stimulation, and just because a particular feed additive caused some yellowfin tuna to eat ten percent more, it doesn't mean that it will obviously be great for carp attraction and feeding. A wide diversity of fish has evolved and it's not possible to talk about fish in general with regards to stimulation, due to the species specific nature of this subject. Not only has taste preference been shown to differ between species, but also between different geographically distributed populations of the same species. Therefore, we can say that taste preference is specific, but at the same time subject to modification based on their location and in the same way those substances that cause stimulation or rejection would be expected to vary according to distribution.

The results of research into this kind of variation suggest that the gustatory response to different substances is genetically specific with only a small amount of variability. Studies which support this have looked at variation between different geographical populations of fish (e.g. Brown trout, *Salmo trutta* (Kasumyan & Sidorov, 2005) and even comparative analysis between species living in the same body of water and sharing the same food sources (e.g. Bridcut & Giller, 1995). It would be expected that the preferences of two species preferentially consuming a shared food item would be the same or at least similar, but that's not true.

In the natural situation, amino acids are important indicators of the presence of food and it's particularly interesting that different fish species display extremely different responses to specific amino acids and these responses show no clear relationship between the natural diet of species of fish, including carp, and the response to particular amino acids. Neither is there a clear correlation between trophic classification (whether the fish is a carnivore, omnivore or herbivore) and the response to different amino acids in the way of active preference or rejection. This would suggest that each species possesses positive and negative preferences for each substance and it's therefore necessary to carry out research of each species and not by family or trophic classification.

The response of carp to different amino acids has been shown to be diverse, depending on the acidity and isomeric properties or each amino. Amino acids include acidic, basic and neutral variants and also D- and L-isomers. General findings indicate that only alpha amino acids are highly stimulatory, that L-isomers are always more stimulatory than D-isomers and the stimulatory effectiveness is not directly related to their essentiality. This means that, despite what anglers might think, a carp will not actively seek out with greater intensity an amino acid that is lacking from its diet or even one that the fish is simply unable to synthesise itself and must be consumed in the diet. Their taste preference has nothing to do with what natural foods are present in the lake or river, what it requires nutritionally or what its body is able to produce. Preference is genetic with some geographical variation. This means that all *Cyprinus carpio* will be turned on and off by the same substances wherever they are found, albeit to different amounts. Between different strains of the same carp, there may be small differences in this respect and there may also be some geographical variation. In both cases, this is not expected to be extreme. This means that in different lakes and rivers in different regions, countries or hemispheres, there is likely to be some degree of taste preference variation. This may be greater if the carp in each place are genetically different strains. However, the general rules regarding substances that cause stimulation or rejection by the carp can be applied to all places.

You might say that I'm wrong, that a bait will work on one lake but not on another. But the thing is that here I'm not talking about bait. I'm not even talking about flavourings. I'm talking about the substances within the bait or within the flavour that have been shown to cause feeding intensity to increase or decrease and I believe those to be generally the same in any lake or river where carp are present and anglers are trying to catch them.

As a result, as anglers we should be guided by these substances in bait choice, bait formulation and what we apply to our bait in the form of dips, soaks and glugs.

The response of carp to different amino acids as well as the detection thresholds of different amino acids have been studied (Marui *et al.*, 1983; Kasumyan & Morsi, 1996). It has also been shown that mixtures of different amino acids can have a synergistic or antagonistic effect. This means that mixing certain aminos can have a cumulative effect regarding their potency or they can counteract each other, nullifying the stimulatory effect. Also, each fish species possesses a threshold detection level to each substance which is particularly variable between species. These thresholds have been found to be highly variable and so have the intensities of responses to stimulation. The reasons for this remain unclear. For example, considering an amino acid shown to be a general positive stimulant to cyprinids, L-cysteine, the threshold detection concentration in common carp was shown to be 10 mM (millimolar), but in tench, a cyprinid that commonly inhabits the same water bodies as the common carp, the threshold concentration was shown to be 25 mM which is two and a half times higher (Kasumyan & Prokopova, 2001).

It was also thought that those substances that are produced by the principal food items of a particular fish species would be those which cause greatest attraction, but it's not the case either. With carp we would expect that the amino acids released by detritus and invertebrates that live on the bottom of lakes and rivers would be the ones to use to attract the fish. The problem with this is that the carp eats such a wide selection of different items, composed of every possible amino acid that it's difficult to know which to consider. Even carnivorous fish consume a similarly wide range of items and no relationship has been found either between the substances that stimulate them in feeding and those that their prey items contain.

Several methods have been utilized for the experimental determination of fish preference to different taste stimuli, such as the orientation of carp to amino acids in a channel (Saglio et al., 1990) by inserting electrodes into the facial nerves of the fish to detect stimulation upon exposure to different amino acids (Funakoshi et al., 1981) and the palatability of pellets impregnated with different taste substances to carp (Kasumyan & Morsi, 1996). Studies with these substances and others have permitted some threshold detection levels to be determined in common carp. However, the availability of a method that allows the standardised testing of general substances that would be applicable to the feed and bait manufacturing industries in a practical manner is lacking. This would provide several advantages over the methods mentioned above including non-invasiveness and greater comparability. Maybe in the future, alternative methods will become available which will help us towards advancement in understanding taste preference in fish. Hopefully, this will enable the responses to different substances to be quantified more precisely and allow comparison between species which will be useful and applicable to both the aquaculture feed and angling bait industries.

However, the information that has been collected using these different methods has indicated which substances are those that cause stimulation and rejection in different species of fish, including carp. The classical stimuli that have been defined and tested in vertebrates are the flavours sweet, bitter, sour, and salty. To these, recent interest has been in 'umami', what the Japanese, who are world leaders in food research of many kinds, have promoted and which is now known as the 'fifth taste'. Umami means 'pleasant savoury taste' with the key stimulating substances for umami being a mixture of glutamates (derived from glutamic acid) and nucleotides (the units that make up molecules like DNA). Umami is considered different from saltiness. If you have eaten Pot Noodle or Doritos, you will recognise umami, since it's a main ingredient of the flavour of those products. Both the internal and external taste buds of the human tongue and those of the carp are able to sense umami.

Of the five basic tastes, the mechanisms of chemosensory signal transduction are understood in greater detail for sweet, bitter and umami. These mechanisms have been decoded through work with mammals and only recently are they being investigated in fish. In the case of sweet, bitter and umami, receptors have been identified that can sense these tastes. It is suggested that for those flavours that are less well understood (sour and salty), taste signal transduction may occur in a different way, using channels instead of receptors for salty and acidification of membranes in the case of sour tastes.

Regarding the classical taste substances, the responses to these have been studied. In an experiment with twenty-seven species of fish, including the common carp, palatability in the form of ingestion or rejection of food pellets containing each of the tastes showed high variability between species, including closely related species such as those of the same family (e.g. cyprinids) (Kasumyan, 1997). The results showed a positive response of carp to citric acid (sour) and to a lesser extent calcium chloride (bitter) and sodium chloride (salty) and a negative response to sucrose (sweet).

Among the substances that have been studied, the majority of these include representatives of these five flavours. However, other substances which have interested workers include organic acids (Kasumyan & Prokopova, 2001), nucleosides and nucleotides (Carr *et al.*, 1996) and betaine (Barnard, 2006).

With regards to organic acids, the results showed similar high variability even between closely related species, with the same tendency also being shown for amino acids (Kasumyan & Morsi, 1996), which have become the group of substances that have now replaced classical taste substances as the most promising candidates for incorporation in both aquaculture feeds and angling baits. In the case of carp, the species showed the highest preference for L-cysteine and L-proline and a total of six amino acids were found to act as stimulants to the fish (alanine, cysteine, glutamine, proline, aspartic acid, glutamic acid). All of these were L-isomers and none of these are essential amino acids. Seven amino acids were found to act as deterrents (tryptophan, arginine, threonine, methionine, phenylalanine, serine and valine).

This study merits further comment since it answers many questions that anglers continue to ask regarding attraction of carp and feeding stimulation. An earlier study by Marui *et al.* (1983) led to the classification of carp as a fish which can be considered as having a limited response range regarding the amino acids that cause attraction. In that study he determined that these were proline, alanine, cysteine, glutamate and glycine. In addition, the investigator considered betaine as stimulatory. Betaine is well known in carp angling and is widely used. It's a methylated amino acid that has been shown to increase food intake in several species of fish including carp and as a feeding attractant in others, particularly in marine species and salmonids (see chapter 4).

Marui *et al.* (1983) included glycine in their list of stimulatory amino acids in carp, but in the later study by Kasumyan & Morsi (1996), this was assigned to list of indifferent aminos, or in other words, those that had no effect regarding acceptance or rejection. However, in both of these studies, there is no doubt about the other amino acids considered.

With regards to L-cysteine, this substance showed highest consumption of pellets and the highest palatability index of any of the amino acids tested. L-proline was in second place. Of these two amino acids, cysteine is detected by both the olfactory and gustatory systems but proline is not detected by the olfactory system .

So, it's clear that the candidates for incorporation in baits should be alanine, cysteine, glutamine, proline, aspartic acid, glutamate and glutamic acid as attractants and in the case of betaine, we could utilise the substance as both an attractant and a feeding stimulant with implications for growth, although information regarding betaine as specific attractant in carp does not go much further than the studies by Marui *et al.* (1983) and Barnard (2006). It must be remembered that all these studies refer to the use of free amino acids, which means not part of a protein and therefore they have greatest relevance for use as liquid coatings for baits or alternatively in the bait itself. However, it's my opinion that the interchange of taste substances between the interior and exterior (water) of a boilie is particularly slow and weak due to the impermeability of the boilie's surface and doesn't allow for important amounts of those substances to be released into the water with the exception of the immediate vicinity of the bait. Chopped boilies, on the other hand, will greatly increase the rate of leaching of whatever the bait contains and any free amino acids included in the bait will be released much more effectively.

In the natural situation and therefore that found in recreational angling, the water column will give rise to a mixture of different substances and therefore the carp has to decipher and process a complex signal in order to feed effectively. The fish is clearly able to do this. However, this means that in order for feed and bait manufacturers to benefit from the understanding of the chemoreceptive response in carp, then it's necessary for them to consider the complexity of the stimulus since their bait has, in some way, to stand out from the rest of the signal.

What is evident is that this complex signal can have an important effect on a bait's own signal, for better and for worse. The complex signal is referred to as background, in the same way as background noise. In our case, let's call it 'background taste'. I have previously described the water found in the places we fish as a 'soup' because of the diversity of chemical substances that make it up, which include much more than the H2O that people associate as being water. There are some very productive lakes and rivers which are not a weak soup but in terms of the substances they contain are much 'thicker'. This myriad of substances obviously infers some kind of smell and taste to the water, to the fish and other organisms with the senses to detect it. You would expect that the more substances that are in there, the thicker the soup, then the 'louder' is the background taste.

This background taste is made up of many substances and maybe many hundreds of substances, even thousands. If I were to fish for carp in a place that was one of the thicker soups, then it's easy to image that it would be more difficult to cause attraction. Even the substances that have been added to your bait or glug in order to cause attraction may be already present, and in higher concentrations to that which you're presenting in or on your bait. This is a problem.

Studies have shown that both the olfactory and gustatory systems of carp can become saturated by an amino acid and that increasing the levels further can result in no further increase in stimulation. The systems become numbed to the stimulant, since, as with any biological system that is based on receptors, there's an optimum range for detection. When that range is exceeded, the receptors become overloaded and any increase in concentration can no longer cause an effect or result in any modification. It's a bit like adding sugar to your cup of tea. As far as sweetness, there's a big difference between no sugar and one sugar and one sugar and three sugars, but the difference between ten and twenty sugars (if for some reason you wanted that many sugars in your tea) is minimal as far as sweetness. That is because the taste buds of the human tongue and those of the carp function based on receptors. And just as yours can become saturated by the sugar in your tea, the same thing can happen to those of the carp for sweetness and other substances including those which we've identified here as important taste stimulants in this particular fish.

As we'll see further on, it's clear that a great bait is strong in two things: nutrition and attraction. Stimulation is a result of the presence of substances that have been shown to cause an increase in the amount of bait ingested or the length of time that the fish are feeding. Both of these have a positive influence on our angling success, since the length of time spent feeding and the intensity with which they feed ultimately increase the amount of bait consumed. This in turn increases the probability that our hookbait, and more importantly our hook, will end up in the fish's mouth.

It's therefore apparent that for attraction to work at its best, it needs to be one of two things. Firstly, the substances that the bait contains and which are used in an accompanying glug need to be proven stimulants in carp. And secondly, that they are used in concentrations that result in the greatest possible stimulation in the carp without exceeding levels that may cause rejection as opposed to attraction. This is not an easy thing to achieve unless you know a carp that talks, but for the substances that I've named here, threshold levels exist. It is also possible to find, among the studies that have already been carried out, the ranges over which the same substances cause stimulation. I have included a summary of threshold levels and these ranges in the appendix (table 7), which will, if you choose to use any of those substances mentioned in your own baits, allow you to know how much is too much and how much is too little.

The use of an attractant on a particular water with success does not automatically mean that it can be used on another with equal success, due to the background taste that we have already referred to. Where the signal is particularly complex, or where the naturally occurring levels of attractant are higher than those used in your bait, then the results are not going to be as expected. This is because this background taste is undetectable by the angler without taking a water sample and sending it for analysis. The other thing to remember is that the background taste levels fluctuate and change throughout the year. This is like saying at some time the soup will be thicker and at others it will be thinner and it won't always have the same flavour. In the same way as the abundance of different aquatic organisms changes throughout the year, the background taste will change accordingly. If there is an algal bloom at some time of the year and that alga excretes a particular substance, then the water might be full of that. As a result the carp may find it much more difficult to distinguish a substance that would normally be a stimulant, even if it's present at the same levels.

On the other hand, a different water or even the same water during a different season is able to result in background taste that is completely different. Particularly in the winter, when all the aquatic plants are dead, only some invertebrates are left to feed the fish through the coldest months. At those times, maybe the signal is not as complex or the natural levels of attractants are lower, then it's maybe possible for the fish to locate the angler's attractant, and therefore bait, more easily. Another example is those lakes that are lower in nutrients. These are referred to as oligotrophic. Because they are lower in nutrients, which includes the free amino acids that might be present, it would, in theory, be easier for the signal from the attractant of an angler's bait to perpetuate and make the carp aware of its presence in a short time, certainly much shorter time than it would for a attractive bait to be located in a lake of river with a high level of background taste.

We began here by talking about the differences between smell and taste and one of those is the threshold level for each substance that is detected by olfaction and gustation. The levels that can be detected by olfaction are lower than those that can be detected by gustation. This makes sense, since when the fish is close to the source of the stimulation, it's exposed to higher concentrations and therefore a higher threshold is sufficient.

Although these concepts have important implications for understanding the feeding response in fish, and more specifically in carp, they require further research. Advances in the understanding of the chemoreceptory system in carp have been based on visually observed responses to external stimuli measured in the different ways described previously. Chemical signals from food items are responsible for causing changes in carp movement, increased or decreased appetite and ingestion of greater or lesser quantities of food as a consequence as they are with other fish. According to studies in this area, it's been shown that important differences exist between substances regarding palatability and responses to stimuli. This is relevant for both carp culture and angling, since it's in the interest of the feed producer to provoke a positive response (increased food consumption, higher growth, etc.) as a result of the food being administered. Similarly, in the case of the bait manufacturer, a positive stimulus will result in a higher probability of bait ingestion and subsequent capture of the target fish which both lead to more bait sales. Other similarities between the two fields exist and as we will continue to see, the research from the field of aquaculture can be applied to many different parts of the recreational angler's world for more successful angling.

Chapter Three

Feeding

Carp feed for the same reasons as we do, with the main one being to obtain enough energy to keep living. There are other consequences of feeding, but as anglers, what we should keep in mind is that feeding is primarily a search for energy.

That energy can be obtained from various sources. Some of these provide more than others and some hardly any at all. And in the same way that food provides fish with energy, it also requires energy to allow the energy that the food contains to be made available to the fish. Also, the fish has to locate that food and doing that requires energy too, just in the same way that in order to get to the supermarket you have to do some walking. But in the wild it's more difficult than a trip to the shops, and locating food may take time and require more energy to do than the fish receives for its efforts.

As a consequence of this, and using the experience that the fish has obtained throughout its life, it frequents the spots (called patches) that it has learned are likely to provide a net energy gain. This reduces energy expenditure and it's for this reason that carp frequent more productive areas. This changes as the abundance and diversity of the food items change throughout the year. If a carp is able to locate energy-rich food easily and quickly, then it's relatively simple for the fish to obtain what it needs, whereas feeding on small, energy-poor disperse food items such as plankton will be counterproductive.

This is relevant for the angler, since if he's able to provide food which is energy-rich, then he'll more than likely be able to attract fish into his swim, including the carp that he's hoping for. Additionally, if the food items that he's offering are relatively large, as is the case of boilies which usually exceed a centimetre in diameter, then energy requirements can be met relatively easily. And in the same way that the fish are able to learn through experience which areas of the lake or river are more productive, the same is true for areas which receive a regular input of high energy loose feed, and the carp soon come to consider it as a natural source of easily accessible nutrients such as protein, fat and carbohydrate.

a. Lake and water types

In Europe and the US the majority of carp fishing is done in lakes. Other popular waters are rivers and canals. River fishing for carp is popular in some areas but these are rivers that are slow flowing and wide since carp are a less common fish in faster-flowing bodies of water and streams. River fishing for carp can extend to tidal sections of rivers such as the Thames and carp have been shown not to have any problem with low salinities.

These days it's freshwater lakes that are the focus for much of our carp fishing. These can vary from small ponds and lagoons to extensive lakes such as the well-known Lake Cassien in France, which covers almost a thousand acres. There are several ways that these can be formed naturally including tectonic, volcanic and glacial activity although it's not my intention to cover these aspects in much detail here since I've done that previously elsewhere. What I would like to discuss here is the range of differences that exist in lakes, their water and bottom sediment types and the implications that these have for our fishing.

Lakes can be formed either naturally or artificially and in recent years the number of waters that have appeared as a result of human intervention by damming and flooding has increased dramatically. This is to some extent due to the increasing demand for drinking water and recreational space as the population increases. Artificial lakes that are made by flooding behind a dam are often called reservoirs and many lakes have been formed as a by-product of mineral extraction such as open pits and quarries. This can result in lakes that vary greatly in terms of depth and size and not all of these are the best design for angling but this depends very much on the foresight of the land owner and what activities are being considered for the site once it's flooded.

Some lakes formed artificially are done so with angling very much in mind. This requires a lake that is shallower than one that people are going to use for water sports. This reminds me of a lake that I fish which is multipurpose and receives everything from anglers to windsurfers and jet bikers, particularly in the summer. It also receives its fair share of campers and people barbecuing. The lake was formed as a result of gravel extraction for building the nearby motorway and the edges of the water are pretty much sheer down to six metres or so. I imagine that it's great for the boating activities that take place but for fishing it isn't the best but the truth is that it was never designed with angling particularly in mind.

However, the growth of angling in Europe has brought about the proliferation of artificial lakes specifically designed for angling. They are purpose built lakes which include features such as islands and gullies which make the lakes more interesting and an additional challenge for fish location as if adding another dimension to the fishing experience. These come with quality pegs which have wood-chips to enable you to get your banksticks and bivvy pegs in the ground.

Maybe commercial fisheries like these aren't for everybody but they are certainly convenient, safe and usually productive places to fish. They're designed for angling and are comfortable places to fish. In many cases, these combine activities for the rest of the family, a restaurant or bed and breakfast. On the downside they're that comfortable that it is often difficult to get on them because they can be very popular. Also, they often don't provide the same detachment and peace and quiet that fishing lakes have traditionally offered.

They are also a sign that times have changed and fishing has become increasingly popular and commercial. At the same time, it shows how our lives have become busier and that spare time is becoming more valuable and scarce. For that reason many people are now starting to prefer these fisheries because they're often within a short drive from where people live and they'd prefer an extra hour on the bank than an extra hour in the car.

Another plus of these waters is that they're well stocked and offer the chance of several fish in a short session. These are often fast-growing strains of carp and because of greater competition for food, the carp are hungry for a longer length of time each day. This gives all levels of angler the possibility of fish with very little travelling and although a day's fishing on a commercial may be more expensive than an equivalent length of session on a season ticket water it's often worth it in terms of emotion. But in the same way, more traditional anglers may still prefer waters that lack any type of creature comforts and if given the choice, would prefer not having to see another soul for the length of their stay.

Naturally formed lakes vary greatly in size and depth depending on the way they were formed. They can also change with time as sediment accumulates in them and may require dredging if that happens too quickly. Silt is formed from the breakdown of organic material and can change the composition of the lake bottom if this is excessive. This natural process is speeded up when there's greater input of bait and disproportionate bait use can change both the water and sediment quality. These kinds of change affect the development and succession of plant and animal communities and the amount of food that's available for the fish in a lake.

Lake water levels vary from season to season and year to year. If rainfall increases, the lake level rises and vice versa. And both light and heat are two other variables that have an effect on the lake and its plant and animal communities, including the carp. As we have already seen, temperature is particularly important because it affects everything from metabolism and feeding rate of the animals in it to the water currents and stratification of the lake itself.

When the light which is absorbed rather than reflected is utilised by plants for photosynthesis, the consequence is we get changes in the abundance and coverage of aquatic plants. Light is also important for determination of feeding and reproductive rhythms in the carp, it indicates to the fish the time of day and year and allows the fish to use its sense of sight to locate, among other things, food and a mate. The transmission of different wavelengths of light through the water of the lake affects the perception of colours. For example in the depths of a lake, since the colour red is unavailable there, a red bait appears black.

As anglers we know that one lake can be very different from another and several factors affect our fishing experience and need to be considered at the moment of bait and technique choice. Obvious visible differences between lakes include practical variables such as the amount of plant life both in and around the lake which has implications for the ease of casting, possible locations for fish to frequent and rig design in order to be able to effectively place a bait in or close to weed beds. Also, much of carp fishing involves fishing on the bottom and the type of bottom, whether silt, clay or gravel means that it's better to consider certain setups rather than others.

The bottom type of a lake is related to the way that the lake was formed, the time that has passed since it was formed and the natural and human activities in and around the lake that have occurred since its formation. For example, a gravel pit that has been recently dug and filled with water will initially have a very hard, rocky bottom with an absence of sediment. However, new sediments can be added to the lake by way of the inflow which, if it's a stream or river, will transfer suspended solids to the lake which are then decanted out. This occurs because a narrow, fast-flowing stream has high energy but a lake is a low energy environment and therefore solids settle, with smaller less dense solids taking longer to do so, and heavy, denser particles such as sand decanting out much faster. Therefore, the composition of the solids will affect the clarity of the water. If they are very fine, then cloudiness can remain for some time.

The input of solids in this way is more probable after rainfall, with heavy rainfall causing not just inflow streams to swell but also the amount of runoff from neighbouring land to transport solids into the lake. Also, any industrial activities in the area which increase the amount of solids on the surface of the land, such as manuring or opencast mining, can mean that there is increased transport of these to rivers and lakes in the same catchment area when it rains. In the same way there's the risk of dissolved substances being transported with them, which may in some cases be toxic to water life.

Solids can be very different in composition and nature. Some are organic which means that they are from once living plants or animals. Typical examples are leaves and sticks which may be whole of fragmented. Others are inorganic and are simply earth and sediment from the erosion of rocks. All these might end up in the lake and decant to the bottom, eventually forming a layer of sediment that with time builds up. Larger solids can be degraded and eroded and particularly those of organic origin can become part of the lake silt.

Anglers are in general familiar with three types of sediment material: silt, clay and gravel. Silt is larger in particle size than clay but smaller than sand. Silt is granular and derived from soil or rock of a specific grain size and it may occur as soil or sediment suspended in the water column. Whereas clay is irregular, silt particles are the same size in all dimensions. Usually silt is black in colour which may be as a result of the type of rock from which it was formed or due to the amount of decomposing plant and animal material it contains. Silt can often have a bad smell for the same reason. One of the gases produced from decomposition is hydrogen sulphide which is the characteristic 'bad eggs' smell that you might have experienced.

Clay is finer in diameter (<4 micrometres) and usually brown in colour. It's derived from rocks that have been weathered over a long period of time. Due to its small size and low density it's more likely to find clay deposits in lakes, which are much lower energy environments than rivers. Another characteristic of clay is its plasticity, which occurs because water exists between the particles of clay and it can therefore be compressed.

The third type of bottom type which anglers commonly encounter is gravel. This is also a product of eroded rock but is of much larger particle size than the others, anywhere from 2 to 64 millimetres in diameter.

Since gravel pits which have been filled with water are one of the types of artificial lakes that are now extensively used for carp fishing, gravel will obviously make up at least some part of the lake bottom of these. However, these three types of sediment are not mutually exclusive and it's possible to find all three in the same place. This is why anglers often refer to a gravel patch which is an area of gravel surrounded by softer sediment which may be silt or clay or a mixture of both.

Whatever the substrate type, the bottom of the lake or river is exposed to deposition from the water column. This may either be from the inflow or runoff as we have already seen, but also as a result of material generated within the water body itself such as excretion by animals and decomposition of dead animal and plant matter. The amount of this will depend on how much life there is in the lake. For example, if there are frequent algal blooms and a large amount of invertebrate and fish life, the amount of sediment build up on the bottom can be significant. However, in an oligotrophic lake where nutrients are scarce and plant and animal growth are correspondingly slow, the amount of sediment build up may be negligible. It's also worth remembering that as sediment is deposited, a part of it, the organic part, is decomposed and nutrients such as phosphorus and nitrogenous substances are released back into the water column and can then be reabsorbed by phytoplankton. If the rate of deposition is higher than the rate of decomposition then there will be a gradual build up of new sediment and the layer will get deeper. The deposition of organic and inorganic material will therefore vary between different lakes and different times of the year with the highest deposition at the end of summer when plankton dies off and sinks to the bottom.

The type of sediment also determines to a certain extent the animals that live in or on it. As the amount of organic material increases, the diversity of invertebrates will increase accordingly. However, when the levels of accumulated organic material become very high, this leads to environmental conditions that only very tolerant animals are able to develop in. This is because the accumulation causes a depletion of oxygen both on the surface of the sediment and within it. The deeper you go in the sediment, the lower are the oxygen concentrations that you'll find there. Some invertebrates need relatively high oxygen levels to survive and develop normally, such as mayfly and stonefly nymphs, whereas others can tolerate and, in some cases prefer low or almost non-existent oxygen concentrations. Animals that fit into that category include snails and bloodworms.

Apart for the preference for low oxygen (anaerobic) conditions, the accumulation of organic matter is associated with higher amounts of silt which are produced by the decomposition of organics. Silt has a fine particle size, which is easier for some animals to move around in whereas others will stay away or will be killed by substrates like that. This is because some use breathing structures which become clogged by the fine silt and as a result they suffocate. These restrictions therefore affect the distribution of aquatic animals in a lake and in doing so modify the food supply of the carp. As a result, there'll be some areas that allow the carp to feed on some organisms whereas in others, different natural food items will be more plentiful.

Each lake is therefore unique because of a combination of the way that it was formed, the amount of water and sediment input from natural or human sources and the age of the lake. These are clearly different if we're talking about a lake that was formed naturally maybe thousands of years ago or an artificially formed lake that was finished last week.

In some lakes, the freshwater input is very low compared with others and as a result the water replenishment (exchange rate) is much slower. This will be a result of the size of the inflow, which might be a river or a spring, and also where the lake is located. Rainfall is directly proportional to this rate of water exchange and it's not the same for a lake located in a rainy part of northern Europe compared with one that's bordering on a desert, which apart from lower freshwater input will additionally experience higher rates of evaporation.

Waters that contain higher nutrient levels, particularly nitrates and phosphates, are able to sustain a higher abundance, diversity and growth of plant and animal life and therefore the carp is able to choose between a larger variety of food items. These waters are referred to by anglers as being 'rich'. One of the positive consequences of high food availability is that the carp in those kinds of lakes increase in size faster than those with a low availability of natural food. On a negative note, this more plentiful and more extensive menu provides the fish with a greater and safer choice of food compared with waters with little plant and animal life and a lack of biomass to sustain carp growth. This can make fish in rich waters much harder to catch than those where there is little natural food on offer.

On more heavily fished waters the input of bait in excessive amounts can change the water quality and sediment profile of lakes. In the same way, this organic input can make the bottom siltier and detrimental for the fauna that lives there, as a consequence altering sediment health and the diversity of the animals that the carp feed on. This highlights the importance of using baits that combine nutrition and attraction as a way of increasing the proportion of bait that is consumed rather than left uneaten. I've spoken here about the combined benefits of nutrition in a bait since if the fish becomes dependent on a bait and it doesn't have to look elsewhere for an alternative or replacement in the form of another angler's bait or natural food, these benefits are fourfold. These are 1) improved health and growth of the fish, 2) improved catch rate in terms of numbers and size of fish for anglers, 3) improved profitability and profile of commercial fisheries where the bait is used and 4) increased sales and improved status of the bait producer(s). To these it's possible to include a fifth benefit which is that of reduced environmental impact by using a nutritionally adequate bait. Compared with other baits, if more of it is eaten and there's less wastage, then there's less chance of it altering water and sediment quality therefore having a direct effect on lake health and appearance and ensuring that the ecosystem is less affected.

b. Competition for food

A lake or river shares many characteristics with terrestrial environments. Both are considered ecosystems, meaning that they're composed of living elements such as plants and animals and non-living parts such as soil, water and air. Both of these are made up of food webs which contain groups of plants and animals of different trophic levels. Examples of these are primary producers (also called autotrophs) that are able to produce complex molecules such as sugars from simple ones using energy from sunlight or other chemical reactions. In the aquatic environment, autotrophs are represented by algae and aquatic plants and on land autotrophs include grasses, trees and other plants.

Autotrophs are consumed by herbivores and then herbivores are eaten by carnivores. These animals that are unable to fix carbon and instead use the organic carbon (protein, lipid and carbohydrate) produced by autotrophs are called heterotrophs. In this way, energy is passed from the plants to animals and then to higher consumers as they prey on other animals. Apart from the herbivores and carnivores, omnivores such as carp which consume a mixture of both plant and animal material also exist.

Because various plants are eaten by the same herbivore, many animals may be eaten by the same carnivore and an even greater selection might be consumed by a particular omnivore, there is a certain amount of overlapping between different groups of animals. This leads to the formation of what are called food webs which is an ecological community representing the feeding links and therefore the flow of energy through the system. After passing to the highest consumer, death and decay of those individuals results in nutrients returning to the environment to be reutilised. Decomposition is brought about by a group of organisms called decomposers, which includes bacteria, fungi and worms and these form a very important part of the food web. On land, decomposers allow nutrients to return to the soil, which are then taken up by terrestrial plants. In the water the same process occurs and these can form part of the bottom sediment where they can be taken up by aquatic plants. Alternatively they remain dissolved in the water column where they are absorbed by algae. In that way energy is able to re-enter the food web.

The links between the different organisms in a food web express the feeding relationships in an ecosystem. They show which animal eats which other plants or animals and at the same time which animal or animals it's eaten by. Trophic levels are therefore formed where an organism's position in a food web is determined by its relationship with the other plants and animals present in a particular ecosystem. Whereas the positions of autotrophs, herbivores and carnivores within a food web can be determined more or less precisely, the position of an omnivore is much less easy to determine because it preys on a larger diversity of organisms and consumption of each may vary with time. This variation is often due to seasonal changes in the abundance of food items in a particular locality.

In the aquatic ecosystem, we are able to observe the presence of both the plants and animals that form part of the carp's diet and also those animals that prey on the carp. The importance of predators decreases as the carp grows. For example when the fish is recently hatched it can be preyed upon by large aquatic invertebrates such as beetles as well as smaller predatory fish of different species, such as perch. As the fish grows it becomes a more interesting food item for larger predatory fish and mammals such as the otter. Although adult specimen carp are more or less out of danger from large predatory fish due to their size, otters will attack even the biggest carp to feed on them partially.

Due to the carp's poorly defined position in the food web as a result of their omnivorous nature, many of the food items that they consume are also eaten by a variety of other animals. This forms the first kind of competition that we will take a look at here, which is competition which results from diet sharing. This means that the available natural food is exploited by several animals that may or may not be as effective feeders on that particular item as the carp are. Therefore, food that can be consumed by the carp will depend on the abundance of competing organisms. The higher the number of competing animals then the greater is the reduction in the amount of food left for the carp. However, this will depend not only on the number of competing individuals but also on the size of the competing organisms.

If competing animals are smaller in size than the carp, then they will probably consume less of the shared food item than the carp but if they are more abundant, then the competitors may eat a larger share.

These competitors include animals of other classes as well as other fish species. In many lakes there is a mixture of different fish species present and many of these can be closely related species of cyprinid such as roach, rudd, tench and bream. These fish not only share a large part of their diet preferences with the carp but also have similar specialisations and limitations regarding feeding and can therefore feed with similar efficiencies. There is therefore a greater amount of competition than there would be if they were very different fish with less similar diet preferences.

Other animals also share the carp's diet either wholly or partially. These include waterfowl and other birds, small mammals, amphibians and reptiles where they are present, but not all of these are able to access the areas of the lake that the carp is able to. Water birds are able to dive a couple of metres below the surface but are not able to reach the deepest areas of a lake or river that a carp is able to without any problem. In a similar way, terrestrial birds, amphibians and reptiles may be able to obtain food from only the shallowest parts of the lake.

However, not only natural food but also angling bait is shared between different fish species and other animals. Carp fisherman know that small boilies can be used to catch tench and bream in particular and other baits such as maggots, worms and bread, which are used for carp fishing are non-selective and the angler can end up catching any of a wide range of species. What this means for a water is that the addition of bait results in the supplementation of the natural food. What percentage of the total amount of available food is made up of bait depends on a wide range of factors including the abundance of natural food, the number of anglers that fish a water, the frequency and duration of sessions and the amount of bait that each angler puts into the water. As we know, the amount of bait used by each angler can vary greatly since different anglers use different baiting tactics.

The amount of bait going into the water will vary with time of the year. This will increase during the summer when a larger number of anglers go fishing and in winter the bait input will decrease according to the lower number of anglers frequenting a water. The total amount of bait input will be eaten by a selection of animals including carp and the other fish species with a preference for whatever bait is being offered. The bait will likely not be consumed equally by all animals and those animals which either prefer the type of bait or are feeding more actively during the period that the bait becomes available will consume more. The amount of bait that is specifically eaten by carp will also depend not just on its availability and how it's preferred over natural food but also the number and sizes of carp that are present and are able to locate the bait when it's added to the water.

So, we can see that a large number of variables affect both types of competition, both between animals for natural food and bait and the competition that exists between bait and natural food. In the most favourable case for the angler, a lack of natural food and the lower abundance of competing species will result in easier fishing and a greater probability of the angler's bait being consumed by a carp rather than another fish.

What can we learn from this that will help us to improve our catch rate? Firstly, our choice of water will affect the numbers and size of carp that we catch. Waters with higher stocking densities of carp compared with other species will mean that there's an increased possibility of the bait being found and taken by a carp. Also, a higher density of carp will mean that greater competition exists between individuals and shoalmates. In this respect, competition means that the available food of either type will be in greater demand and ration size will be smaller. As a result, carp will feed for longer as they continue to satisfy their energy requirement.

Water choice also has an effect on the catch rate due to the amount of natural food present. Where this is lower, carp angling can be more effective because the fish will be on average more motivated to feed and will also be more likely to think that angling baits are natural sources of food, although this will depend on the amount of bait going into a water, its frequency and type.

Then there are the tactics that the angler can use to increase success. The angler can choose from a wide range of baits, some of which are more specific for carp. This is mainly due to the size of the bait and its texture. The use of boilies as a hookbait reduces interest from other species although the softer the bait, the easier it is for them to be whittled away by other species of fish and crustaceans. Harder baits last longer in the water, prevent water soaking into the bait more effectively and the external texture is a better deterrent to competing fish.

Not only bait choice but also rig design influences angling success in this respect. Smaller hooks and finer hooklengths may result in catching smaller fish and greater numbers of other species. Therefore, using a larger hook size in accordance with the larger size of the carp's mouth gape will tend to exclude individuals of non-target species.

Another technique is to make the bait more attractive to carp and at the same time less attractive to other species. This means using those substances that have been shown to be proven to cause a positive stimulatory effect in carp as far as attraction or the amount of feed consumed. These substances are discussed in chapters 2 to 4 of this book and information regarding their chemosensory properties has been included in the appendix. These substances can be included to the bait mix itself or the finished bait can be dipped in or mixed with the substance as the case may be. These increase the attractiveness of the bait or in other cases they increase the amount or feed that the fish consumes by increasing the fish's appetite. Some of the commercially available baits and groundbaits include these substances.

An alternative that anglers have to using these is to make their own. In that way an angler has greater control over which stimulants the carp in a particular water are exposed to. These substances have been shown to be specifically stimulatory to species and even between closely related species of fish there can be important differences in attraction and rejection (for a review of this subject see Kasumyan & Døving, 2003). Similarly, different strains of the same species of fish and the same fish in different geographical locations can react differently to the same substance. However, some of these have shown undeniable stimulatory responses in carp independently of location and strain.

Particularly in recent years, the number of alternatives for dipping, soaking and glugging baits has increased dramatically. In some cases these will increase the interest of carp and reduce those of other species. In others, there will be little if any discriminating effect between different species and all species will experience attraction, rejection or indifference depending on the substances that the dip, soak or glug includes.

Where the amount of natural food is lower in abundance or diversity, it makes sense that there will be a better reaction to our baits, especially if the angler is able to optimise both attraction and the nutritional properties of the bait. If this is done and the bait allows more optimal foraging in terms of energy then it's probable that the bait will be preferred over natural food despite it being a less safe option compared with natural food.

In this respect, specific conditions can greatly affect angling success. Among these, fish age, size and experience can have a bearing on the reaction to baits. On the positive side, carp are relatively fast-growing fish that in optimum conditions are easily able to consume five percent of their body weight per day. The fish that we are interested in catching are generally fish over ten pounds. This means that they're foraging for a good part of each day in order to satisfy their energy requirements and avoid discomfort. This benefits us because feeding fish are fish that can be caught and the more fish that feed can mean more fish on the bank. Additionally, carp are fish that are able to gain experience and as we have already seen, they feed in patterns, made up of repeated feeding in certain locations, at specific times of the day when the right environmental conditions present themselves. Consequently we can learn where to find them and by trial and error or by our own knowledge and experience we can increase the probability of capture by using certain baits and rigs.

The ability of a carp to use its experience in feeding has resulted over the years in anglers trying every tactic possible to capture them. They have climbed trees, used every ingredient imaginable in their baits and spent marathon periods of time by the water trying to achieve their objective. Carp learning has caused marriages to end and grown men to cry and go grey and bald. This learning can therefore work very much against the angler, especially when being caught previously has influenced the knowledge and experience of the carp that the angler is after.

However, the other way that an angler can affect his success is by good planning. This usually includes some kind of prebaiting strategy, at least on those waters that allow it. Prebaiting has several positive effects on angling. Since it means that bait is added regularly to the water, the carp are more likely to consider it a natural food and therefore a safer alternative to a novel bait that they have rarely or never encountered before. Also, if the carp consumes it and recognise its attractive or nutritional properties, then the fish is more likely to accept it again when the angler begins fishing. And if the carp is able to recognise that the bait is an energetically advantageous alternative over natural food, then it's more likely to prefer it, which would obviously be a huge benefit for an angler in such a situation.

Regarding competition, prebaiting increases the presence of a bait in a water and has the potential to form a 'natural' alternative to the real natural food items on offer. In that case, the feeding balance can move away from natural food and towards bait. This of course will depend on the characteristics of the bait. If prebaiting and fishing occur with baits that select for larger carp rather than smaller fish or other species, then this will also help the angler's cause.

Finally, it's necessary to summarise that competition between natural food items and bait and between different species of fish for the same food items, including bait are just two considerations that an angler has to consider if he's to improve his catch results. Undeniably these are important considerations since they determine to some extent bait and rig choices and tactics and if they can be understood for each water where an angler fishes, then their comprehension and interpretation can have a direct effect on catch rate. Additional important considerations are the environmental and internal factors that affect feeding and appetite in the fish as well as how the carp feeds, which are covered in the following sections.

c. Feeding response and rhythms

No animal feeds continuously 24 hours a day but rather as a result of a motivation to feed. In the natural environment feeding motivation, or what we would refer to as hunger, is a result of two things. The first is the physical discomfort caused by the emptying of the gut and the second is the fish realising that it lacks energy and it needs to be replenished. This is achieved by fish ingesting food and thus beginning to fill the gut, providing the fish with the energy that it requires at the same time which will depend on the type and amount of food ingested.

You may think that the carp feeds whenever it feels hunger, which is true to a certain extent, although the timing of feeding motivation is not solely dependent on hunger and a number of factors affect when the fish is motivated to feed. These are described as coming from the carp itself (endogenous) or from environmental factors that affect both the motivation and timing of feeding (exogenous).

If the angler is able to understand both how the carp internally reacts to hunger and how the changes in environmental factors affect the feeding response, then it's possible that we are able to anticipate carp feeding and obtain better catch results. Some anglers may already know the best times to fish on the lakes they fish, both at different times of the day and different times of the year. Even so, I'll provide you here with some additional information which shows how the rhythms that feeding is dependent on are related to our fishing and how we can take best advantage of them.

The carp's environment is filled with variables that change hourly, daily, monthly and seasonally. Even during a single session we're able to notice how the lake changes in certain respects but some of the environmental (abiotic) parameters such as light, temperature and oxygen concentrations fluctuate according to very specific times and periods. Also there are biological (biotic) factors such as the abundance of food items and interactions with shoalmates and other species that can affect the timing of feeding.

For example, if the fish in a lake feed during the day and at night but the pike are more active during the day then the fish might prefer to feed at night because there is less chance of being eaten. Also, if the carp feeds on a particular invertebrate that is easier to locate during the daytime, then feeding during the day might be preferred. These two examples are a result of the activities of other animals (predator and prey) but the determining factor is the effect of light intensity on their activities (day/light or night/dark).

Apart from the fluctuations caused by exogenous factors, fish maintain an internal control of feeding, in particular related to increased appetite (the need to feed) and satiation (the need to not feed), which is controlled by hormones and associated with an internal pacemaker. This has the job of processing the information from various biological sensors and receiving feedback from the fish itself to determine whether it should feed or not. Therefore the feeding response is a result of both exogenous factors and endogenous ones which are detected by the sensors.

These sensors include 1) the pineal organ that we have already mentioned, which is able to sense light intensity and also temperature, 2) the retinas in the fish's eyes, which also determine light intensity and changes in it, and 3) other photoreceptors that are not located in the pineal organ or the retina. Each of these is able to be stimulated by the corresponding external influence and vary daily or seasonally. For example, the central pacemaker will receive signals from all three but the amount of feeding is determined not by just one of the signals but the combined signal of all three plus the information that the carp receives from the gut and brain telling it how much food is in the gut and what the energy levels of the fish are.

The external influences are therefore detected by the pineal organ, retinas and other receptors and these allow synchronisation of a central pacemaker. This receives information from the exterior stimuli and places a demand on the fish to fulfil an energy requirement. Since the pacemaker is in touch with both what the fish contains (the energy stores) and the brain of the fish, it's able to tell it how much energy is required. If it requires a lot, the fish will feed and once the energy demand is satisfied, the fish will stop feeding.

Also, when the fish has little or no food in its gut, then it feels hunger in the same way as we do. As it eats, its gut begins to fill and hormones are then released, which tell the fish that it's becoming fuller. These cause a slowing of the food leaving the gut and therefore the fish feels satiety (full) for a longer length of time and is forced to stop feeding. As time goes on, and the gut is emptied, another group of hormones are released, which tell the fish that hunger is returning and feeding activity begins again and the external influences of light and temperature influence the intensity of the activity that occurs.

Since the fish is in touch with the external environment by way of these sensors, these are involved in controlling the amount of feeding done by the carp and since temperature and light fluctuate daily and seasonally, so too does the feeding of the fish accordingly. The forces that affect these external factors, and therefore the behaviour of the fish, are in some cases unpredictable, such as coming across a predator or a competing shoal of fish or the amount of cloud cover which can affect both light intensity and temperature. However, others are predictably associated to certain times of the day, the seasons or even phases of the moon. These fluctuations are termed cycles because, like any cycle, they return to what they were (to an initial level) after a certain amount of time. For example, during the year, the hours of daylight change. In winter the days are shorter and in summer they are longer and then as winter approaches they grow shorter again. Since the fish is able to sense these changes it knows what time of the year it is and as a result knows when to spawn and when to eat more as it prepares for the lean months of winter. Also, since temperature varies during the year, this also affects feeding and as the water warms up in spring and continues into summer, we see both the activity of the carp and the amount of food it eats increase.

Cycles occur not just seasonally but also monthly and on a daily basis. Particularly in sea fishing, the tidal cycle which, depending on location, can result in two or more high tides in each 24 hour period, has been shown to influence the times at which fish feed. In freshwater lakes and non-tidal rivers this is less influential but we have already seen that carp are able to detect near infrared light and since this is produced particularly when the moon is fullest, then it may permit longer periods of feeding at those times of the month. Therefore there is another influence over the carp's feeding, in this case monthly.

Similarly, daily cycles affect us all, not just carp but humans too. If we look at how we spend each day then we can immediately relate our activities to the time, even in the absence of a watch or clock. Although we usually eat at the same time each day we don't do it just because the town clock is striking six and we know we should be having dinner. If we don't eat when we feel the need, we'll begin to suffer the discomfort that hunger can produce. Similarly when we wake up in the morning, we know that if we go without breakfast, then during the morning we'll begin to experience the same effects of hunger and lack of energy. We've therefore selected certain times of the day to eat based on the physiological effects that the absence of food in our stomachs and the lack of available energy produce. So, although using a clock or watch to remind us to eat is a safeguard, in the absence of those ways of measuring time, we would use the environmental indicators such as the sun coming up or going down and the heating or cooling of the earth's surface during the day to tell us when is a good time to eat, combined with the way we feel internally as the day progresses. In this respect there is little difference between the carp and us.

In the same way as for humans, fish can feel the days getting longer or shorter as the year progresses and they can detect the average daily temperature getting warmer or cooler accordingly. In view of that they're able to adjust their food intake. At some times they require higher food intake such as when winter is approaching because that tells them that the ability to locate food will become more difficult in the near future. And there are other times when the temperature is the main factor determining food intake. Even in winter, a mild period may cause the fish to become unusually active and begin to feed because they think that spring is on its way when it isn't. Temperature is also a very notable influence in summer when at midday, when the water may be the warmest, the fish stop feeding because they are out of their comfort zone. In winter the opposite is true and midday can be the most productive time of the day. All these fluctuations are sensed by the carp and it's able to translate the complexity of several interacting cycles into a single signal to feed or not with varying degrees of intensity as the case may be.

It's also beneficial for the prey or predators to understand the daily, monthly and seasonal rhythms of their respective predators and prey since this will enable them to feed or avoid being fed on more effectively. Living organisms use two main ways of measuring time. One is to use the periodicity of the environment to gauge the time of the day or year and the other is to use some kind of internal clock. The carp uses a combination of both of these. The biological clock of a fish provides it with three kinds of information (Brady, 1982). Firstly, it allows the fish to set some processes so that they are 'on time' with respect to the environmental time. For example if it's getting dark and the carp in a water are preferentially nocturnal, then they know that it's time to begin feeding. Secondly, the internal clock allows the fish to determine the length of certain events such as day length which lets the fish know the season of the year. And thirdly, this allows local time fixing which has relevance for fish which migrate, which is to say that by registering time they obtain information about their location.

For the angler, these cycles are important because the fish's hunger is directly related to catch rate and it's these cycles that influence when the fish will feed. However, although the carp may feel hunger, it's the translation of the environmental signals as well as the knowledge of its energy status that will jointly determine how intensely the fish will feed.

The external and internal rhythms of the fish lead to a combined result, which is that which can be observed by the angler in terms of feeding activity and bite and run rate and therefore the number of fish that he's able to put on the bank. Carp are not migratory but they are probably underestimated with regards to their understanding of their local environment. I think that a fish may be just as aware as we are with respect to the time of day and time of the year without the aid of a wristwatch. By synchronising their central pacemaker and sensing the environmental changes in light and temperature, an experienced fish has the potential to anticipate periodic events such as increased predation risk or times of greatest food availability, which have adaptive value and increase wellbeing and survival rates.

In fish, the most frequent types of feeding rhythms that have been observed are circadian which means that they are 24 hour cycles (daily). Other studies of feeding cycles in fish have shown the presence of feeding rhythms that are annual or concur with lunar or tidal cycles. Many of these studies have been carried out with fish farming as the objective. In this respect fish are exposed to very different conditions compared with the natural situation since they don't need to search for food. At least in intensive aquaculture, the fish receive feed when the fish farmer decides that it's feeding time. However, the feeding regime including the amount of feed per feeding and the number of feedings per day, are selected in order to maximise feed intake and growth so that the fish reach harvest size in a shorter time with maximum economic gain. In aquaculture the conditions are often controlled, including photoperiod (light duration and intensity) and temperature with both of these allowing the fish's biological clock to be readjusted with the objective being higher feed intake and growth.

The natural situation is different because the fish have to search for food and their activity is more dependent on environmental changes. Food availability and complications such as food deficiency and the existence of predators may mean that it's necessary for a fish to adhere very much to environmental change and indicators regarding the optimum times to feed.

Despite the importance of these environmental influences on fish, it has also been shown that fish do not exactly repeat feeding on successive days. This means that if a carp feeds in a particular spot one day at a particular time, then it might not be found there the next day even if the water is the same temperature and the light intensity is the same as the day before. This is because feeding is a very complex activity to understand and as we have already seen, it depends on both biotic and abiotic factors as well as endogenous and exogenous ones. Patches become depleted and the carp will need to find alternatives and this means that a fish might not return to the same place on successive days. Similarly, it's unlikely that the amount of food ingested on one day is exactly the same as that of the day before and that the composition of the food is the same either.

We have already covered optimum foraging theory in chapter 1. This gives us an idea as to the intentions of the carp and other animals that need to forage are and what they are trying to achieve by foraging. If we consider OFT and the rhythms that we've mentioned here, then it's clear that the feeding response is dependent on a wide range of factors and these affect the behaviour we're able to observe at certain times.

In a practical sense, if we're able to spend enough time on a water, we add our observations on the bank to the theoretical and develop an idea of where and how fish will feed at different times of the day and year. Although the fish in a lake or river may respond differently to those in other waters, all the information that we're able to obtain will help us to better understand new situations on each particular water. These local differences might be down to different strains of carp being present in the different waters or simply variability between individual carp of groups of carp. Even in the same water, fish of different ages or sizes will react differently to the same environmental variables and generalised feeding might not always be as generalised as we think. And if we are after one particular fish, then it may be the case that that fish reacts very differently to the others as a result of size, age or experience. Where most of the carp in a lake might be more active in the daytime, the fish that most interest an angler, which are more often than not the largest individuals, can show a preference for night feeding or vice versa. Different fish may also show preferences for a particular food type or a certain area of the water. Usually this will offer the fish some kind of advantage over other fish regarding foraging or survival but deciphering the reason or reasons why is the job of the angler, which can often be difficult.

The differences between individuals or groups of individuals in the way that they react to biotic and abiotic change is not the same and this is one of the reasons why there's still a lot to be learned in this area and research regarding feeding rhythms has shown not only a wide range of effects but in many cases contrasting findings. It's therefore hoped that in the years to come we'll be able to clarify some of these contrasts and find out exactly how fish react to their changing environment and why different species, ages and sizes may react differently to the same variation.

But progress doesn't only depend on scientists. Each of us is able to make a contribution to the understanding that can be obtained on any water by fish observation and correlating our catches with different climatic conditions. Anyone who fishes on a regular basis at the same water develops what anglers refer to as watercraft. This means that the angler is able to anticipate the movements and activities of the fish based on previous experience. In the same way as an experienced carp that's able to know more certainly where the best patches for foraging can be found at different times of the year or where the most comfortable conditions can be found in a lake or river at different times of the day, the angler with watercraft is able to optimise his own activities and objectives in order to catch the fish he wants to catch.

d. Factors affecting feeding and appetite

In all animals, food is ingested in order to satisfy energy balance. Some might think that animals eat to grow, but the truth is that growth is merely a consequence of feeding. Repair of tissues, replacement of lost scales, or defence against disease are other consequences of feeding. The reason for feeding is to obtain and provide energy.

This means that carp feed to satisfy their energy requirements and the fish must eat enough every day to live, to repair tissues and remain active. If those are satisfied, then growth may occur. However, it's important to remember that the carp, as with any living organism, is subject to changes in growth capacity throughout its life. Humans grow fastest when they're born as long as they are provided with the correct nutrition. Growth then slows as the child grows and usually by adolescence we reach our maximum height. Adults grow very little and it's during this stage that more energy begins to be used for repair than it was previously. Activity is also reduced and as we move into old age, there's even more repair, less activity and hardly any growth.

The same thing happens in fish. They grow fastest at the moment of hatching and then as juveniles they continue to experience fast growth. This slows as they become adults and then as old fish, growth may be minimal, there is more energy used for repair and they're usually much less active than they were as juveniles. These changes, observable in both fish and humans, have important implications for both the quantity and quality of food that fish consume both in the wild and that which they're fed on fish farms.

However, despite the similarities between fish and humans described above, many anglers will be surprised to learn that protein is the preferred source of energy for fish. This is because protein is used very efficiently to provide energy by fish compared with what happens in other animals and it's possible that excess protein ends up being used as energy rather than for growth. Protein is also the most expensive nutrient used in fish feeds. As a result, in manufactured diets for fish farming, protein is often kept at a minimum that economically ensures good growth and feed conversion. Since there is little excess, this keeps fish production profitable, and energy needs are met through the use of carbohydrate and fat.

In carp fishing, the use of High Nutritional Value (HNV) baits suggests the provision of high quantities of protein in the bait. If we consider the above, then it would appear that these baits would be an expensive way of providing energy for the fish. We can also propose that it would be less effective to use HNV bait if what we want to achieve is the fish becoming used to our bait. In order to do this, the first step is obviously to include everything it needs nutritionally in order that it has no need to look anywhere else for what it needs. If the bait is too high in protein, apart from it being an expensive waste of protein and it lacking other, equally important ingredients, we're increasing the possibility of the fish having to go elsewhere in search of what it requires.

The different quantities and qualities of food required change with each developmental stage of the fish's life, but it makes sense that higher protein should be required during the part when the fish is growing faster, so particularly as a juvenile and into the early adult stages. It's also as a juvenile that the fish is more active and it's therefore desirable to ensure adequate provision of an energy source at that time, whether that's in the form of protein also or as a less effectively catabolised energy source such as fat or carbohydrate.

The energy that the fish ingests in the form of food in whatever composition contains an amount of what is called gross energy, which is the sum of the energy of all the different constituents. Those include the macro-nutrients (those which are required in larger quantities including protein, fat and carbohydrate) and micro-nutrients (those which are required in smaller amounts such as vitamins and minerals). All those added together gives a number, which is the energy content, which is the same as what you see if you look at the nutritional value on the back of a packet of biscuits or a tin of beans. This amount, which can be calculated for both fishing baits and aquafeeds, is represented in the form of calories or joules. Both these refer to energy.

Of the food that is eaten by the carp, some of that is digestible. This means that it can be broken down in the fish's gut to simpler molecules and can pass into the body of the fish. Therefore of the total energy that is ingested not all of it is completely available to the fish because not all of the food is digestible. Some will be excreted as faeces at this stage and what is left, that which is absorbed by the fish from the gut, is referred to as digestible energy. This digestible energy is then metabolised in the fish, which means that each of the different fuels produced during digestion are used. This results in losses of energy in urine, primarily excreted by the gills as ammonia, and loss of energy as heat.

Fish are cold-blooded and their body temperature depends on that of their surroundings. If the temperature of the water rises, then so does the internal temperature of the fish. On the other hand, we humans have to maintain our bodies at a constant temperature which requires energy to warm us up and also to cool ourselves down. We therefore use more energy for temperature control than a fish does, but even so, the fish, as a result of breaking down the food, produces a quantity of heat that is lost to the environment in the same way as it is in our case.

So, of the total amount of energy originally ingested as food, we're left with a quantity of energy that can be utilised by the fish according to its needs. Those needs, as we saw before, are related to the life stage of the fish but also to particular activities on a day-to-day basis. For example, you have probably noticed that when you eat a large meal, you fancy a nap afterwards. This is because all that food needs to be digested and absorbed and for that, your body needs energy and that's why you feel tired. The same thing happens with fish. After eating, the fish needs to rest, and this might happen several times each day. And each time, although the fish is gaining energy through the amount of food that it's eating, there is also a loss of energy in order to deal with the food that's ingested.

After all of these processes, the energy that's left over is referred to as production energy and this may have various fates. Firstly, it's used for maintenance, which is basically that which is needed by the fish to live and breathe. This is sometimes separately referred to as maintenance energy. Then comes repair of cells and tissues that may be damaged or naturally need replacing. And finally, what is left over can be used for growth.

What we find is that the composition and constituents of the food have a great deal of relevance regarding what the fish is able to do with what it ingests. Quite often, the fish is unable to satisfy every requirement. Therefore, it has three alternatives. The first is to convert excesses of what it has ingested into what it's lacking. This is possible with some substances, but it's impossible with others. The second alternative is to locate and ingest what it's lacking which may be a possibility if a food item is available that contains what it needs. And the third alternative is simply to go without it.

Carp anglers talk about amino acids a lot of the time. But how much do they actually understand about what they are and what their relationship with the fish is? And a more important question still is how much do the bait producers understand about them in order that the product we buy from them can help us to catch more fish?

One thing that is discussed frequently is the importance of providing the right amount of each amino acid, because as any fish farmer will tell you, fish don't need protein, what they need are amino acids. And each one of these must be provided in the correct amount so that there are no deficiencies and the fish, in theory, should eat more of that diet, grow better (since good nutrition is related to good growth) and have a lower probability of getting sick. This sounds complicated, but in reality there are only ten amino acids that you should really worry about. These are the essential amino acids and they're called essential because the fish is unable to make them from others. They must be provided in the diet.

This concept will be covered more extensively in chapter 4, but the advice of celebrity anglers telling you to make sure that your bait includes the amino acids that a fish is lacking is just tosh. How are you supposed to know what the fish is lacking? That would include science that is beyond the technical and economic means of 99.9 percent of anglers. The easiest way to do that is to simply find out how much of the total protein that the carp requires should be made up of each of the essential amino acids and use that on the lake. In that way, the carp will receive all of its amino acid requirements from your bait and if the rest of the nutrients that it needs are provided too, then, hypothetically, it wouldn't have to search anywhere else for alternatives, including other anglers' baits or natural food items.

To make this part of the quest easier, let me help. The ten essential amino acids are the following and for each of the these, the requirement as a percentage of total protein is shown in brackets after each one: arginine (4.3), histidine (2.1), isoleucine (2.5), leucine (3.3), lysine (5.7), methionine (3.1), phenylalanine (6.5), threonine (3.9), tryptophan (0.8) and valine (3.6). These values are from a study by Nose (1979). Similarly, the optimal percentage for carp has been shown to be 38 percent using a casein based diet (Ogino & Saito, 1970). This means that if you want to ensure that none of these amino acids are deficient, then these percentages should be present in the mixture of protein sources used in the bait, which should be 38 percent of the total weight.

Excess protein in the form of essential or non-essential amino acids will simply be used as energy or transformed into something else that the fish needs if that's possible. However, these kinds of transformations require energy.

Similarly, it's not just amino acids that are essential. In the case of lipids (fats and oils), there are many different types. As well as falling into similar essential and non-essential categories, these have different structures. Some are short molecules and others long. They also have different amounts of saturation, which is a property that's important for their fluidity. If you think of a common fatty material such as lard, it's solid when you take it out of the fridge. That's because it's 40 percent saturated fat and 60 percent unsaturated fat. In comparison, olive oil, contains only 20 percent saturated fat and 80 percent unsaturated fat. That consistency means that olive oil is liquid at refrigerator temperature. In order to increase the fluidity of lard, it's necessary to increase its temperature by heating.

These are only two examples of fatty substances and both are mixtures of several types of lipid. These lipids can be produced synthetically, but they're all found naturally. Some are produced by plants and others by animals. For example, fish oil is extracted from fish and coconut oil comes from coconuts. The lipids found in lowest quantities naturally are those which are longer and more highly unsaturated. These are most plentiful in marine organisms, including fish species and for that reason, the benefits of highly unsaturated fish oils have been publicised because they are important constituents of cells and in both humans and fish are health promoting. Fish use more energy to synthesise these highly unsaturated lipids than shorter, more saturated lipids and some fish are unable to do this. This means that they are essential in those fish and it's therefore beneficial to provide these in a diet or bait in order to avoid deficiency.

The second option that the carp has is to find what it needs, which it might be able to. If the lake is productive with a high diversity of invertebrate and plant life, it may locate the missing nutrients quite easily, but in other bodies of water that are barren of life, this might be much more difficult. If that's the case, then the presence of anglers throwing all manner of different baits into the water increases the probability of adding substances to the carp's world that are there naturally in much lower amounts. Also, the addition of bait will indirectly increase productivity through the fertilisation (nutrification) of the water, which will increase the amount of animal and plant life and as a result the substances they contain and which the carp may require.

In order to obtain the total requirement for a particular nutrient, what a fish might do is eat more than usual. If it's fifty percent deficient in a particular food, then it makes sense for a fish to eat double that, if of course that's physically possible.

A similar thing can be seen in humans. If a balanced diet is eaten, then we feel well fed and not lacking anything. However, when we get a craving for something, it's usually because we haven't eaten that particular thing for a long time. Try it for yourself. Start eating nothing but salad for lunch and dinner from Monday onwards. Most people would probably be able to get to Thursday, or maybe Wednesday, before they felt a craving for fat and protein in the shape of a burger, a steak or something similar. In this respect, there's no reason why the same thing shouldn't happen in fish. It's part of the evolution of both fish and humans to feel the need for what they aren't receiving. And this, in a practical manner, is a biological safeguard to avoid us not receiving what our body needs. In the same way, we're pretty sure that fish feel the same urges. They more than likely don't know that they are specifically lacking, say vitamin C or arginine, but they probably know what they have to eat, even at the level of plant or animal, in order to satisfy the urge.

The third option is simply not to receive what they require. This means that the carp will lack them permanently and this will have a negative effect of their development, depending on which substances are lacking and in what amounts. In general, the deficiency of a particular nutrient manifests itself by decreased growth, which may be more noticeable in fish that should be growing more rapidly, such as small and juvenile carp. The other way that the carp's development is affected is by causing disease. This can commonly be observed when vitamin and minerals are lacking from the fish's diet. It's true that only very small quantities of these micro-nutrients are required by the fish, but if the fish has little or no access to them for a period of time, then the deficiencies can manifest themselves in form of reduced biological functions, growth abnormalities and malformations. This is because, despite the small amounts required, these substances are required for very important reactions and functions within the fish. These often act as co-enzymes which are basically substances that attach themselves to enzymes so that reactions occur more effectively.

These three options differ depending on the characteristics of the lake or river where the carp lives and obviously what substances are present and what is being added by anglers. How the fish develops and whether that happens optimally will have something to do with the absence of certain substances. If all the fish's requirements can be satisfied, then we would expect normal development. That's why a bait that contains everything that a carp needs is particularly relevant and important, since there are four-fold benefits for fish, angler, bait producer and fishery owner of a complete bait.

Apart from quality, the amount or quantity of food that a fish ingests throughout its life also changes. As a proportion of its body weight, a fish eats daily a greater amount when it's smaller. As the fish increases in size it requires proportionally less. A carp of 100 grams or so may eat anything from three to five percent of its body weight per day, which would equate to two to five grams. A 30 pound (13.6 kg) carp might eat one to two percent per day or less of its body weight per day. Although this is proportionally less, considering the size of the fish it's obviously an important amount of food. Two percent would be equivalent to 270 grams of food, which would vary depending on a number of factors including energy content and composition of the food and water temperature. Highest weight gains both in aquaculture and in the natural environment occur when the fish is able to feed several times during the day and night and this can be responsible for increased daily consumption.

121

Increased consumption has various implications for the angler. If the bait being used is both nutritionally complete and is additionally attractive for the carp and is also available many times each day or permanently, this clearly means that the fish will eat more. Greater bait consumption means two things. Firstly, the fish will feed more confidently and secondly, there's more probability of the hookbait being sucked in.

Having already familiarised you with the importance of food quality and quantity and the supply of energy that the fish needs, we'll move on to the subject of appetite. Once again it's easier to understand these concepts if we use humans as a model rather than fish and I always find it's easier to understand certain things if I think about it in a human context or even a personal one. This should not be a general rule though.

The biggest mistake that anglers make is to think of fish as they do humans. That's why the first thing they'll do when they pick up a bag of boilies is crush one and smell it. By their reasoning, if it smells good to them, then it's going to catch carp. Similarly if it makes the angler feel hungry, then it'll have the same effect on the fish. Unfortunately it doesn't work like that but because we have placed so much faith in the bait companies, we trust them that what we're buying is what gets the carp motivated to feed and provides exactly what it needs nutritionally in order to develop normally.

I have just finished working on a bait that I've designed for my own fishing. It looks similar to other baits in texture and size and it has some of the same ingredients. How it differs though is that it doesn't smell of fishmeal or strawberries or chocolate or an Indian takeaway. In fact it smells of very little. That is because I'm interested in the carp's opinion rather than that of anglers, I'm able to differentiate between the two and the bait has been formulated with that objective in mind. That's not to say that smell isn't important. On the contrary. But what I'm interested in is a smell that's attractive to the fish rather than the angler. This particular bait just has the smell of the ingredients but in particular that of two amino acids that I've incorporated. These are in order to boost the levels of one to that required by the fish and the other as a way of increasing attraction due to the positive chemosensory properties of that particular amino. But there's nothing in the way of additional flavourings or essences. To accompany that I've included a palatant but even that is odourless.

Maybe it is an unusual bait because of this lack of scent for most anglers but I've a lot of faith in it. It's been developed to be nutritionally complete and to be used in conjunction with a glug that contains a high concentration of the same amino. Tank tests of both the bait and the glug have provided very positive and promising results and the glug, in the same way as the bait, has very little smell to us but is highly stimulatory to the carp because what it contains is effective in water and not air and also specific for carp.

The common mistake made by anglers of thinking that the carp's response to something is the same as ours is understandable. We share many common characteristics including feeding for the same reason and much of the internal workings of the carp with respect to feeding and appetite. For example, the hormones that tell the fish that the gut is filling or emptying and those which increase or decrease the motivation to feed are in nearly all cases the same as the ones we have in our bodies. They may differ slightly structurally but functionally they are the same as ours and they carry out the same purposes. Some of these increase appetite and others have the opposite effect as a result of increased satiation.

The mechanisms that control feeding are complex. Even in mammals, where scientists have been studying these for many years, not everything is understood yet about how the mechanisms work. In fish, although there have been fewer studies carried out compared with humans and other mammals, the amount of research in this area is on the increase as fish farmers realise the importance of the potential to manipulate feed intake of fish. This could solve a problem for fish that are inappetant or sick and through generally increasing intake it may be possible to achieve more efficient conversion of feed to biomass and better growth rates.

Up until now they have worked out the that the fish's brain is very important in this regulation and a large number of different hormones are responsible for communicating between the brain and some of the fish's other organs, including the gut, the liver and the pancreas as well as fatty tissue. These similarly produce hormones that are responsible for communication with the brain. The majority of these are inhibitory, which means that their secretion causes an overall reduction in food intake but some are stimulatory and cause an increase in food intake.

But before you try to get your hands on these hormones with the plan to add them to your bait you should know that they are not currently produced in very high quantities and for that reason are very expensive. Also, they're proteins so they are generally broken down in the gut of the fish and absorbed as not much more than amino acids and so are rendered inactive. A similar thing happens with biologically active protein-containing substances that anglers might add to their bait such as enzymes.

However, in practice, the mechanism of control of feeding and satiation means that as a carp eats and its gut begins to fill, there's a decrease in the hormones that are involved in appetite and an increase in those that are involved in satiation. In this way the brain of the fish is kept informed of the amount of food in the gut and is able to work out how much energy that is going to provide. Therefore, if the fish thinks that there's still going to be an energy deficiency, it will continue to feed and ingest food until it works out that the deficiency will be effectively satisfied.

Carp are opportunistic to a certain degree, meaning that they will feed when they have access to food. In some lakes and rivers, the scarcity of food will mean that fish feed more readily when they eventually find food but in others, where there's a much greater abundance and diversity of food, the carp can afford to be more selective. The latter fish will be more difficult to catch. For the angler, it's these that will provide the biggest challenge since their motivations for feeding will not be as simple as those of fish that are lucky to be able to find food at all and are basically interested in filling their gut and meeting maintenance energy requirements in order to keep living.

This situation is a result of not just the amount of food but the presence of other carp and competing fish populations. If competition is higher, the amount of food that's available per fish is lower and if the number of fish in a water increases dramatically, either through the natural disappearance or artificial removal of predators, then the population explosion can result in the collapse of the food supply as natural food is depleted and the fish begin to starve. It's under these kinds of conditions that anglers notice a very different response to their bait and easier fishing compared to what regularly happens.

Appetite depends on a large number of factors. We have seen that feeding is influenced by environmental variables such as light and temperature. We have also mentioned the importance of the carp feeling comfortable in its environment, which will to some extent be conducive to feeding. This might include abundant oxygen or low levels of metabolic products such as ammonia and carbon dioxide. We have also seen that the ability to feed is related to the transparency of the water, which is also an environmental factor and consideration. Carp feed most effectively when they can combine their senses of sight, smell and taste and this may be affected if the water is particularly turbid.

Apart from the abiotic factors, the biotic factors such as competition with shoalmates and other fish for a finite amount of natural food are important factors regarding the feeding response. Increased or reduced food availability will clearly decrease or increase hunger and therefore appetite. Other factors such as the presence of predators will affect whether a carp feeds or not. Even though feeding motivation is high and food is abundant, the presence of a predator may deter the fish from feeding if it means that it has to leave the security of the shoal or shelter and become exposed to the threat of predation.

Not only the abundance of food but its composition, texture, size, taste and smell are also important. The food items may have to be what the carp requires at a particular moment due to a specific nutritional requirement such as energy or another nutrient deficiency. The safeness of the bait is also important. Although the fish might prefer a particular type of food over another, it will not consume it at any cost and not only predation by other animals is a consideration but so is being caught by an angler. The perception of a threat and the ability to determine if a food is safe to eat or not has a lot to do with a fish's experience. This means that it's more likely that fish that have been caught previously will be able to determine safeness more effectively and will be more likely to avoid a bait than a younger, less experienced individual.

As we have also seen, the balance between appetite and satiation is regulated internally in the fish by hormones. These are associated with the central nervous system of the fish and it's the brain of the carp that ultimately processes signals from several organs of the fish with respect to the amount of food that has to be ingested in order to satisfy energy requirement. At the same time, the brain processes information regarding daily and seasonal cycles such as changes in day length and environmental temperature, which provide an additional influence to feeding motivation in the form of a biological feeding rhythm. Both appetite and feeding are therefore a function of all these factors and they determine the response to both natural food and bait.

Because these factors are almost all dependent of the fish itself and changes in its environment, the angler can have only a limited amount of influence over the feeding response of the fish. The ways that this can be done are 1) understanding when and where the fish are more likely to feed and fishing there, or 2) using substances in or on the bait that improve feeding stimulation, which may be through attraction or increasing the amount of food ingested.

e. Feeding phases

In many fish, including carp, the systems that these animals possess to locate food based on a combination of smell and taste are highly developed. This includes a high concentration of taste buds both inside the mouth and on the external surface of the fish, particularly on different parts of the head and surfaces that are in contact with the lake or river bed.

The concentrations of these taste buds in carp vary from as little as 15 taste buds per square millimetre on the top of the head, which has relatively little to do with feeding, to 359 per square millimetre on the small barbels to 385 taste buds on the large barbels (Devitsina, 2006). Suffice to say that the fish has a very high capacity to both detect and identify the type and source of chemical signals in the water. And compared with humans that have a mere two to three taste buds per square millimetre of their tongues, this ability is quite overwhelming.

As human beings that utilise daily the senses of smell and taste hundreds of times, it's surprising to learn that the system associated with these senses is so poorly understood. In fish, it is less well understood because of the comparative amount of research that has been carried out specifically in fish species. As carp fishermen, this system in fish should interest us even more than our own, because our success as anglers is directly related to the perception of the bait we are offering to the fish.

A similar thing can be seen in fish farming. Here, the success of the activity is related to how much food is ingested, how digestible the food is, how well it's converted from feed to flesh and how quickly that can be achieved. In this respect, an important part of how suitable the feed is to the fish is the fish's reaction to it. At that moment, which is variable between species as far as how the feed is detected, at least in those species that depend greatly on chemical signals in the water, it's the stimulation of those taste buds that causes the intensity of feeding activity that follows. This determines the length of feeding and the amount of feed ingested, which in turn affects growth and the economic viability of the activity.

In the carp fishing industry, it's in the interest of several parties to ensure that the stimulation produced in the fish is long and intense. Increased bait intake promotes growth, which can be improved by using a bait that is nutritionally complete and attractive. The owner of the lake benefits because a nutritionally superior bait means less waste and also results in healthier, faster-growing fish. The fish benefits because of the increased health associated with nutritionally complete food and growth results in improved capacity to compete with other fish for food and other resources. But the real winners are the bait companies who sell more bait as a result of the good publicity that intense feeding provides and the angler who is searching for more and bigger fish and is very interested in stimulating the carp's olfactory (smell) and gustatory (taste) senses, since this is a key to his angling success.

The smell and taste systems that have been studied in greatest detail in fish are those of the catfish and the carp. In these, the distribution of taste buds over the different surfaces in contact with the water is not haphazard. It's organised in a way so as to optimise the search for food and feeding by including higher densities of taste buds on and in different regions of the head and pectoral fins. This surface organisation makes it easier for carp to find food since they're in contact with both the water carrying chemical signals and the river or lake bed that contains chemical signals of its own.

The taste buds are connected to two important nerves which end in the brain of the fish. The signal that is transduced along these nerves, just as if it were an electrical signal from one caller to another down a telephone wire, is translated by one part of the brain. As a result, the signals are processed and the fish makes a decision as to what it should do. If the signal is from a substance in the water that is positively stimulatory, then it means that the fish will probably move towards that stimulus and if it is negatively stimulatory or causes rejection, then the fish will likely do the opposite.

The brain of the fish is not much different from ours in the sense of being able to process complex stimuli. Rarely is a chemical signal in the natural environment a pure one and it will usually be a mixture of many signals, of varying intensities and types and a range from positively to negatively stimulatory. It has been shown, for example, that for each fish species each different amino acid can produce some kind of stimulation. This may be positive or negative. Some have no effect at all, but these, obviously, are a much less interest to us as anglers.

If you take a non-specific commonly sold attractant such as minamino, which was developed for a completely different reason than some other 'attractants' and you look at the contents, you'll find that it does include some of the positively stimulatory amino acids. But at the same time, it contains several of those which have no effect at all, and in a more worrying sense, several of those found to produce rejection in carp. It's therefore counterproductive to use a wide range of amino acids in a preparation as compared with only those that have been proven to attract, due to the fact that you may be adding as many or more amino acids that cause rejection in carp as those which result in attraction. It's not simply a matter of adding amino acids to a bait, but including only those which have been shown to be positive stimulants in carp.

Feeding behaviour in fish as a result of the stimulation produced by external substances, including many amino acids, is composed of three phases. The first stage begins with the stimulation of the sensory system in carp by the presence of substances in the aquatic environment. This is the case in carp although in other fish which use alternative sensory systems such as food detection by the use of electrical pulses, visual detection, or a mixture of these or others, the stimulation trigger will be through those. This first phase is characterised by the fish entering a state of arousal or alert. This consists of an increase in muscular activity of the mouth, throat and appendices such as the fins and barbels and the flank and has been described as including twitching or exaggerated movements.

This is followed by what is called the appetitive phase, which, as its name suggests, is where appetite is increased by the presence of positively stimulatory substances in the water. Here, the brain of the fish has translated the signals that it has received and the fish is urged to identify and localise the source of the signals that are received. Continued chemical stimulation results in searching behaviours in order to find the food. Those behaviours which are typical of the appetitive phase of feeding usually include swimming patterns or others with the objective of localisation. Species such as carp, which are equipped with barbels, respond to the existence of taste stimuli by increasing swimming activity. This is done in order that barbels in particularly are used optimally in the search for the source of the stimulation. However, as we have already seen, the stimulation can be received by the fish superficially in several areas of the head apart from the barbels, although they are particularly sensitive. In fact direct contact between these areas and food has been shown to cause greater arousal, which suggests that at close range, the fish's sense of taste is much more important than smell , which is thought to be more useful when the stimulus is further away.

The final phase, referred to as the consummatory phase, consists of ingestion or rejection of the food items. This decision is usually based not just on the influence of the chemical signals which brought the fish to that spot, but also based on testing of the food item, either wholly or partly. This involves the taste buds located on the lips and inside the mouth and those of a structure called the palatal organ towards the back of the mouth, which has the highest concentration of taste buds with as many as 800 per square millimetre. This organ is the place where food is separated into acceptable and non-acceptable and also food and non-food which will be described further ahead, along with the option that a carp has for physically dealing with different food types of varying degrees of palatability.

f. Food intake

As we've seen, the amount of food ingested is directly related to the amount of energy required by the carp. Food in excess of that energy requirement is either excreted or stored. The regulation and control of energy in organisms is called homeostasis. When more energy is required, the fish feeds and when energy needs are satisfied, then it doesn't.

Both external and internal factors affect the 'need to feed'. Among the most well know external influences are daily, monthly and seasonal variations in light and temperature. These are so important that anglers can sense their effects on the fish during a day's fishing and fishing at different times of the year. Fishing is never hectic from arriving at the lake or river until leaving. There are always more intense periods at particular times of the day. This is because changes in both light and temperature are detected by the fish. In the case of light, this is done by the pineal organ, which is basically a light sensor close to the surface of the fish's head. However, light is also detected by the retina inside the eye because the fish can of course visually tell the difference between day and night. Also, there's a collection of what are called photoreceptors which, as their name suggests, are capable of detecting changes in light intensity.

The pineal organ can also detect temperature changes and so can the fish's internal appetite control centres. Since fish are poikilothermic, which means that their body temperature may vary considerably as the external temperature (that of the surrounding water) increases or decreases, the temperature of the fish's insides is the same as its environment. As a result, sensors within the fish tell the fish what the temperature is and many processes are adjusted accordingly.

Other external factors affect the energy requirement and the need to feed. These can include the health of the fish, its stage of development, relationships between the fish and others and the quality of the feed that's being ingested. More specifically, if the fish is healthy, then it may require less energy than one that's unhealthy in order to fight off infection. If it's growing quickly, then the energy demand will be higher and if it's competing against other fish for food, as is the case with weaker and smaller fish, then it will receive less energy. In the case of food quality, if the food being ingested is nutritionally inadequate, then much of it may be excreted instead of being incorporated into the fish's tissues.

Another alternative for an inadequate food is that a greater amount is required in order to satisfy energy needs. However, as we have seen, of the gross energy ingested, a number of energy needs have to be satisfied, and many of these, such as digestion and metabolism, actually require energy themselves in order to occur. Therefore, an inadequate diet or bait that is nutritionally inadequate is particularly wasteful since it doesn't provide the fish with what it needs and what it does provide could well be used simply in dealing with the same in order to make it useful.

You might think that the fish eating a greater amount of a bait is a good thing. It may be, but in the long term, in the same way as the response that we described earlier of a human eating nothing but salad every day, it's likely that sooner or later the fish's body is going to tell it that what it's eating is not providing it with what it needs. It's likely therefore that such a bait will be much more short-lived than one that is nutritionally complete.

As we discussed in chapter 1, it's necessary to spend time on a water in order to understand the feeding rhythms that occur both at different times of the day and night as well as different months and seasons. Also, not all carp in the water will feed at the same time. This is because appetite is variable between different individual fish in the same way that it is between different people. Appetite is also determined by both endogenous (internal) and exogenous (external) factors. This means that unless two fish are exactly the same biologically, meaning that they are biological copies of each other regarding such things as weight and stomach size, and apart from that they react the same way to the environmental stimuli of light and temperature, then they will feed at different times and intensities.

Fish of the same age in a water may look very similar, but they might not all feed at the same time either. Not all areas of the lake or river will be the same temperature and receive the same light intensity all the time and therefore the external stimuli will provoke feeding at different times depending on where in the lake the fish is and where it's been moving around. Additionally, the size of the fish has a great deal to do with the variety of feeding times.

On a lake that I fish frequently, the larger carp feed on and off at different times but in general this occurs during the daytime and these larger fish are therefore diurnal. On the other hand, the small carp feed at night (nocturnal). This is not a coincidence. As we have seen, feeding is not a random process. It's determined both internally and externally and is dependent on daily and seasonal rhythms as well as interactions with predators and shelter and also other fish. Smaller carp in particular like to move around in groups but it's advantageous for them to shoal with fish of a similar size rather than much bigger fish. Similar sized fish offer greater protection, especially if there are many of them and when food is found, it's shared by many small mouths rather than a few large ones.

In the case of the lake that I'm referring to, the small fish feed at night because there's a lower abundance of fish-eating predators at night and also not feeding at the same time as the larger carp provides them with an advantage regarding food detection and ingestion. This is probably not a unique case and you might even know a lake with a similar 'phenomenon'. But there are no hard and fast rules. The situation might be reversed and the big fish feed at night. It might be some other pattern that's advantageous to different groups of fish, but as an angler, your job is to fathom out that pattern.

There are many other environmental factors that have been shown to have some affect on feeding and appetite. Examples of these are turbidity and the amount of solids in the water, something that anglers refer to simply as 'colour'. The number of fish in a particular area may affect feeding. Larger fish often prefer to be and feed alone whereas smaller fish might not feed if they aren't accompanied. Other water quality parameters that can affect feeding apart from temperature are dissolved oxygen and pH. Carp prefer to be comfortable and variations in water quality can affect feeding dramatically. This is true not only for carp but for other fish too. Ask a salmon angler if the colour of the water has anything to do with how good the fishing will be and get ready for a long conversation.

Another important factor affecting feeding is stress. As with humans, stress reduces our appetite. When we are under pressure at work or are worried about something at home, our appetite becomes reduced and our priorities change regarding eating. In fish, it's not clear whether they worry as such, but increased levels of stress hormones in fish, such as can happen if a predator is nearby or the water quality changes drastically or the fish are sick, have been shown to have a negative effect on feed intake. So when a fish is stressed, it might even stop eating altogether. This is called inappetance.

One other well-known cause of inappetance is reproduction. Again, comparisons can be made with humans in that when they are involved in courtship, priorities change and in the thrill of the chase, the last thing on our minds might be eating. In fish, including carp, the hormones that we mentioned that are involved with appetite and satiety in many cases have more than one function and may be directly involved in reproduction. In other cases these are indirectly involved and cause other hormones to be released which play an important role in reproduction. So, in the same way that the appetite and stress systems are closely linked, so are those of appetite and reproduction.

For the angler, this means that during certain periods the fish may be off the feed. This may be a short or a long time, but rest assured that the fish must feed sooner or later. And all that stressing and all that reproduction will likely result in fish that are very hungry when all the worrying and mating have been completed, which is a plus for any angler by the water at that moment. Similarly, before the breeding season begins, it's likely that carp ingest food in larger and more frequent meals and that's another period that the angler might want to be prepared for.

g. The feeding mechanism

In the same way as the variety of food and preference that can be observed among the fishes that inhabit the planet, evolution has provided us with a wide range of structures that fish use to obtain or capture their food. Capture is usually associated with predatory fish, since it is living and moving organisms that require the fish not only to adopt certain behaviours to capture them but also to employ teeth to prevent their escape or protuberance of the jaws to engulf the animal whole.

However, we know from the carp that exclusively carnivorous fish species are not the only ones to capture live food, and omnivores, due to their highly varied diet, also deal with live food. However, in many cases, the consumption of living prey does not require any additional specialisation regarding the structure and behaviour of the carp. This is because living prey can be obtained and consumed as a consequence of their typical feeding behaviour, which is that of vacuuming the bottom of a lake or river, or by any other use of the extendible mouthparts that it possesses. In fact, in the case of the carp, the material may be alive or dead and can be treated exactly the same much of the time. Vacuuming ensures the fate of living and dead organisms and therefore we are led to believe that the feeding mechanism of the carp is unspecialised. In fact by assuming that, we are committing a very big mistake.

A method which is unspecific, such as suction, provides benefits for an omnivore. If it were equipped with the same feeding apparatus as the pike, a fish that often shares the same body of water as the carp, we can imagine that it would find it difficult to consume small invertebrates and detritus, which make up a large proportion of its diet. The pike's jaws would be more useful for the capture of larger invertebrates which the carp may spot and engulf individually or small fish, which although they are not a principal or preferred part of the carps' diet, can be included at certain times or when the availability of alternatives is low. This has been shown by the capture of carp by anglers on artificial lures and flies which simulate small fish and which might come as a surprise to some.

The other food source that can at times be an important one for carp is that of plankton, which the fish can extract from the water column. I think it's pretty clear that the pike's feeding apparatus would be no good at all for that and it helps explain why diet type is related to the feeding structures that a fish possesses. This is because, in the past, meaning millions of years ago, the number of feeding adaptations were fewer and the diversity of food organisms fewer than they are today too. As time went on, also over millions of years, the number of food organisms increased and so did the opportunity for fish to feed more effectively if they possessed an adaptation to a particular food type, or alternatively to a wide range of food types as in the case of the carp. The adaptation which led to the provision of protrusible (or protractile) jaws is a form of cranial kinesis and led to greater volume inside the mouth, which increases the suction that the carp is able to achieve in conjunction with the movement of other bones in the head.

Cranial kinesis is not uncommon throughout the animal kingdom, and examples can be found particularly among insects, amphibians and reptiles. In mammals it's less common and in humans is non-existent. Instead of protrusible jaws, we have a complex system of facial muscles in order to achieve activities such as sucking and blowing. We also have hands with which to grab hold of food items, a luxury that fish don't possess.

The earliest fish were jawless (called Agnathans, meaning 'no-jaws' in Latin) and modern day examples are the hagfish and the lamprey. Evolution led to the appearance of cartilaginous and bony fishes, which both have mouth adaptations. For example, when sharks bite their jaws (maxillae) can be pushed forward in order to increase the size of the bite. This is perhaps the earliest example of cranial kinesis in fish. With the appearance of the ray-finned fish (Teleostei) in the Triassic period, some 250 to 200 million years ago, a larger number of specialisations and adaptations occurred. Carp belong to this infraclass (order Cypriniformes). Teleosts have a moveable maxilla and premaxilla as well as modifications to the muscles of the jaws in order for them to perform specific tasks. In most cases, this involves some kind of protrusion, even if that adaptation allows capture rather than sucking. In the case of some, such as the John Dory (genus Zeus), which is equipped with highly protractile jaws, they are used not in a random, probing fashion as with the carp, but in a predatory manner, with the fish able to shoot out the hinged mouthparts at the small fish which form its diet.

It's likely that since the Triassic period and the beginning of domestication of carp in Europe by the Romans more than two thousand years ago in south-central Europe, the carp's appearance remained very much the same. However, the growth of aquaculture for food and recently for stocking recreational fisheries has resulted in a wide diversity of carp strains that have been produced through artificial as opposed to natural selection. These fish differ in a number of ways from the original wild carp and have become modified mainly due to a combination of being enclosed and being fed artificially.

The physical changes that have occurred and which can now be appreciated in the modern carp include a deeper body, a reduced number of scales (in the case of variants) and variation in colour. Also, the intestine of the domesticated carp is 15 to 25 percent longer than that of the wild carp, probably due to the utilisation of vegetable food not normally consumed as extensively by the wild common carp. Several other physiological differences exist, including greater vascularisation (more blood vessels) and a greater concentration of red blood cells in the wild fish, which explains why these fish fight better once hooked. This characteristic may perpetuate to different degrees in stocked fish and may be the reason why some fish fight better than others.

Another external difference, particularly relevant to our discussion, is that of mouth gape, which is the size of the mouth opening. This has been used to differentiate between wild and domesticated fish when other characteristics are similar, with the wild fish having a much smaller gape than domesticated varieties. This has been explained as being a result of diet change and it's this larger mouth that the majority of anglers are used to and what we usually consider when we think about rigs and baits.

There's no difference in the way that the carp's mouth works these days compared with the Middle Ages when carp domestication began to occur on an even larger scale. It's just larger. This adaptation has a number of implications, with a larger size means more efficient feeding, since more substrate can be processed in a given amount of time and, as long as the food is nutritionally adequate, it will lead to faster growth. This may be more evident in particular strains of carp and in recent years, a number of 'fast-growing' strains have become available for stocking. These have been artificially selected due to possessing desirable characteristics for the table or for fishing since the destiny of a reared carp is almost always one of these.

As a result of evolution and domestication, the carp that we encounter in our fishing is as prepared as ever for feeding. Although the amount of time spent feeding each day is indirectly proportional to the availability of food and its nutritional adequacy, this is thought to be considerable, at least in the natural environment. Food items eaten by the carp as we saw in chapter 2 are very varied. They differ in size and shape as well as the characteristics of the places they are found, how they move or don't as the case may be, or the chemical and mechanical properties of each food item. They may be easy or difficult to grasp or catch and in some cases require a structural adaptation in order for the fish to consume them effectively.

Carp are not real graspers as some other fish are, although a limited amount of grasping can be achieved by the rough surface of the fish's lips. And since fish have no claws as mammals do, the alternative is to obtain their food by the use of their combined mouth and throat structure (called their oropharyngeal apparatus). This varies from species to species, but in carp it forms a pump which uses suction and pressure in order to achieve its objective, that of initially moving food from the outside into their mouth and then swallowing it. This is referred to as the feeding mechanism.

The carp has one of the most complex feeding mechanisms of any fish, which is made up of a sequence of different feeding actions. These are based on changes in oral volume of different parts of the oropharyngeal apparatus, and by adjusting the timing of individual volume changes the carp is able to fulfil each of the different feeding actions and feed effectively. The different movement patterns in carp have been studied and their functions in food processing identified (Sibbing *et al.*, 1986). In total there are nine movement patterns. These are 1) particulate intake, 2) gulping, 3) spitting, 4) selective retention, 5) rinsing, 6) transport, 7) filling of the chewing cavity, 8) crushing and grinding, and 9) deglutination (swallowing).

The first two are particulate intake and gulping, which are the two methods by which the carp transfers food to the mouth. Particulate intake is used for food items of any size up to a maximum which may be on the lake or river bottom. The maximum size of food that can enter the carp's mouth is nine percent of its body length for fish up to 25 centimetres long and seven percent for larger fish. The fish is able to 'aim' the suction at the item that it intends to ingest by manoeuvring of the body in order to alter its position and then particulate intake occurs by the fish quickly opening its gill flaps (opercula) and mouth, which creates a fast oral suction along with protrusion of the upper jaw. This forms a tube through which the item passes into the fish's mouth. The maximum speed of suction has been recorded at 60 centimetres per second. Particulate intake is an especially effective method of feeding although it requires a relatively large amount of energy to carry it out. The fish is able to use it for sticky or heavy items that may be in difficult to reach places such as crevices.

This method of intake must be variable, since the particles that are ingested this way are diverse and vary in size, weight and density. Therefore, the fish must apply varying amounts of suction in order for them to be transferred into the mouth cavity. Otherwise, energy would be wasted if too little suction were applied to move a heavy item and the procedure had to be repeated or an unnecessary amount of suction were applied to a small, light item. This variation occurs by the fish adjusting appropriately the expansion of the head and the amount and timing of the opening of the gill flaps. These factors have an effect on both the velocity and volume of the water entering the mouth cavity and similarly the particles that it contains. The expansion of the upper jaw has another advantage for the fish, which is that the lips are brought closer to the food item, reducing the amount of suction required and therefore saving energy.

The other method for food intake is gulping which is used when the fish is feeding on suspended items such as plankton and found in the water column rather than on the bottom. This is also used for items that might be stirred up from the bottom. Whereas particulate intake would be expected for baits such as boilies, luncheon meat, corn or breadflake, which are individual items and relatively large in size and dense, gulping might well be used for bait suspensions like a cloud of groundbait or even finely chopped boilies that may be lifted up from the bottom and sink so slowly as to hang in the water column. Gulping is achieved by limited protrusion of the mouth in order to enclose the most water possible. There's no suction as there is with particulate intake and it's comparatively less selective. This means that instead of an item being located and aimed at, it's a general area that contains food that moves little and which is enclosed and then processed within the mouth. Compared with particulate intake, gulping uses less energy, although the net energy gain for the fish will depend on the amount of food ingested with each gulp and its energy content.

Following intake, the food is processed. This involves first of all the separation of food from non-food (referred to in the literature as selective retention). At the top of the mouth, the carp possesses something called a palatal organ, which is a pad that the fish pushes against the gill rakers by compression of the head. This pushing clamps the food and the non-food can be flushed out through the gills. The palatal organis particularly rich in taste buds and has a function in taste selection. The organ therefore has a physical function which is that of separating food from non-food and is additionally responsible for deciding whether food should be swallowed or rejected. We know that the palatal organ possesses chemosensory functions because it has the largest number of taste buds of any of the feeding structures of the carp, including the barbels, which most of us would expect as being the most sensitive to taste. These can be as many as 800 per square millimetre, which is the highest number recorded in any fish. The fate of non-food items is expulsion through the gills, not as would be expected through the mouth by spitting. The palatal organ and the gill rakers interdigitate, which allows easier flushing of the non-food items through the gills.

However, spitting is another food processing action which is used to expel items from the mouth. It's less subtle than expulsion from the gills as a result of selective retention and is the preferred method for food items that are to be rejected. It's also used for waste and non-food items and can be seen to occur particularly when the fish is feeding on the bottom when muddy mouthfuls are commonplace.

The carp also uses the method of rinsing to concentrate or separate food inside the mouth cavity. This often uses back-washing of the food and non-food mixture and occurs by the fish protruding the upper jaw with the mouth closed which is referred to as 'closed protrusion'. By doing this, the mixture which is being separated at the back of the mouth is resuspended and brought back into the anterior part of the mouth cavity. Following resuspension, selective retention is repeated with food being trapped again by the palatal organ and more of the non-food portion is separated and expelled through the gills. If closed protrusion and back-washing is repeated several times, then selective retention based on taste and composition allows gradual purification of the mixture.

Once the food has been separated from non-food, the food part is moved by muscular contraction from the palatal organ to the pharyngeal teeth. These are located at the rear of the mouth in what is described as the chewing cavity and consist of two jaws, left and right. In many fish species, including other cyprinids, these interdigitate in a similar way to the fingers of either hand if you clench them together. In the carp, this doesn't occur. Instead, these are made up of flattened teeth which do not interlock although, as with other fish, the teeth oppose a chewing pad at the base of the skull.

The chewing cavity is only large enough for food items up to four percent of the length of the fish. On reaching this cavity, food is chewed and ground by the combined action of the teeth and chewing pad and the material is mixed with a type of mucus in order to form balls of food, which are then swallowed. The mucus is an important part of the mixture since it lubricates the balls and makes their transport easier. A similar thing happens in humans.

The apparatus that the carp possesses to chew the food is particularly important due to the varied diet of the carp. Being an omnivore, this needs to be able to deal with a wide range of different foods, including such difficult to chew foods as seeds, grains and mollusc shells (e.g. snails) and tough plant material such as stems and roots of aquatic plants. In the same way as our own teeth, the pharyngeal apparatus not only breaks up food items into smaller pieces, but chewing actually breaks apart the cellular structure of whatever it is and allows the contents to escape. This mechanical rupturing means that the material is exposed to digestive enzymes and fluids and their later digestion is made easier.

Different food items have a range of properties, both mechanical and chemical. The mechanical properties means that they react differently to the pressure applied during chewing. Unlike other animals, the carp's chewing apparatus is not designed for cutting, shearing and lacerating.

Alternatively, it's been shown that the carp is able to deal with hard, brittle and stiff materials very effectively although tough, elastic and fibrous objects are often just flattened. The objective of passing through the chewing apparatus is to increase the surface area of the food. The larger the surface area, the more effective digestion is expected to be.

Chewing and suction cannot both occur at the same time. They are therefore alternated. If you watch a carp feeding you'll see that it doesn't suck never-endingly and it in fact stops, chews and then returns to sucking. This is because these two processes do not use the same movements of head bones and muscles. You'll also see the fish close its mouth in order to grind which prevents the loss of suspended material.

Chewing and grinding require a large amount of pressure which is achieved by the fish transferring large forces to the pharyngeal jaws by way of different muscles above and below them. Although pressure is effective for dealing with the majority of food items, the relatively large and smooth surfaces of the pharyngeal jaws do not provide shearing forces and as a result, a few materials are left intact. Similar muscular compression eventually closes the entrance to the chewing cavity and moves the balls of food into the entrance of the gut (called the oesophagus). The following diagram shows food processing in the carp from intake to swallowing.

The velocity, direction and destination of food and non-food particles that are ingested are determined by a number of factors. These include the timing, amplitude and velocity of the opening of the mouth, protrusion of the upper jaw and opening of the gills . They affect the volumes of the different parts of the mouth covered here, such as the oral and gill cavities. For each type of food, different patterns of feeding actions can be observed. These sequences show that due to differences in the properties of each food type, these cause changes in how the foods are processed.

As anglers, what we have recently been discussing is highly relevant. This is because we should be interested in how feed is handled by the fish because this has implications for both how the fish reacts to our loose feeding or groundbaiting as well as to the hookbait itself. The feeding sequence for some baits is not the same as for others and knowing and understanding the alternatives will help us to know what the fish are feeding on or whether they are feeding at all.

Experiments with different food types have determined the sequences that are used for dealing with each. In the case of pellets, particulate intake is used, followed by rinsing. Pellets are repositioned in the mouth and then backwashed, then transported, crushed, ground and eventually swallowed. Due to the relatively hard texture of pellets they are crushed before being ground whereas softer foods such as earthworms (another

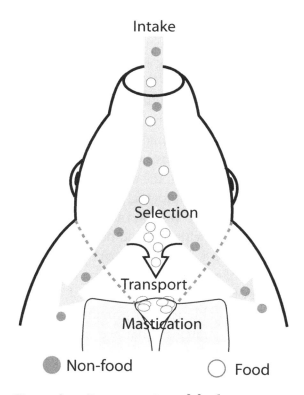

Figure 8: Representation of food processing showing the fates of food and non-food and flows of water and particles (modified from Sibbing, 1988).

of the food tested by Sibbing *et al.*, 1986) are only ground. It would be expected that a pellet that has been exposed to water for a longer period of time would be treated in a similar way since it would have lost its hardness and as a result could be ground rather than crushed and ground.

A different sequence can be observed for food items that are suspended in the water column. Instead of particulate intake, these are consumed by gulping. This can be observed when carp are feeding on a cloud of groundbait, or plankton (Sibbing *et al.*, 1986 used cladoceran zooplankton). Here, the gulping is followed by back-washing and gathering which refers to the process of concentrating the food again. This is followed by crushing and grinding in the same way as for pellets before swallowing occurs.

In the angling context, these sequences are employed by the fish to deal with the baits we use. Gulping is preferred for finer, suspended foods and it has been shown that the separation of food particles can be carried out as fine as a quarter of a millimetre in diameter (250 microns). That diameter includes more or less everything that we throw at the fish. It may however be difficult for the angler to distinguish the actual item that the fish is feeding on, unless observation at very close quarters is a possibility. In that kind of situation, the angler should be at least able to determine whether the fish is employing particulate intake or gulping. Since the feeding sequence involves internal processes, the angler will not be able to associate those with the food being consumed. However, some food such as seeds (e.g. hemp and barley) require considerable repetition of crushing strokes which is something that can be recognised from the angler's point of view.

The ways that a carp is able to feed provides us with a great deal of information regarding strategies that we should employ in bait making, bait choice and rig design. For example, we know that within the mouth of the fish there are several things going on, often at the same time. The carp is interested in testing the food that's on offer and so if it's palatable and a candidate for consumption, meaning that it consists of food rather than non-food, then it's separated and then mechanically broken down by crushing or grinding, or both, before

144

finally being swallowed. As anglers this concerns us since we want our bait to be accepted by the fish and to be taken into the mouth of the carp although not swallowed. It's difficult to say exactly how long a baited hook can remain in the fish's mouth before it's rejected, but it's safe to say that the more palatable a bait is and the more confidently the fish is feeding then the more chance it has of being sucked in and staying in there long enough for the angler to react or, in the case of bolt rigs, enough time for a hook hold to be found.

Modern bottom rigs work based on the bait on a hair being sucked in and the hook pricking the fish and causing it to run. In this case, fish will suck up the bait by particulate intake as opposed to gulping since groundbait or chopped bait are not used on the hook. From what we already know from this chapter, the speed with which that bait is sucked in depends on several things including the size of the fish and therefore the force of suction that can be applied and the density of the bait, which will mean that the fish has to adjust the force to the characteristics of the bait in order to suck it in efficiently. Remember that the fish is concerned primarily with net energy gain, which is a result of energy intake minus the energy used to obtain it. This means that it's beneficial for the fish to use only just enough energy to suck the bait in.

The heavier the bait is then the stronger the suck will need to be in order to get it into its mouth. That heaviness depends on the size of the bait and also its density. A bait that is close to the density of water will require the least amount of force to move and the smaller that bait is then moving it will be even easier. Therefore, two baits of different densities and sizes will not react the same way when exposed to the same force of suck from a carp. Bait ingredient choice has a lot to do with the density of the finished bait, but it's in the angler's interest to produce a bait that has a similar density to water. This means that for the sucking force applied to it, it will be more easily sucked in. In fact this weightlessness has been achieved using combinations of baits with pop-ups (either corn or actual baits) to form snowman setups and their variations with the intention being the presentation of a neutral bait held down by the hook.

We should remember that the boilie is not the only bait out there.

There are plenty of alternatives and each has its own density. Although baits with a similar density to water may make it easier for them to be sucked into the carp's mouth, this is not to say that that characteristic alone is enough to merit their use. As we will see in chapter 4, a bait has to satisfy a small number of criteria for it to be a great bait and low density is just one of them. Palatability and attraction are two others that are important if the fish are to feed confidently. This confident feeding means higher consumption of free offerings and an increased probability of the hookbait being ingested. One part of the feeding sequence involves separation of food according to size and taste and therefore it's important that a bait is attractive and the fish recognises its palatability. If so, this will add to the fish's confidence and there will be less reluctance for the bait to be rejected once it's been sucked in.

Although the palatal organ has been shown to influence the decision to swallow or reject a food, more recent studies than those by Sibbing into this subject have suggested that the palatal organ serves a localised taste sensory function rather than a mechanical one (Callan & Sanderson, 2003). This means that it's involved in tasting materials to find out which is acceptable, but apart from retaining the larger food particles, this study showed that it's not particularly active in sorting the smaller ones, which is instead carried out by the concentration of particles in the pharyngeal cavity. Non-food particles are expelled through the gills and by spitting as thought earlier.

The length of time that an item of food spends in the mouth of the fish depends on a number of factors. If it's palatable, meaning that the taste is agreeable to the fish, then it's likely to be maintained for a longer length of time in the mouth since there's less probability of rejection. Also, if the fish is feeding confidently, then it's unlikely that the item will be expelled due to it being suspicious. When the bait is eventually blown out, then if the bait is palatable, it's probable that this occurs due to the detection of the hook or other rig bits rather than the bait itself. The natural behaviour of the fish is to separate what it can eat from what it cannot. It's therefore understandable that the rig be expelled in this process and unfortunately for us that's the part that we don't want to be blown out.

The feeding mechanism allows the fish to obtain the energy that it needs from the food part of the material that it ingests. We have seen that the mechanism is complicated and the sequence of feeding actions used to deal with the food depends very much on the type of food and its properties. If it's soft, it will be dealt with differently from one that's hard and the time taken to deal with the food will depend greatly on how contaminated it is with non-food particles and how much crushing and/or grinding is required. The time that we have to be able to hook the fish is between the moment of our bait entering the mouth and the moment of it leaving it and since our rig is attached to the bait, it only gets as far as the palatal organ before it is rejected by spitting. Large, inorganic items are spat rather than ejected through the gills and a hook falls into this category.

In the same way, the rejection of a bait can be for other reasons, with suspicion by the fish ranking highly. This is particularly true in clearer waters where a carp may be relying more on visual detection than chemoreception. In those cases, it will be more difficult to get the fish to take the bait because it will be paying more attention to anything that is attached to the bait. At the moment that it sucks a hookbait in and its suspicion is aroused because the bait reacts unusually to the force of suction applied by the carp, then it may be expelled before it's even tasted. Therefore, it's important that rig design is optimised for each situation in order to avoid premature expulsion of the bait. Although rig design will not be covered here, there's plenty of information available on the subject and I'll leave this area to anglers who are more expert on the subject. Suffice to say that the objective of rig design is to hook the fish effectively. Although this does not necessarily mean that the longer the bait is in the mouth the better, what we do want to achieve is confident feeding, which will reduce the probability of premature expulsion of the bait and I'm convinced that bait design can make a big difference to this. On the other hand, the longer the bait is in the mouth, the greater the probability of an effective hook-hold being found.

The carp's feeding mechanism is complex and can deal with a wide range of food items with the structure and function of each part of the fish's mouth specialising in different actions, from separation to crushing and grinding, to suction and expulsion. The carp has a great ability to be successful when they are introduced to or when they naturally relocate to a new environment. Carp are rarely unsuccessfully introduced and they have acquired fame as troublesome invasive species in many parts of the world. This shows on the one hand how hardy a species they are and on the other how adaptable they are to different ecosystems. One of the most important reasons for this is the effectiveness of the feeding specialisations that the carp possesses. And this doesn't just apply to the internal structures but also the chemosensory feeding specialisations such as the taste buds on the exterior of the fish which connect the fish with its environment and allow it to locate food so effectively.

However, these specialisations also result in limitations, mainly because as the effectiveness of feeding on the most commonly available items is increased, which is something that is favourable for the fish, the ability to feed on some other items decreases. There are some examples of this in the carp. One of these is the inability to deal with organisms smaller than 250 micrometres in size (a quarter of a millimetre) since they cannot be concentrated by the branchial sieve, which is the filter-feeding organ possessed by the fish. Also, the fish is able to filter larger phytoplankton, but these are still too small to be effectively broken apart by chewing. Other fish use their acid gastric juices to open up phytoplankton in order to get at the contents, but since carp don't possess a stomach, this is not possible and the fish is therefore restricted in that respect.

Although seeds can be dealt with effectively by carp, the plants themselves are much more of a challenge. These plants (called macrophytes), which are usually aquatic, are available to the fish in the form of roots, shoots and leaves, but the feeding apparatus of the fish is not designed to deal with those which are particularly large in size. The carp is unable to bite or scrape because its jaws lack teeth and any plant material that is ingested, such as smaller pieces that have broken or rotted off the main plant, cannot be damaged much by chewing because of the smooth surface of the pharyngeal teeth.

It has also been suggested that as cyprinids grow in size, the size of items that can be retained by the branchial sieve also increases proportionally. This means that it's easier for smaller fish to feed on smaller items such as plankton than it is for larger fish.

In comparison, the carp's ability to feed on animals that live on or in the lake or river bottom (benthic invertebrates) are dealt with very well as a result of their relatively large size and the structural specialisations that the carp possesses with which it processes them. This is true too when these items are contaminated by non-food particles or when they are very tough. Even so, there are limitations associated with this regarding the size of organisms that can be processed. Although a carp can ingest items up to nine percent of its total length in diameter, only those up to four percent in diameter can enter the chewing cavity. The carp has been classified as a feeding specialist regarding hard food particles and also for dealing with mixtures of food and non-food although other options exist for it in order to obtain foods which do not require specialisations.

Regarding the capture of items as opposed to 'accidentally' vacuuming them up, the carp is only reasonably talented. The carp must find both the capture and processing of live food such as small fish difficult, not only during the act of capture which requires precision suction, but also the steps that follow, since even within the mouth, live prey continues to writhe, wriggle and swim around until it reaches the chewing cavity. This is also made more difficult by the lack of teeth, which could at least incapacitate the prey, making transport easier. It is therefore possible to summarise that the carp is highly effective at selection and feeding on hard particles such as invertebrates and seeds, but is less effective with plant material, extremely small items and large live food that may move fast.

Another important food item in the carp's diet is detritus. This is composed mainly of the remains of dead plants and animals, which may take the form of whole or fragmented material. As we have already seen, carp are not as efficient dealing with plant material as they are that of animals. Since detritus can often be composed of large quantities of plant rather than animal material, it's likely that in that case, detritus does not provide continued sustenance. In the same way as other food items, only detritus over a quarter of a millimetre can be processed due to its retention by the branchial sieve.

In the same way as feeding effectiveness varies from item to item, seasonal variation in item abundance can affect the fish's ability to find the food items that it needs to satisfy energy requirements. Total energy intake will therefore depend on the abundance of different food items and the energy they contain. It has been shown that seasonal variation affects the abundance of preferred food items, including a variety of foods of plant and animal origin.

In winter, feeding activity is reduced and in the case of the carp, when the temperature is below six degrees, they may stop feeding altogether. At that time of the year, midge larvae (bloodworm) may be the only food available or ingested. In spring, water temperatures are already rising and zooplankton begins to become more abundant. Carp may leave the bottom as bloodworm numbers decrease and search for plankton in the water column. Larger types of crustacean become the preferred diet at this time. Then in summer, the numbers of zooplankton become depleted mainly due to consumption by young fish. Plant growth is high at this time of the year and carp may graze on the softer, more edible parts of macrophytes. Between these plants live a variety of animals both in the water column and on the lake or river bottom, which may include such organisms as molluscs, worms and insect larvae and pupae. Following the summer, vertical mixing and lower temperatures leads to higher oxygen levels and carp may leave the plentiful margin areas and move back to bottom feeding in open water. Here, both planktonic and benthic organisms may form important dietary components of the fish.

Most reports refer to carp feeding on either planktonic or benthic organisms, vegetation or detritus throughout the year in differing proportions. Rarely are smaller fish an important source of food unless there is a lack or absence of other alternatives. It is also thought that herbivory (the eating of plants) is not the preferred feeding strategy of the

150

fish and may be employed only when there's an absence of invertebrates. The energy that the fish receives from eating plant material may barely sustain it. As we will see further on, the carp requires an average protein content of 38 percent. Although plants may provide the fish with some nutrients that other foods do not, plant material in general contains at most five percent of its wet weight as protein. What that basically means is that a carp would have to eat an awful lot of plant to obtain the same amount of protein that it obtains from insect larvae, which is generally in the region of 26 to 34 percent protein as wet weight.

Some foods also require that the carp expend more energy in their handling, which is particularly true for some hard invertebrates as opposed to soft ones. If we consider some of those found in our lakes and rivers and which we come into contact with regularly, examples are the caddis larva which builds its 'home' out of sticks and stones and different types of mollusc, including various species of freshwater mussels and snails. Relatively speaking, these require large amounts of energy to crush in order for the fish to get at the contents of their shells. With those types of animal, there's a relatively large amount of energy used in order to obtain a comparatively small amount of energy because even large molluscs which are able to be consumed by the fish contain only small amounts of edible material.

The places where you fish have their own characteristics regarding the flora and fauna and in no two lakes or rivers do the carp eat exactly the same selection of natural food items at the same time. This means that their diet will consist of a variety of different organisms. Fish such as carp are opportunist feeders and in the natural situation they will eat whatever is most readily available, with that depending very much on seasonal variation. It's part of the angler's job to determine what the fish are feeding on since that will give him an idea of how to fish, with types or food often indicating where the fish will be feeding and therefore providing the angler with a greater insight into locating the fish.

Chapter Four

Bait

Carp fishing has changed immensely since real interest in the species began some fifty years ago. Several things have been responsible for this including improvements in tackle, the appearance of specialist books, magazines and then more modern media and the hard work and dedication of experts and innovators. Whether carp fishing has changed more than any other areas of the sport is difficult to say, but its position as one of the fastest growing branches of angling is undeniable.

Apart from the factors mentioned, interest in the species is somewhat due to the biology of the common carp and its variants; it's generally a fast-growing species, omnivorous in nature, which can, to varying degrees, be found feeding at different times of the day and all year round. These conditions make it an interesting and often willing target species for the angler. Let's face it, if carp were a species with a maximum weight of half a pound that fed exclusively on plankton at a certain time of the day during one month of the year, it wouldn't receive anywhere near the interest that it does.

However, one of the things that stands out among the current information available on the carp is the amount of supposition and uncertainty surrounding carp feeding and behaviour. Understanding these two variables is directly related to our successes or failures as anglers and guessing or not knowing the facts behind why a carp does or doesn't do something is counterproductive to our activity.

People sometimes ask me why I do so much thinking about my fishing and principally carp when angling is supposed to be relaxing. For me it's because of the unknowns. These are those which when you read articles or talk to other anglers are all too glaringly obvious and commonplace in carp fishing, that stress the fact that our knowledge of the species as humble anglers is still very limited and that without certain changes, particularly in the field of carp bait development, we will never be able to reach our full potential as carpers. That would be a shame, since reduced potential is usually equivalent to reduced enjoyment of the sport.

These days it's easy to speak about bait and think of boilies. Although there are now more types of carp bait available than any time in the past, the boilie is the one that has been given more thought than any other and is the one that most money is spent on by anglers. The subject of boilies is a book in itself. There's an awful lot of information available, mainly because it's such a widely used bait, as well as being versatile, durable and successful. Boilies are responsible for continuous catches of monster fish in any country that carp inhabit, independently of water type or ecosystem. What began as a simple solution to the problem of the bait being devoured by smaller, non-target fish has revolutionised the sport and in conjunction with the hair rig has provided an extremely effective manner of catching big carp.

However, this dramatic change in carp-fishing has resulted in two less desirable consequences. Many anglers would probably not give these a second thought, but the appearance of the boilie has meant that 1) traditional baits and techniques are overlooked when they could prove more effective and, 2) new anglers are often plunged straight into the use of boilies without experiencing other carp-catching baits and methods.

Both of these modern trends are unfortunate and for those of us who have come through the 'carping school' for two or more decades, it seems a shame that newcomers will miss out on arguably less technical carp fishing, which has been replaced in many cases by long-range standardised tackle and tactics. There was a time before the boilie and before you were able to cast anywhere on the lake from one swim. But I suppose that there are still a large number of unknowns and despite advances in tackle and bait design, the angler still needs to pit his wits against the fish and also that independently of the advances in modern carp fishing, the techniques that the angler uses will depend not only on modern trends but on the preferences of the angler himself and his mentality in general.

Often the type of fishing that an angler will prefer is not a result of a trend but as a consequence of personal experience. If he's been successful using a particular method, then it's often the same one that he uses repeatedly even when it might not be the most productive on a particular day or in a specific situation. In that respect, many anglers prefer the tried and tested as opposed to the method of the moment, which is basically an attempt to keep confidence levels up. The same thing is particularly true in the case of bait.

New baits appear all the time. With every issue of one of the angling magazines it's possible to find a new type or at least flavour of bait and the selection is not only daunting but it can have an impact not just on confidence but these days also on your pocket. The majority of anglers aren't millionaires and a difficult economic climate doesn't favour those with little to spare. Years ago you could quite happily leave home with half a loaf and a tin of sweetcorn, but now it seems that if you're not carrying at least five kilos of bait that appeared in the latest magazine and the dip to go with it, then you're not worthy of a place on the bank.

That of course is rubbish. As we know, a carp can be caught on the simplest of baits. You can catch one on a piece of coloured foam, a dog biscuit or an earthworm. I met a lad a while back who said he'd once run out of bait and ended up fishing for and catching a carp on a Wotsit. When you're able to locate the carp and they're feeding, they're not a difficult fish to catch. The trouble is when the fish don't show themselves, when they're not interested in feeding then even the most dedicated angler begins to wonder if he's wasting his time.

The bait industry is huge. When I was a child, the only manufactured baits were groundbaits and the early packs of shelf-life boilies. Sometime in the eighties, the number and diversity of manufactured baits began to increase. The packaging became more elaborate and, with time, the presentation seems to have become just as important as the contents.

This of course is wrong and the majority of the best-known boilies are now packaged in the same quality packaging or even better than some of those used for human food. They're made with foil and are often shiny and resealable to keep the freshness in. On the one hand the ability to keep bait freshness, texture and moisture levels as they were intended when the bait left the factory is progress, but the gaudy, shiny package could be done away with, since it does nothing more than distract the angler from the contents, which is what his real concern should be. It reminds me of lures and flies that don't catch that many fish but they certainly look good.

The additional costs associated with bait advertising and packaging add up and it's the angler who eventually has to pay for these. Several pounds of every kilo of bait are costs associated with getting you to hear about the bait, getting the bait to your nearest fishing shop and getting you to buy it. Most well-known bait costs ten pounds sterling or more per kilo, which is an amount that anglers seem willing to pay for results and not having to go to the trouble of making the bait themselves. If you take off the fishing shop's profit, shipping from the factory, the manufacturer's profit, the cost of the packaging, how much is there left for research and development and using high quality ingredients? Bait manufacture is not something that I currently know that much about, but what I am familiar with are the costs associated with feed production for the aquaculture industry, an area from which some of the concepts associated with bait production have come.

In aquaculture, feed costs for a fish farmer can represent 50 percent of all costs on an intensive fish farm such as those where salmon and trout are produced. These are carnivorous species and as a result they receive a diet with a large percentage of fishmeal, which is a relatively expensive resource even if the feed producer buys in very large quantities. It's also a resource that's running out as a consequence of overfishing of the pelagic sea fish stocks from which it's obtained and fishmeal will therefore continue to increase in price as time goes on. Although fishmeal incorporation in carp baits is usually less than the 40 to 55 percent average used in aquaculture feeds for carnivorous fish, it's still considered an important ingredient for bait, for both boilies and pellets . There's no doubting that fish like fishmeal and this is due to the similarity of amino acid profiles making conversion from feed to flesh more efficient. Also, the smell of fishmeal comes from the substances which it's composed of, with those apparently causing a positive feeding reaction.

Aquaculture is very different from angling in many respects. For example, the objectives of each differ, with that of aquaculture being the production of the highest amount of fish biomass in the shortest possible time with the highest possible economic gain. This sounds a very negative way to describe my profession but it's the honest truth and is no different from other agricultural activities that owe their existence usually not to quality but to quantity and profitability.

Angling on the other hand is not about fish biomass production, although fish growth is a desirable characteristic for the angler and of course the fishery owner, but about capturing the fish. In the angling situation, the objective of bait design is improved capture efficiency of the target species with consideration of the attractive and nutritional properties of the bait. It often doesn't require a lot of thought, scientific knowledge about nutrition and growth or even large amounts of resources or bait. It's possible to catch a big carp with anything from a natural bait to a state-of-the-art boilie from a foil packet or an artificial. In some cases you don't need more than a handful of bait to get the fish interested. Sometimes one single hookbait will suffice.

Bait companies are doing a job just like any other business, trying to sell as much as possible and increase their market share. I think that if carp fishing development were to stop today, as a community I feel we've achieved a great deal in a relatively short time and a lot of that has been as a result of the efforts of bait producers. At the same time, only time will tell who we should continue to place our trust in. Only recently have some bags of bait begun to include an ingredients list and we are just now finding out what the bait that we have in some case been buying for years actually contains.

As with many products, it's those companies that have become the biggest that are able to influence the market more and since they are able to buy ingredients in greater bulk, they're able to incorporate more of the more expensive ingredients without it affecting their profits as it would a smaller company. In the same way, it's these larger companies that are able to carry out a greater amount of testing, whether that occurs in tanks or in the field. They're able to provide more free bait to testers and as a result the chances of capturing more big fish are improved. The bigger companies are able to get big name anglers on board more easily and that leads to more pictures of monster carp that can be used to fuel their publicity.

However, I believe that there's room for more companies in the bait industry. There's still a great deal that we don't know about carp nutrition and behaviour and I would imagine that with time, further advances will be seen in the areas of bait development and manufacture. Science is only recently being applied to angling. This is also occurring indirectly since the aquaculture budget is much greater than that of recreational angling and carp fishing is still much smaller and much less lucrative than carp farming. Therefore, it's likely that research into carp for angling reasons will occur much more slowly than advances as a result of funding for aquaculture reasons. This is because research is funded by state, private and public institutions and this usually happens on the basis that at the end of the project, some hypothesis will have been tested, some problem will have been solved and the financers will own some new technology or product or an industry will be better off as a result of the research.

There's room for companies that can bring something new to carp fishing. One way to do that is to apply knowledge of carp nutrition to the sport, using what the aquaculture world knows to ultimately improve the angling experience. Maybe there's even something beyond the mighty boilie, just waiting to be discovered, something that will revolutionise the sport once again.

Bait is what is most talked about in angling circles, mainly because it's the part of the tackle that offers maybe the most variety and it's the point of contact between the fish and angler. Also, a change in bait sometimes requires a change of rig and a change of rig often warrants a change in bait. The two are connected (no pun intended). Bait is also the main reason why an angler might lose confidence in his approach. If he hasn't had a run, then the first thing he blames is his bait, when the cause might be something else. In the same way as the fly fisherman, the first change he makes when he hasn't had a fish will be the fly. Then again and again, until eventually he will probably come back to the one he started with.

There are anglers who are consistently successful. There are some who will catch no matter what. Whether they are just lucky or are truly more talented than the rest is debatable. It's true that a lot of the well-known carp anglers are just that because at one time or another they spent or even still spend an unnatural amount of time by the water. In their case, maybe bait choice isn't as important as it is for someone who's only able to fish for a couple of hours each week or fortnight but that's debatable. Perhaps for the short session carper, attraction is more important than nutrition as far as bait goes. He wants a fast response in the form of a big fish and for that reason his approach won't be the same as that of the angler who can spend a week on a water without a second thought.

This chapter is the most extensive because of the importance of bait and for the reasons I've already mentioned. Bait is central to the fishing equation and is in a constant state of development. Whether you're the angler who lives by the water or the one who only has a short time available to fish, it's likely that you spend a large proportion of your time thinking about bait and what's happening to it in the water. If you've got this far than you're hopefully well versed in carp location and feeding (if you weren't already) and what remains is to put the bait on the end of the line and catch yourself a new personal best.

Carp Fishing Science looked at all different baits from naturals and standard baits to elaborated baits and artificials. However, since the nutritional compositions have already been presented there and any further information is available on the web from such sites as the USDA Nutritional Database, here I'll concentrate initially on the main food groups and their relationship to carp nutrition before focusing on boiled baits due to their continued and growing importance to the sport. Although a wide range of standard baits are available, their composition doesn't vary too much. Sweetcorn and even bread doesn't change too much between brands. This isn't to say that they can't be made more or less attractive to the carp by the addition of other substances. Those are not part of the standard bait itself but are covered here because they are highly relevant to the effectiveness of any bait, from bread to boilies.

a. Requirements

In carp bait development, as a result of several theories appearing regarding terms such as HNV, instant attractor and food bait, more recently there has been greater interest in providing baits which consider the nutritional requirements of the fish. This is because, as we have already mentioned and what should be considered the central message of these chapters, the benefits of using a bait that is nutritionally adequate is beneficial in several ways. It's a benefit to the fish health-wise, to the fishery owner because of the increased growth and health of the stock, to the angler who is catching healthier and bigger fish and of course to the bait manufacturer who'll sell more bait as a result.

There are many variations on the general description of 'nutrition' that you can find, but the majority of these mention the provision of nutrients for organisms or the cells of organisms. These nutrients take different forms, with the most common and well-known being the fats (also referred to as lipids), protein and carbohydrate . These are also the nutrients that are most frequently spoken about by anglers. These three are macro-nutrients, meaning that they're required in larger amounts and, along with others, allow the bodies of all organisms to sustain life since the intake of these nutrients allows the fish, the human or whatever other organism that we might be talking about to provide the energy necessary to keep the organism alive. It's therefore understandable that without food intake and the supply of the nutrients that the organism needs, life sooner or later ends.

If the supply of nutrients and therefore the source of energy is stopped abruptly, then life may end quite quickly. If nutrient supply is slowly reduced, then life can continue for longer. This depends on the organism. Fish can survive for several months without food with bigger fish able to last even longer. In contrast, humans without food usually die within ninety days. This is in part due to the ability of fish to modify their metabolic rate to use energy resources more slowly and the fact that the amount of energy required by a fish is much less than that of a human due to the fact that they are cold-blooded (poikilothermic).

This means that their internal temperature is not kept constant and instead varies according to changes in the temperature of their external environment. This is to say that if a carp is moved from water of ten degrees to water of twenty degrees, the internal temperature of the fish does the same, whereas a human being moved between different environments of ten and twenty degrees would experience no internal temperature change and it would instead remain at normal human body temperature of about 37 degrees.

Carp, in the same way as other animals, feed in order to obtain energy. The nutrients that are ingested may be used directly for growth or the repair or body tissues, but the majority are made available by the breaking down of long molecules composed of chains of nutrients in the gut, which are then passed into the body of the fish where they're used to construct new molecules, which form the structural and functional parts of the fish.

The different macro-nutrients can all be used as sources of energy. In humans, energy is more efficiently obtained from fats and carbohydrates. This is because fish, despite their many similarities with humans, have evolved differently. Land animals, like us, have evolved in an environment filled with a plentiful supply of carbohydrate, mainly in the form of plants. Likewise, the aquatic environment is abundant in protein and fat but scarce in carbohydrates. As a result, fish have adapted to this background of nutrients and have evolved to use protein as their preferred energy source, followed by lipids. Although they are able to extract energy from carbohydrate sources, fish do so inefficiently, so much so that they've been described as being intolerant to large quantities of carbohydrate in their food. This has been shown with some species of fish that have been injected with glucose and the time recorded for the blood glucose level to return to normal. Compared with humans, fish are much slower at doing this and their capacity for dealing with carbohydrate is related to the way fish have evolved, which means in an environment in which the primary source of energy is protein.

This has a number of implications for the angler. Although we haven't yet looked at protein in any detail here, we already know that protein should be an important consideration for any bait. It serves as both a preferential energy source and a valuable resource for the construction of structures such as muscles in the fish. Effectively, protein is what is often referred to as a building block for increasing the body mass of the fish. This is one of the main principles of fish farming . However, more specifically, it's the units that make up the proteins that the fish ingests, the amino acids, that are used to build the proteins that make up muscles and other structures in the fish.

Muscles are the largest collections of protein in the body of vertebrates, although proteins are present in many other tissues and fluids in the fish's body. Proteins are extremely diverse. Often they are not only made up of amino acids but can also be combined with non-protein material, which is called conjugation and in that way it's possible to form substances such as haemoglobin, which includes iron, which is used to carry oxygen in the blood, or enzymes which catalyse biochemical reactions and glycoproteins formed from protein and carbohydrate and which are used to construct antibodies used in protection against disease. Proteins can have other uses, both structurally and in reactions in our bodies and those of fish. Also, they're involved in signalling (message sending) between cells in different parts of the body in the form of hormones and other substances. Protein is therefore very important in animals and even more so in fish. In comparison, a fish's daily requirement for protein is usually double that of a human.

However, what fish need for all these different structures and functions is not protein. What a fish needs are amino acids. It's from those that the fish is able to construct everything protein-based that it needs to live, grow and reproduce. Unfortunately, we're unable to make baits and aquaculture feeds out of amino acids because of the cost involved. Pure amino acid is quite expensive, but it would signify an important energy saving for the animal if protein were provided in the form of amino acids rather than the long chains of aminos that crude protein is made from. Instead of having to break them up into their constituent amino acids to be passed from the gut into the blood and then constructed into the proteins it requires (both these processes require energy), they wouldn't need to be broken down.

Amino acids can be used for boosting levels (supplementing) when the natural levels of a particular amino in the protein source used is lower than that which the fish requires. This works out cheaper because it's often not a particularly large amount. We will examine this concept in greater detail in a while.

There are many protein sources available for consumption by animals and these are of plant or animal origin. Many of these have been evaluated for incorporation into aquaculture feeds and some appear frequently in carp baits. Probably the best-known protein source is fishmeal, which is obtained from pelagic sea fish such as herrings, sardines and mackerel. Fishmeal is basically a flour made from the processing of these fish with the process consisting of cooking, pressing and drying of the meal to produce a dry solid product. This may then be ground or milled to produce the finished meal. The pressing and drying or the fishmeal is in order to remove oil and water. The fish oil is retained for use in a variety of industries including the production of pelleted aquafeeds where the oil is added back before pelleting to provide the fat source of the diet. Other animal protein sources that have been used in aquaculture and which may appear in carp baits are meat and bone meal, blood meal and poultry meal.

Plant protein sources are more diverse, with common alternatives being soybean, potato, wheat, maize or corn and lupins. Protein content varies, as do the amino acid profiles of each of these. The profile refers to the amount of each of the amino acids in the protein. These are present as units of the protein chains that make up each source. I've included a selection of plant and animal sources in the appendix (table 1). For each you can see that the amounts of each amino acid present can vary considerably, which has implications for bait formulation.

Optimal total crude protein for common carp diets has been shown to be 38 percent using a casein based diet (Ogino & Saito, 1970). This means that 38 percent is a good guide for anyone formulating a nutritionally adequate bait for carp. However, this percentage cannot be made up of just any combination of amino acids. Instead, to ensure adequacy it should be composed of the corresponding percentages of each one that have been determined.

Amino acids may be essential or non-essential. An essential amino means one that the fish is unable to synthesise from another amino acid or from something else and it must therefore be obtained from the diet. Of the 23 amino acids that have been isolated from natural proteins, ten have been found to be essential in fish and have been defined regarding the percentage of each of these that must be present in a feed or bait if a deficiency of one or more of these is to be avoided.

The requirements for the ten essential amino acids have been evaluated for common carp (Nose, 1979) and are summarised in table 2 of the appendix. Therefore, to avoid deficiency, we should ensure that our bait consists of 38 percent protein and also that the percentage of each of the amino acids is satisfied. To give you an example, if we were making a kilo of bait, then to arrive at 38 percent protein, we would adjust our mixture so that 380 grams of that kilo were made up of protein. Our protein source should contain considerably more than 38 percent protein or we will never arrive at that percentage in the finished bait. However, it's unlikely that the protein source will be a hundred percent protein. Therefore, we need to make an allowance for that. If for example it's 50 percent protein, then we'll need to double the amount (760 grams) in order to be able to arrive at the correct value.

It's better to include more than is required than less. Excess protein can always be used for energy. However, it's also likely that although we're ensuring the value of total protein, if we look at the amounts of each essential amino acid included, then there'll probably be several that are below the required amount. There are two options to solve this deficiency. The first is to increase the amount of the amino acid that is deficient by supplementation. This means obtaining the amino acid and adding the required amount to the mix. This is not the cheapest alternative. Protein is the most expensive of all the food groups and specific aminos are even more expensive. I'd therefore suggest the second alternative, which is to combine your principal protein source with another. This means that by mixing the two, or more than two if need be, the profiles complement each other. Such an example would be a source that is rich in amino A (150% requirement) but deficient in amino B (50% requirement) and a separate source that is deficient in amino A (50% requirement) but rich in amino B (150% requirement). By mixing the two in equal quantities we would have twice the amount but the excesses and deficiencies would, in this case, cancel themselves out and the presence of both aminos A and B would be 100% in the new mixture.

Carp anglers talk about amino acids a great deal and often make mistakes when they're discussing them. Some anglers are under the impression that amino acids are free within the bait. If they are, then they are in extremely low levels. The vast majority of amino acids are found in bait as part of the proteins of the sources that have been used in its formulation. Others think that supplementation is used to replace an amino acid that is absent or in low quantities in the carp's natural food. This is a fallacy. In the same way that the amino acid profile varies from source to source, it also varies from food item to food item. But you can be assured that the lake contains all of the naturally occurring essential amino acids in one form or another. If the carp wasn't receiving all of them in the correct amounts, then it would either be dead or heading that way. The angler cannot know how much of each amino is present in a lake or river or how much of each one a carp has received in its diet without extensive research and a very large number of analyses. It's therefore impractical to find out. Therefore, trying to supplement a 'missing' amino acid is rubbish.

Supplementation allows the bait producer to provide the amino acid profile that the carp requires, independently of what the fish is receiving from its natural diet. This supplementation can result in two important benefits for the angler. Firstly, it allows the deficiency of a particular amino acid to be avoided. Secondly, if the amino acid is one of those responsible for a positive feeding response, then its incorporation in free form can increase the attractive properties of the bait. These two benefits are the main reason which supplementation occurs. However, I'd avoid supplementation with free amino acids that have been shown to result in a negative feeding response. To help you with this I've included a list of amino acids in table 3 of the appendix, which has been modified from Kasumyan & Morsi (1996) and are specific to Cyprinus carpio. Rather than including free amino acids that are deterrents, it makes sense to use a protein source that has relatively high levels of the deficient amino. This will be present as part of the crude protein molecules and not in its free form, therefore resulting in little if any chemosensory activity for the fish.

There's an additional complication to the addition of protein to our bait. Although we provide the required amount of one or more protein sources or amounts of amino acids that satisfy particular requirements in the fish, the amount that's available to the fish will usually not be a hundred percent. This is because digestion is not a totally effective process and it's almost impossible for an organism to digest all of a particular substance. The same principles apply not only to protein but also to the other major food groups (fat and carbohydrate) and the micronutrients (vitamins and minerals). We have already seen that food intake is how a fish obtains energy and of the total energy ingested (gross energy), some of this is excreted as urine and faecal energy. This excretion is made up of undigested food as well as bacteria and metabolic products. Digestible energy is therefore the energy that can be obtained from the food that is actually absorbed from the total energy (or food) ingested.

Digestion is the breaking down of large molecules in the food into smaller ones, which as a result can pass into the bloodstream of the fish. This movement of small molecules is called absorption and occurs in several parts of the gut depending on the structure of the animal's gut. We've seen that carnivorous fish possess a true stomach (e.g. trout, salmon, bass, pike) and others don't. The latter are referred to as agastric fish and include the carp. They may have an enlarged front part of the intestine but not the stomach that we're familiar with. As a result, absorption can occur in many parts of the gut, whereas in fish with a true stomach this is more common for the stomach to be used for digestion and the small intestine to be used for absorption. The lack of a stomach is not a problem for the carp and the absorption of larger molecules has been shown to be several times greater in the carp than in fish with a functional stomach (McLean & Donaldson, 1990).

Since carp don't have a stomach and don't produce the acid that fish with stomachs and humans do, the pH of the carp's intestine is relatively high in comparison (7.0-8.2). Even though carp don't feed principally on fish, they still have to deal with high levels of protein from other food items and in the absence of stomach acid they use a combination of enzymes produced in the pancreas and the intestine to reduce complex proteins such as those used in bait (e.g. casein) to amino acids, which can then be absorbed. These digestive juices are also not just used for dealing with proteins but also carbohydrates and fats.

Many factors can affect the efficiency of a fish to digest food and digestibility can be dependent on many things, which include specialisations of the digestive system of the animal and the characteristics of the food being ingested as well as characteristics of the environment where the carp lives. Evolution has led to particular animals being able to deal better with some food groups than others due to the higher availability of those in the animal's environment and their importance to the animal. In comparison, an animal in an environment with low food availability of the preferred type may opt for ingesting an alternative but the efficiency of digestion may be much lower than the other.

Also, the ability to digest a food can be affected by the food's texture, such as its hardness and particle size. This means, in the angling sense, that a bait that a fish is able to grind and crush (see chapter 3) effectively before swallowing will be better digested than one than can only be split before swallowing. This is because one of the objectives of the feeding mechanism is to increase the surface area of the food item. Greater surface area means more contact between the digestive juices and the food particles and more effective breaking down of the food. For example, if you think of a boilie and the fish chewed it only just enough to swallow it as chopped boilie, then a large proportion of the contents of those chops would remain on the inside and would only come in contact with the digestive juices once those on the outside were broken down. On the other hand, if the boilie was chewed more and reduced to basically powdered boilie before swallowing, it's understandable that a greater proportion of the ingested food could be exposed to the digestive juices from the start.

Digestion is a function of not just surface area and texture, but also of temperature and time. Temperature increase means the fish will be more active. Greater activity means that the fish will eat more and as a result the food has a tendency to pass more quickly through the gut. This faster speed of passage means that absorption of digested food is reduced since contact times between the food and enzymes in different parts of the gut are reduced and become less effective and therefore there is less digested food produced that can then be absorbed. The general rule is that with increased feed (or bait) intake, the efficiency of absorption is lower. That's why fish on farms are usually fed small ration sizes but several times per day since this optimises digestion, absorption and growth. As anglers we want the fish to eat more but overeating can mean reduced growth due to reduced digestion efficiency and growth and increased food wastage. However, considering our priorities as anglers it's reasonable to assume that despite these consequences, we would still prefer the fish to eat more.

Environmental temperature can affect not just the activity of the fish but also the effect of gut enzymes. Increased temperature means the food is broken down faster. Therefore, as temperature increases, the amount of food effectively digested is a trade-off between increased digestion and reduced absorption as a result of increased passage times of food through the gut.

In a practical sense, bait ingredients will be better digested and absorbed if their texture is finer. This means that the surface area is already greater even before mastication and digestion begin. Examples of this are the flours and meals that are produced and are often incorporated in baits. They come in a range of textures, from very coarse to very fine and although they are chemically the same, they are physically different. They are dry and in the case of coarse meals such as maize meal, they consist of hard fragments of dry maize, which is understandably difficult for the carp to digest as well as the same ingredient provided in fine powder form. We have seen that carp are effective at grinding, but this still might not be as efficient as consuming the meal as a finer flour.

There are other factors that affect the ability to digest a food item, which include such things as the age and size of the fish. As with other animals, as individuals age biological processes become less efficient. Therefore, a juvenile to adult carp will probably have more effective digestion than an old or very old fish. Carp larvae also have reduced digestive effectiveness due to them not yet possessing full digestive capacity including all and enough of the digestive enzymes of older fish.

Studies of feed digestibility in carp have been carried out. For example, Degani et al. (1997a) compared the digestibility of three different feed ingredients (wheat, barley and corn) according to their protein, carbohydrate and fat contents. Wheat meal protein was found to have a digestibility of 92 percent and wheat meal fat a digestibility of 80 percent. Corn protein showed a digestibility of 81 percent and fat digestibility of 90 percent. For barley, digestibility of protein was 73 percent and fat was 67 percent. We can see that depending on the type of ingredient, digestibility can change. If the study were to be repeated with coarse and fine examples of each meal, it's likely that other differences would be found.

In a separate study by Degani et al. (1997b) the researchers focused on three different protein sources and also found the digestibility of these to vary. Of the three, fishmeal protein showed a digestibility of 83.8 percent, followed by soybean meal at 69.8 percent and finally poultry meal at 47.2 percent. The same study was used to evaluate the digestibility of the energy of each protein source, which resulted in values of 93.4, 74.7 and 63.9 percent energy digestibility for fishmeal, soybean meal and poultry meal proteins respectively. This study highlights the fact that carp are efficient and effective utilisers of protein, despite being omnivorous. This is probably related somewhat to the abundance of protein in most aquatic environments. This available protein, as we have already discussed, has been responsible in part for the dietary evolution of the carp, its capacity to deal with protein effectively and the structural and functional specialisations that it has developed in order to cope with aquatic organisms and other food items which often contain large amounts of protein. Not only that, but the most important substances affecting the chemosensory feeding response in carp are amino acids, which are the building blocks of proteins. Similar studies are available for different fats utilised by carp. In general, freshwater fish are very effective at digesting fats with values of 90 percent or above not uncommon.

There are a number of implications of digestion for anglers and bait formulators alike. We should keep in mind that not all of the food the carp eats will be utilised by the fish. A variable percentage, depending on the composition of the food and a range of other factors that affect its digestibility, will be excreted. From a bait formulation standpoint, it's therefore necessary to know how much of what you are putting into a bait is not being utilised. You can go into this point in any depth depending on how important this aspect is for you.

Bait companies should consider this aspect most seriously, basically because they're providing bait in larger quantities and publicising its effectiveness. As we'll see, a successful bait is a combination of what's in it and how you use it. Obviously the bait producers can't influence how you use it very much. That depends on the angler. However, the 'what's in it' is their responsibility and it would be nice to think that they were actually concerned enough about the two key aspects of bait manufacture, attraction and nutrition, to put in not just the physical work necessary to produce a well-rolled bait but also the mental work required to solve questions regarding biological issues such as that of digestibility.

The simplest solution to digestibility is to ensure that the fish eat more of the bait. For example, if the digestibility and absorption of a particular ingredient is 50 percent, then if the amount ingested is doubled, then in theory it will absorb 100 percent. That is possible if the digestibility is relatively high. If the digestibility is low, say 10 percent, then it might not be physically possible for the carp to eat ten times the amount of a food or bait in order to absorb the amount that it requires.

Another solution is to give the ingredient a helping hand in the form of predigestion, which can occur naturally by the use of an enzyme. An example of this is the enzymatic digestion of the milk protein casein by trypsin which, as with other forms of predigestion, cuts the long crude protein molecule into much smaller parts (peptides and amino acids), which are more easily digested and absorbed by the fish's gut. What predigestion achieves is basically a reduction of the work that needs to be done by the fish to bring about complete digestion.

Predigestion occurs by hydrolysis, which means that by adding water the bonds are broken between the building blocks of food materials. Hydrolysis sounds scientific but it's something that humans carry out whenever they boil a potato or pasta. The heat that we apply and the water we use for boiling causes the hydrolysis of starch to produce shorter carbohydrates in the form of sugars. The process changes both the texture and the flavour of the food. In nature, hydrolysis uses biological catalysts (enzymes) which speed up the reaction at lower temperatures so unlike the heat required to boil foods when we're cooking, not as much energy is needed for the hydrolysis to take place.

Hydrolysis is possible with all three macro-nutrients. Commonly, enzymes are used and it's possible for the angler or bait formulator to use enzyme preparations to assist with digestion. However, enzymes have a weakness. They are made ineffective (denatured) by heating, which means that boiling or steaming of bait will halt the enzymatic process. Therefore, enzymes can be considered as a way of hydrolysing ingredients before mixing but once boiled will cause little or no further activity in the bait. Anglers may think that by adding enzymes to a mix they are improving digestion in the gut of the fish. I don't agree with this unless the enzymes are not exposed to heat and their integrity is preserved such as mixing with particles at low temperature or in a paste which is not steamed or boiled. In those cases, enzymes may be longer-lasting hydrolysers and, depending on their nature and characteristics, their activity might persist even in the fish's gut .

I've previously compared the composition of natural food with the protein content of boiled baits in order to show how natural food items 'compete' with our baits. Based on the composition of natural food items in the stomachs of carp from three different sites (from Crivelli, 1981), I estimated the total protein content of food ingested by the carp to be approximately 44 percent. This is higher than the 38 percent determined by Ogino & Saito (1970) experimentally using casein. I suggested at that time that this had implications for the development of a bait which completely satisfies the nutritional requirements of the carp since formulation will depend not just on the amount of total protein but also its amino acid profile and the digestibility of the protein sources used. I've also presented here several solutions for solving problems of digestibility and another of these is obviously to increase the amount of the digestibly deficient ingredient in the bait in terms of percentage. If natural food is effectively higher in protein than the value that the carp actually requires in its diet, then this may take account of insufficiencies in digestion and absorption in order to eventually fulfil the protein requirement.

The evaluation of natural food was done using just a sample from one of the many places that carp inhabit and for that reason might not be the best representation of the carp's diet or the amount of protein that it ingests. However, as an indicator of how adequate our baits are in terms of protein it has enabled comparison. This is because a nutritionally adequate bait, as well as having to fulfil requirements in terms of not just protein but also the other macro- and micro-nutrients, has to compete with both natural food and the baits of other anglers. In this respect, I also suggested that the energy expended in locating one gram of natural food is much higher than that required to locate a gram of loose feed which the angler usually distributes over a small area of the lake, usually a few square metres. In this respect, it's energetically favourable for the fish to feed on bait as opposed to natural food.

I can add to this that a nutritionally adequate bait is the best way to compete with both other anglers' baits and natural food items in the long term. In the short term, increased bait attraction will improve catch results. Nutritional adequacy means that energy as well as each nutrient meet the levels determined by different studies as being required by the carp. In the case of protein, this has been shown to be 38 percent (Ogino & Saito, 1970) although other authors have suggested lower values (e.g. 31 percent, Varghese et al., 1976).

It should be remembered that temperature is the parameter that affects to the greatest extent digestibility and the amount of feed or bait consumed by the carp. Temperature can affect the total amount of protein required since at higher temperatures, growth is faster and so therefore is the synthesis of proteins in the fish. Studies have demonstrated that the individual amino acid requirement can increase according to temperature. For example, Viola & Arieli (1989) showed that the requirement for lysine, an essential amino acid, is 5.3 percent of the total protein content of the feed at 20 degrees Celsius but that this increases to 8.4 percent at 25 degrees Celsius, which is equivalent to an increase of about 60 percent. By the same measure, as the requirement for one amino acid increases, the requirement for others has to decrease as a percentage of total protein, although specific data for this in carp is still lacking.

According to a study by Niesar et al. (2004) where the authors evaluated the composition of different types of baits used by anglers including both ready-made (commercial) and self-made (homemade) boilies . Additionally they separated commercial boilies into two groups, which were those that were relatively rich in crude protein and fat and the others that were rich in carbohydrate and fibre (nitrogen-free extracts, NFE). The first group were shown to contain higher levels of fishmeals whereas the second had a composition much closer to that of cereals.

Only three of the 26 boilie types tested showed crude protein levels above 38 percent dry weight. This suggests that protein is present in the majority of boiled baits in amounts inferior to the nutritional requirement of the fish. In this study, crude protein of commercial boilies ranged from 11.2 to 40.4 percent protein with one exceptionally high value in a bait with 62.5 percent protein. With regards to fat, this ranged from 0.9 percent to 14.8 percent and NFE ranged from 14.7 percent (in the bait with the highest protein content) to 86.8 percent in one of the lower nutritional quality boilies.

This study was carried out not as a nutritional study to look at the growth of carp or the effect of nutrient deficiency on the fish but in order to evaluate the environmental impact of bait use, since uneaten bait has the potential to affect water and sediment quality. Pollution is greater in the case of baits with higher nitrogen and phosphorus content. Even so, the results of the study are very interesting to us as anglers and bait formulators since we can get an idea of what's going into the baits that are being produced and compare these figures to those of requirement for each nutrient by the carp.

In the same study of Niesar et al. (2004) the different baits (ready-made boilies, self-made boilies, particles, ordinary groundbait and a commercial pelleted feed) were fed to groups of carp. The pellet was used as a control diet with which to compare the other baits. The results showed that growth was highest in the control group fed the pellet (specific growth rate (SGR) 1.30 ± 0.18) followed by self-made boilies (0.98 ± 0.15) then commercial boilies (0.41 ± 0.16). The lowest growth was shown by ordinary groundbait (0.18 ± 0.18) and particles (0.08 ± 0.11). The best feed conversion rate (FCR) was shown by the pelleted feed (1.50 ± 0.25) followed by self-made boilies (1.94 ± 0.33) and the poorest conversion was shown in the case of particles (34.34 ± 34.19).

The same researchers also carried out a carp angling survey as part of the study. This was a mail and internet-based survey that asked specialist anglers in Germany a number of questions regarding the types and quantities of bait that they used each year. The results showed that of the total amount of bait used on average per angler each year, some 40 percent consisted of boilies , 48 percent was particles and 12 percent a mixture of other types, principally groundbait and commercial fish feed. Of all the boilies used, 45 percent of these were ready-mades, 36 percent were self-mades and 19 percent were made from commercial base mixes. If this represents the tendency for the rest of Europe it would mean that more than half of the boilies going into lakes and rivers are self-made from individual ingredients or from commercial base mixes.

A second study by Arlinghaus & Niesar (2005) looked at the same five baits but in the context of digestibility. They found that the digestibility of both protein and fat in all cases was approximately 84 percent. NFE digestibility was lower and ranged from 52.2 percent in the case of commercial fish pellet to 81.6 percent in the case of groundbait, which was, surprisingly, the highest NFE digestibility of all those studied, including ready-made boilies in second place with 78.9 percent. The authors suggested that carp are able to digest all of the baits tested very effectively. Also, there is clearly little difference in the ability of the carp to digest angling baits compared with commercial aquaculture diets, which as well as being used on a large scale for carp farming and on-growing for stocking are also used by carp anglers as bait. In recent years the use of pellets of all kinds has become very commonplace in the angling community and nowadays it's rare for a carp angler to leave home without a bag of pellet of some description among his tackle.

One important question that we have not covered yet is that of the digestibility of natural food. This is not something that there's much information about, mainly because the diet of carp is so varied that figures for digestibility would be very general indeed. Also, in order to obtain information about digestion, it would be first necessary to know exactly what the fish has eaten and compare that with what it has excreted. In that way we could in theory measure the protein content of the food and the protein content of the faeces and work out how much has been digested. However, the problem is that what we're interested in is the digestibility of natural food in a natural situation. However, it's impossible to determine exactly what a wild fish has been eating without opening the fish up and doing that ends any possibility of further digestion taking place. For this reason there's no information that I've been able to find about digestibility of natural food items in juvenile or adult carp.

Energy, on the other hand, is a parameter that was measured in tank tests by both Niesar *et al.* (2004) and Arlinghaus & Niesar (2005) for the five baits with the highest energy content was that of self-made boilies with an average of 19.65 kilojoules per gram (kJ/g). The lowest energy content was that of ordinary groundbait with an average content of 18.95 kJ/g.

In *Carp Fishing Science* I was able to evaluate the protein content of natural food using data obtained by Crivelli (1981). Here, data of carp stomach content analyses over a period of more than two years was used. Three different sites were sampled and the occurrence of each invertebrate group was recorded, which included examples of insects, crustaceans and molluscs as well as vegetable matter, detritus, seeds and algae, which formed the rest of the types of food ingested in the three sites. In order to calculate average protein, I considered the abundance of each organism in each site, the proportion that each one represented in the diet of the carp, the protein content (dry weight) of each one and the relative protein (protein content multiplied by proportion) gave an average protein content of natural food as 44.35 percent.

The energy content of aquatic invertebrates has been shown to change seasonally. For example, with the onset of winter, some planktonic species increase their fat content and therefore their energy content. However, during some stage of their development during the year, aquatic invertebrates fall within the range of 21.3-24.7 kJ/g. Driver *et al.* (1974) arrived at an average energy content of 21.9 kJ/g and other workers have suggested that the energy content of aquatic invertebrates is around 20.9 kJ/g (Richman & Slobodkin, 1960).

If we compare this range of values with the energy content of angling baits, we find that commercial pelleted feed and self-made boilies are within this range. However, all the baits tested are relatively close to the lower limit and this means that if we consider the energy that a carp has to expend to find the same amount of natural food, then it's very probable that feeding on any one of the baits analysed, including that with the lowest energy content (groundbait), is energetically favourable to the fish. Therefore, feeding on our bait as opposed to feeding on natural food quite likely results in a net energy gain for the carp. This is due to the greatly reduced amount of swimming that a carp has to do to satisfy energy requirements if it's feeding on bait. However, this is not the key to increasing catch rate, since it's vital to ensure that the bait is nutritionally adequate. Also, when feeding on bait the carp must evaluate the advantage of this higher net energy gain against the disadvantage of the higher probability of being captured.

Much of the previous discussion has centred on proteins and their importance in our baits. There is no doubting that protein is maybe the most important consideration as far as ingredients and bait composition. For that reason it's protein that's spoken about most regularly when anglers get together and the focus of many magazine articles. For both bait manufacturers and home formulators, a great deal of thought goes into selecting and blending different protein sources. It's important that this is done objectively and using a certain amount of understanding of what proteins are and why they're important to the fish. Hopefully I've been able to give you enough information so far regarding proteins for you to be able to continue to work on your bait or even to enable bait companies to improve their products for the benefit of many of us who depend on the baits they produce. I'll continue to mention protein when we discuss formulation.

However, protein is only one of the nutrients that should be effectively incorporated into bait and only one of those that we should consider if we are to develop a bait that fulfils every type of nutritional expectancy. I'm a firm believer in nutritional adequacy and the benefits that a complete bait can bring to both fish health and growth, fishery status and angling success. Additionally, a nutritionally adequate bait results in less waste since more is used by the fish and therefore less is excreted. As a consequence there is less environmental impact from recreational angling through baiting.

Busy commercial fisheries with low volumes of inflowing water are often the first to suffer when large quantities of bait are used. Bait that is nutritionally inadequate, poorly digestible or not attractive enough to ensure that it's consumed can be left uneaten on the lake bottom and can lead to the water becoming coloured, smelly and unsightly. Excess nutrients can lead to algal blooms and eutrophication and as a result our fishing experience is affected.

Nutritional adequacy is a big step forward and can have a diverse number of benefits for our sport. However, as with other industries, there are many more claims to have produced a nutritionally adequate product than there are truths.

The next macro-nutrient that we'll discuss is fat, also referred to as lipid. In the same way as protein, lipid is vital for the fish but for different reasons. Lipids are soluble in fats rather than in water and this is why you can see oils floating on water because they are immiscible, which means that they don't mix. Lipids are a very diverse group of substances and some of these provide us with ways to solve everyday problems in our homes and lives. For example, some oils are used for cooking and others for industrial applications in engines and other machines. Lipids are present in a great many foods and we consume several of them daily such as vegetable and olive oils and butter and margarine, which contain important amounts of lipids. Also, waxes are modified (esterified) fatty acids with a wide range of domestic and industrial uses.

In the same way as proteins, lipids come from both vegetable and animal sources. The diversity of lipids is very large and many of these have been used in both aquaculture and recreational fishing. The most commonly used is fish oil, which is usually obtained from the same species of fish as fishmeal, including mackerel, herrings, sardines and anchovies. The oil is separated during the stages of pressing and drying of the meal and is often added back when the fishmeal is made into pellets, which we are familiar with as anglers or cakes, which are fed to a range of other farmed animals.

As with fishmeal, a great amount of research is currently taking place in order to find substitutes for fish oil. This is mainly because over the last few decades aquaculture has grown so much due to an inability of capture fisheries to feed the masses that it's now at the point of overtaking capture fisheries as the main source of global fish production. Fishmeal and fish oil from capture fisheries is therefore on the decline as stocks continue to be overfished and as a result has been described as environmentally unsustainable. The cost is expected to increase even more with time and therefore farmers of aquatic species are trying to find replacements.

Replacement of fish oil is difficult since, in the same way that amino acid profile varies from protein source to protein source, the lipid profile of different oils can also vary greatly. And since fish oil and fishmeal come from fish, their incorporation back into fish through the feed, whether that's for aquaculture or recreational angling purposes, is more efficient. Therefore it's usually the case that an alternative protein or lipid source from another animal or plant results in a lower conversion rate and slower growth, which are two parameters which interest both the fishery owner and the fish farmer. However, there are some alternatives that have shown promising results as far as fish oil replacement, which is usually partial rather than complete. These include such inclusions as rapeseed oil, palm oil, linseed oil and sunflower oil.

Fats are the primary energy reserves of animals including fish which are used as long-term energy supplies when the animal is extensively active or when food and energy intakes are insufficient. This can occur when the fish is unable to find enough food. Fish are unusual in one respect among animals in that they are able to readily use fat as an energy source and are also able to go for long periods without food, certainly longer than mammals such as humans who generally start to grumble if they aren't receiving three meals each day on a regular basis. But energy supply is not the only function of fats and another important one is structurally in the composition of cell membranes.

Fats are a group of lipids called triglycerides, which are made up of glycerol and fatty acids. These fatty acids are diverse and vary in their lengths and degree of saturation. When people talk about unsaturated fats, these have a larger number of double-bonds, which make the fat more liquid at a lower temperature. The more highly saturated the fat is, the more liquid it is at a particular temperature. In the kitchen we talk about fats as being those that are solid at room temperature and oils as those that are liquid. The ones we add to angling bait and aquaculture feeds are usually liquid at water temperature and are therefore termed oils.

If we look at a particular oil, it can be made up of one, several or many different fatty acids that might be free or present as triglycerides. And in the same way as amino acids, fatty acids can be essential. This means, as with aminos, that an animal is not able to synthesise them (make them) from some other fatty acid or other substance. In the case of some fish this is a problem but in the majority of freshwater fish, including carp, there are no fatty acids that the fish is unable to make, including those that other fish need to receive in their diet. However, the synthesis of fatty acids from others is not energetically optimal and obtaining them from the diet (or providing these in a bait) can be beneficial for the fish energetic ally.

Salmon and trout, while they're in freshwater, are also able to synthesise all the fatty acids that they might need themselves, but once they migrate to the sea, the system that allows them to synthesise the most highly unsaturated fatty acids (HUFAs) appears to switch off and as a result, they have to receive these from the diet. These HUFAs come from phytoplankton, which are consumed and concentrated by marine fish from which we obtain fish oil. And that's why fish oil is so important to the aquaculture industry because it's in these fish alone that large amounts of highly unsaturated fatty acids can be obtained, which has been shown to provide many health benefits to humans and other animals.

The HUFAs are important structurally in cells and their liquidity provides the fluid composition of cell walls. As a result it gives us healthier cells and more flexible arteries and other vessels. The most important of these are DHA and EPA, which are present in cod liver oil in important amounts. DHA is also the most plentiful omega 3 fatty acid in the mammalian brain. These are also important in similar ways for fish but apart from making membranes more fluid and being structurally important in the central nervous system, they are involved in the immune response (protection against disease) and reproduction.

You will probably have heard people talk about omega 3 and omega 6, fatty acids. The name depends on whether the first double bond is at position three or six in the carbon chain. These are present in both marine oils Xand plant oils and apart from fish oil, which contains principally omega 3 but also omega 6, many cereals, nuts and plants contain mixtures of both or either. Not all of these are highly unsaturated or even polyunsaturated (PUFA) and just because the fatty acid is an omega 3, it doesn't necessarily mean that it's as exceptionally healthy for the consumer as EPA and DHA are. In fact, many common oils such as olive oil contain quantities of omega 3 but these often not in very large amounts and not of types that are highly unsaturated.

Freshwater fish contain higher levels of omega 6 than marine fish, but fish in general contain more omega 3 than omega 6 polyunsaturated fatty acids. This means that their dietary requirement for omega 3 PUFAs is greater than for omega 6. Also, coldwater fish tend to have higher levels of HUFAs than other fish since this increases the fluidity of cell membranes and this is particularly valuable during the colder months.

In carp farming in warmer waters, the fish tend to grow better when fed a mixture of omega 3 and omega 6 PUFAs. Also, the lipid content of the fish has been shown to be affected by the lipid being fed to the fish. Therefore, if carp are fed higher levels of omega 3, then their body will contain higher levels of omega 3.

Lipid requirement in common carp has been shown to depend on the stage of fish development and to vary seasonally (Kminková et al., 2001). In this study, a total of 14 fatty acids were analysed in five different carp tissues (hepatopancreas, soft roe, hard roe, muscle and fatty tissue) during spring, summer, autumn and winter. Between these tissues and seasons the lipid content varied significantly. The concentration of fat in muscle was almost constant during the year (5.03-5.92g per 100g of tissue) except in spring (2.08g per 100g of tissue), when the reproductive activity of the fish starts prior to increased food availability. The maximum fat values were found in the hepatopancreas, which were found to reach their maximum during spring (11.72g per 100g of tissue), but to be high even in summer (10.01g per 100g of tissue).

The content of fat in the hepatopancreas decreased during autumn and winter (5.09 and 4.75g per 100g of tissue respectively), approaching the fat level of the muscle. It was concluded from the study that the hepatopancreas is the principal site of carp fat synthesis, particularly during spring and summer. The relative concentration of omega 3 to omega 6 polyunsaturated fatty acids was found to be even more important than total lipids. This ratio, favouring the presence of omega 3, was found in all tissues except the fat tissue itself.

Particularly in hard roe and soft roe, the high level of omega 3 polyunsaturated fatty acids suggests that higher omega 3 is a requirement of carp prior to spawning. In carp, the concentration of individual fatty acids changes during the year particularly according to the reproductive activity of the fish and the availability of food items. Based on the same study, the most abundant fatty acids in carp were found to be palmitic, palmitoleic, oleic, arachidonic, eicosapentaenoic (EPA), docosahexaenoic (DHA), α-linolenic and γ-linolenic.

This information has implications for anglers and bait formulators since the variation of fatty acid requirement, both in quantity and quality is a consideration for bait making. The evidence suggests that we should use higher lipid levels and higher levels of omega 3 in spring and summer and at those times, the ratio of omega 3 to omega 6 was on average, considering the fatty acid content of all the carp tissues sampled, 1.59:1 in spring and 1.18:1 in summer. Additionally, the eight fatty acids named above as those being the most abundant in carp tissues should be considered as bait ingredients or at least lipid sources that contain these. In table 4 of the appendix I've included a summary of some lipid sources and the amounts of the principal fatty acids types they contain.

As already stated, the carp is very effective at synthesising all the fatty acids that it might need, therefore reducing the amount of essential fatty acids that it has to obtain in the diet. But as already mentioned, this is maybe not the best strategy for the fish, especially if they can be obtained in the diet. The capacity for PUFA synthesis is also greater in adult fish than it is in larval or juveniles, mainly because smaller fish experience higher growth rates and therefore require relatively higher levels of fatty acids. Although information regarding adult fish is lacking, the amount of essential fatty acids (EFAs) have been determined for common carp in both early juvenile stages and older juvenile and preadult stages. These are 1% (0.25% linoleic acid) omega 6   PUFA and approximately 0.5% PUFA (Radunzneto et al., 1996) and 1% omega 6 (linoleic acid) and 0.5-1.0% omega 3 (linolenic acid) (Takeuchi & Watanabe, 1977) respectively. Despite the fact that this information is applicable particularly to juvenile carp, the growth of carp in modern fisheries is relatively high due to the large amount of food available to them. In commercial fisheries this is even more the case although for large lakes with low stocking densities this information may be less useful since natural food will provide more of the fatty acid requirement of the fish. However, these fatty acid incorporations are still a guide for bait formulation in the absence of more extensive or specific data.

In aquaculture, lipid is an important constituent of fish feeds. In general terms, the objective of this is not only to provide the right amount of lipid for the species being reared in terms of structural lipid and lipid for biological function but also to help meet energy requirements. Fish farmers employ something called protein sparing which is feeding with a diet that contains levels of fat and carbohydrate that reduce the amount of catabolism (breaking down) of protein into amino acids to be used for energy production. This is done to shift the preference of the fish for energy production from protein to fat or carbohydrate.

One of the consequences of protein sparing is that aquafeed producers are able to reduce production costs. Since protein is the highest priced component of both aquaculture feeds and bait, it makes sense to include sufficient protein but not excess, with the idea being that the fish uses cheaper energy sources for energy production, namely fat and carbohydrate, while the protein is used for growth. This is a strategy that's used not just in fish production but also other types of animal production and even in bodybuilding.

On the downside, protein sparing can sometimes backfire. It's only an effective technique if the right amount of alternative energy is used for the amount of food that the fish is ingesting. If too much energy is ingested, then it's stored as fat and that's why a farmed salmon has a different texture from a wild salmon, usually with fat deposits in and on the internal organs and the flesh will have a higher fat content. The same thing can be seen in the carp that we catch and those with huge bellies have obviously been doing too much protein sparing. If the fish continues to eat an excessively high energy diet (or bait) for the amount of activity that it's doing then it will begin to change shape a bit like humans when they ingest too much fat and sugar and don't do enough (or any) exercise.

The final thing that I'll say for now about fat is that it has another property apart from being structurally important in the carp's body, biologically important in cell signalling and reproduction and as an important energy reserve - it's tasty. Fats are included in many foods for the sole reason of making them more palatable or more agreeable to the consumer, in this case the carp. We've already spoken about certain amino acids that increase the feeding response and cause a positive stimulation when they are sensed by the fish. These can involve both the gustatory and olfactory systems (taste and smell) but can also affect the palatability of the food. If a food is more palatable, then there's more chance of it being consumed. Both taste (or flavour in humans) and palatability involve contact with the food item, but the difference between taste and palatability is that palatability is a measure of how desirable that food item is to the individual.

Palatability is therefore something more personal to the consumer, more self-indulgent, with another difference being that palatability changes as the state of mind of the consumer changes. This is to say that it depends on several factors such as appetite size, how long the individual has been without that particular food, or whether the individual is depressed or not. So, where tastes remain the same, palatability is dependent on other things and variable with time.

One of the nutrients that have been shown to increase palatability is lipid in the form of fats and oils. This occurs because fatty acids are supposedly able to be detected by taste buds . This has been observed in humans and the human tongue has been shown to become stimulated by certain fatty acids and cause the release of endorphins, which are well-known for creating a feeling of well-being. Eating chocolate and falling in love have also been shown to cause endorphin secretion. In fish, the taste response to fatty acids has not been well investigated and specifically for carp there's currently no information available.

However, what is clear is that lipids, especially fish oil, are used extensively in aquaculture and as far as I know, there hasn't been a negative report of it causing rejection of the feed it's used in and it's commonly known as an ingredient that increases appetence and palatability. It's likely that fish and humans share some characteristics in this respect but whether or not they react in exactly the same way as humans do to lipids coming in contact with their taste buds is difficult to ascertain without more evidence.

The third macro-nutrient that we will discuss here is carbohydrate, which includes a wide range of substances from simple sugars such as glucose to complex polysaccharides (meaning 'many sugars') such as starch. In carnivorous fish, including the majority of marine fish, carbohydrate has little importance as an energy source. However, omnivorous species such as carp consume plant material containing easily digestible sugars as well as complex, more difficult to digest polysaccharides made up of maybe hundreds or thousands of sugar units. Although carbohydrate can make up an important part of plant material, it's present in the bodies of animals in relatively small amounts. One of the most common forms of carbohydrate present in the bodies of animals is glycogen, which is an energy source stored for periods of activity, fasting or starvation. Common sources of carbohydrate include different flours and meals such as cornmeal, cereals and in angling what we would call particles and the golden oldie semolina, which is made by coarsely milling wheat.

Aquatic plant material in the same way as that of terrestrial plants is a major source of carbohydrate for omnivorous or herbivorous fish. These contain different carbohydrates, some of which the carp can digest easily and others such as cellulose, chitin and lignin which are more difficult to digest. The ease of digestibility, as with fats and proteins, decreases with increasing size of the molecule. In some cases, digestion of these is aided by the bacteria that live in the fish's gut. Common aquatic plants such as waterweed and duckweed contain about 30 to 40 percent carbohydrate measured as dry weight.

Digestion of carbohydrate in animals including carp requires amylase, which is an enzyme that causes hydrolysis of the molecule in order to break it up into smaller sugars which can be more easily absorbed. It's similar to the hydrolysis that we mentioned earlier regarding proteins and also the boiling of pasta and potatoes to break up starch. Experiments have shown that carnivorous fish are ill-equipped to deal with large amounts of carbohydrate but omnivorous fish such as carp can handle significant quantities. Also, in carnivorous fish, the amylase is found principally in the gut near to the pancreas where it's produced and where there is greater enzymatic activity but in the carp, although it's produced in the pancreas, it can be found more or less throughout the gut. As we saw in the studies by Niesar, the digestibility of carbohydrate in fish feeds and baits consumed by carp can be high but this will always depend on the quantity and quality (type) of the carbohydrate that's involved. For example, it's not the same including polysaccharides in a diet or bait as it is including simple sugars such as sucrose, fructose and glucose. These can be dealt with and absorbed much easier and it is energetically favourable for the fish to consume these rather than polysaccharides.

However, since carbohydrate is the most abundant and cheapest source of energy for animals, it's easy to understand why carbohydrate is present in all baits to some extent and many ingredients include carbohydrate although it may not be one of the main ingredients. I've previously shown the carbohydrate contents of natural baits, which are summarised as follows: white bread 50.6 percent, sweetcorn 20.8 percent, luncheon meat 3.0 percent, mussel 3.7 percent, tiger nut 58.1 percent, hempseed 34.0 percent, earthworm 17.6 percent and maggot 19.6 percent.

In boilies , the amount of carbohydrate included can vary greatly, with figures for nitrogen-free extracts (carbohydrate plus fibre) in the study by Niesar *et al.* (2004) of the 26 boilies analysed as anywhere between 14.7 and 86.8 percent. The amount of carbohydrate included in a bait is down to the formulator and manufacturer. In the case of carbohydrate there is no specific requirement as there is for amino acids and fatty acids. This means that carbohydrate is included for other reasons, with protein sparing an important one. Also, the addition of carbohydrate, although it can be considered an energy source, has the effect of 'watering down' a bait. This sounds negative but the inclusion of higher levels of carbohydrate and lower amounts of protein and fat means that a fish would, in theory, if it were feeding exclusively on the bait have to eat more of the bait in order to obtain all that it requires. On the other hand, in order for a carp to eat a larger amount of a bait we have to ensure that the fish is feeding confidently, which is sometimes not an easy thing to achieve. In fact sometimes it's difficult to get the fish to feed at all.

Our objective should be to provide a nutritionally complete bait and also one that is as attractive as possible. In order for this to be achieved, we have to consider a large number of factors and aspects both regarding the place where the bait is to be used, the behaviour of the fish and the chemical, biological and technical characteristics of the bait. It may be possible to create a bait with almost 90 percent carbohydrate (or NFE) in it that catches carp, even big carp, but I wouldn't knowingly use it. This is because some part of the other 10 percent might be attractive to the fish, but it will not by any stretch of the imagination be able to satisfy the nutritional requirements of the carp.

I imagine that the excessive and unjustified use of carbohydrate would be the end of a bait company if their baits were analysed and it came to light that that was the case, even if it wasn't the norm for all of their products. However, since we pay good money for bait we would hope that we're getting the best value for money. Maybe it's not in the bait company's best interest to produce baits with the amounts of the three important macro-nutrients (protein, lipid and carbohydrate) that I've described here and not only that but also the correct types and inclusions of amino acids and fatty acids , but it should be. However, if you look at what separates different bait companies today, then it appears that it is nutritional inadequacy and the inability to include the right attractants and stimulants.

In my opinion, a good bait should reduce the risk of a carp having to look elsewhere for food and a nutritionally adequate bait does that. If it's possible to increase the attraction of fish to the place you're fishing and intensify the feeding response , then that would be fantastic. However, the four-fold benefits of a nutritional bait cannot be caused by high levels of carbohydrate.

If we move away from the macro-nutrients now and look at those required by the carp in much lower amounts, then there are two that we'll deal with here. The first are the vitamins and the second are the minerals. Both of these are obtained naturally in the diet of the fish and we can incorporate them both in bait in order to ensure that their requirement is met. Also, these two groups of substances are needed in organisms for a wide range of vital biological functions despite the small amounts required and the partial or complete lack of each are well-known for causing diseases associated with their deficiency.

A vitamin is an organic compound required by an organism that it is unable to synthesise in amounts which satisfy its requirement for that substance. These are separated in two groups according to their solubility; the water-soluble vitamins are eight vitamin B vitamins as well as ascorbate (vitamin C) and choline which are often referred to as major dietary nutrients. The fat -soluble vitamins are vitamins A, D, E and K.

Both types of vitamin can result in deficiency syndromes and in the case of the fat-soluble ones, which can be easily accumulated in the organism's tissues, too much of a vitamin can result in hypervitaminosis, which is due to an excess of a vitamin. Therefore, if we are to incorporate vitamins into a bait, it's important that we know what the carp's requirement for each vitamin is and try to match that. It's likely that a carp will obtain some amount of the vitamin from its natural diet but it's impossible to know exactly how much. However, if we use the guide for the vitamin requirements of carp (Halver & Hardy, 2002) that I've included in table 5 of the appendix, as you can see, the amounts of these differ greatly between some vitamins and many include a range rather than a value. If you are formulating a bait, then it would make sense to aim for the middle of the range. For example in the case of Vitamin B3 (niacin) with a range of 30 to 50 milligrams per kilogram of bait dry weight, a value of 40 milligrams would suffice. This may not sound too scientific, but we're talking about substances that are required in very small amounts and, as I've already stated, some of the requirement will always be provided by the carp's natural food.

The sources of vitamins are also very variable. Vitamins A (retinol) and E (tocopherols) are found in invertebrates and form an important part of the fish's diet. Vitamin B12 is found in phytoplankton and vitamin C is found in fruits and berries, which can find their way into the carp's environment from bankside trees and bushes. Vitamin K is present in plant material, which as we know also forms part of the carp's diet and vitamin D can be produced by a reaction between ultraviolet light and cholesterol in the skin of some fish, but this has not been observed in carp. The majority of vitamin D in fish, including carp, is thought to be obtained from the diet and phytoplankton have been shown to be source of the vitamin.

The signs of vitamin deficiency vary according to the degree of deficiency. These are extremely diverse, from barely noticeable loss of appetite to the malformation of the skeleton. Common effects of deficiency include poor growth, anaemia and nervous disorders. These can be resolved using ingredients that satisfy the fish's requirement for each vitamin. After a period of deficiency, the intake of food containing the required amount of a vitamin will halt the deficiency and may partly or completely reverse the deficiency symptoms. Some of these may be irreversible such as more severe malformations.

Bait makers should remember that some vitamins are particularly sensitive to changes in temperature during storage and the formulation process. This will affect their biological availability in the carp once the bait is ingested. This is particularly relevant considering that boilies are produced, as their name suggests, by boiling or steaming. Since this is an integral part of the bait manufacture process, care should be taken regarding the boiling time since excessive heating will denature any enzymes that have been purposefully included or, in the case of vitamins, they will be partially or completely transformed and rendered biologically unavailable. One solution to this is to use antioxidants, which reduce the possibility of this.

The other important group of micro-nutrients are the minerals. As with the vitamins, these also have a great diversity of functions within the body of animals including carp. The carp obtains the minerals it requires from two sources; from the diet and from the water column (uptake by the gills or in water that is ingested). The minerals that have been shown to be essential for fish (not specifically carp) are shown in table 6 of the appendix. Again, these are relatively wide-ranging values and as far as bait formulation goes, an attempt should be made to ensure an amount that lies between the limits. Minerals are required by fish as constituents of skeletal structures (e.g. calcium and phosphorus) in the metabolism of other nutrients (e.g. magnesium) or in digestion (e.g. chlorine). Mineral deficiency symptoms include appetite loss, poor growth and anaemia but a great many of the symptoms have not been determined yet in fish. The levels of some minerals required by fish have not been defined but it's clear that they should not be excluded from diets that are used exclusively and for long periods of time (e.g. fluorine, see table 6).

From the standpoints of some bait formulators, the inclusion of vitamins and minerals may not seem as important as that of protein, lipid and carbohydrate. Maybe vitamins and minerals are not required in the same amounts as the macro-nutrients, but their incorporation is just as important. By developing a nutritionally complete bait we are trying to ensure that the carp doesn't need to go elsewhere and if the bait lacks a required nutrient, then it will be forced to go elsewhere and depend on natural food or another angler's bait for at least some of its nutrition. If we can keep the fish eating our bait for longer, either in the short term such as the length of a session or in the long term, by which I mean the length of a season or several seasons, then we have to get the fish to become dependable on the bait and recognise what we can refer to as nutritional attractiveness.

But don't panic. In order to incorporate each of the vitamins and minerals it's not necessary to go searching for sources of each one. There are commercially available preparations and premixes available to use. It's also important to remember that the other ingredients often include micronutrients in sufficient amounts to satisfy some requirements. For example, eggs are rich in choline, cereals are rich in many of the B vitamins and liver contains vitamin C. However, if you include ingredients such as these in a bait and they cannot be included in amounts large enough to satisfy a vitamin or mineral requirement, then supplementation is therefore required.

On the previous pages we've seen what the carp's requirement is for the different nutrients. The values presented are useful when it comes to formulating a bait and using it. Also, understanding the factors that affect such biological processes as digestion, absorption and the fate of the different nutrients that we provide in a diet can help us to improve baits and modify them for different situations. We have also seen that all of these are relevant for nutrition and that they should all be considered in a bait, especially if the objective is to completely satisfy the dietary requirements of the fish.

However, the values presented are not the be-all and end-all of inclusion rates. They can guide us, but as with any biological system, the numbers will vary depending on external and internal factors. These can therefore be a result of both changes in the fish's environment and those related to the carp's nutritional or developmental status. Nutritional status refers to whether the carp is underfed or overfed, or whether it presents a deficiency in one or more of the nutrients we've already mentioned. Developmental status refers to whether the fish is in a state of maintenance or growth. As we saw previously, bigger, older fish grow more slowly than smaller, younger fish.

Values for maintenance can be very different from those for growth, because this means that the fish requires only enough to keep living as opposed to living and growing. We have seen that the total protein as a percentage of dry weight of the bait should be around 38 percent. However, this is a figure taken from a growth study and is therefore the amount that the carp requires for maintenance plus growth. If we examine the values for just maintenance, we see that the requirement is 1 to 2 grams of protein per kilogram of body weight. This would mean that a carp weighing 20 pounds (9.1 kgs) would require between 9 and 18 grams of protein per day. In theory this could be satisfied by a hundred grams of bait with a protein level between 9 and 18 percent. In other words, much less than what we have been talking about up until now.

However, maintenance is not the typical state of a fish and as we know as anglers, on waters with a normal stocking density, the carp are continually increasing in size. Growth is commonplace. And it must be remembered that carp growth is something that is desirable not just to us, the fishery owner and the bait manufacturer, but also the carp itself. Being of a larger size than the rest of the shoal, as we saw in the first chapter, is beneficial to the fish as far as exploiting patches of food and avoiding being eaten by a predator. Anyone who has observed fish in a tank will tell you that the larger fish usually eat more than the smaller fish, and when fish of different sizes are placed together, a hierarchy forms which gives preference to the bigger fish during feeding.

In comparison with the figure for daily protein requirement, high growth rates in carp have been achieved by feeding up to 10 to 12 grams of protein per kilo of body weight per day. In the case of our 20 pound carp, this would signify a protein requirement of 91 to 109 grams of protein per day that could, in theory, be provided by the fish consuming more than two kilos of bait with 38 percent protein per day. However, it would be impossible to do that since two kilos (4.4 pounds) of bait will not fit inside a 20 pound fish, even during a whole day, and as we know, the faster the passage of food through the gut, the lower is the relative amount digested and absorbed. The only option would be to increase the protein content of the diet in such a case, but at the same time there is the risk of excluding other nutrients that the carp requires just as much, especially if it's growing quickly.

It's therefore very probable that the normal situation is somewhere between these two extremes. Most carp are not in a state of just maintenance and neither are they growing at the highest rate. This is why I've suggested the 38 percent protein level since it is at the higher end of the values suggested as being required by the fish. And if the fish in a lake are growing slower and therefore require a lower amount of protein than this, then there should, in theory, be an excess of protein that can be used for energy.

In a similar sense, the energy requirement of the carp is also related to both its level of activity and water temperature. Since increased temperature results in increased metabolic rate, more energy is required to meet that demand. Therefore, if you observe active fish as opposed to those that are looking almost dormant, there's more of a chance that they will feed since they will require energy levels to be replenished sooner rather than later.

In resting carp, when they are particularly inactive, the metabolic rate has been shown to be extremely low. This usually coincides with low water temperatures and as the water temperature becomes even lower, such as below 10 degrees Celsius, the amount of activity can become so low that energy used is almost nothing. At times like those, since energy used is so low, the amount of food that's required is almost nothing too. It's for that reason that catch rates are lower in winter and you can go many sessions without a fish.

Studies have looked at the effect of temperature on the maintenance energy needs of the carp, which is the energy that's needed simply to keep the fish living. This was shown to be 45 kJ of digestible energy per kilogram of body weight at 20 degrees Celsius but at 10 degrees Celsius, the energy requirement fell to 19 kJ of digestible energy per kilogram of body weight. This means that the energy requirement over those ten degrees of temperature more than doubles and at 20 degrees we can expect both activity and food intake to be more than twice as much as at 10 degrees (Schwarz & Kirchgessner, 1984).

Fat is something that anglers often talk about as the water temperature falls in autumn and reaches its lowest in winter. One consideration is the reduced efficiency of digestibility of fats as the temperatures fall and another is the reduced fluidity of fats at the same time. However, the main types of lipids used are oils, which remain liquid at very low temperatures and in many cases even below freezing. This concern over digestibility should not be a serious one since, as we have already seen, the amount of food ingested by a carp at very low temperatures is particularly low. Therefore, the practice of prebaiting and getting fish accustomed to your bait is less applicable than when water temperatures are high. In winter, things become more haphazard. Less bait is eaten and although the bait may be nutritionally adequate, the amount ingested may not be enough to see the full benefits of the bait. In that case, digestibility of fat becomes less important and not the main concern regarding the acceptability of the bait. In those conditions, attraction can become as, or if not more important than the nutritional aspects.

b. Attraction and nutrition

The two key aspects of a successful bait are attraction and nutrition. In some circumstances, one can be more important than the other but in this section I aim to discuss how both can be improved using current knowledge and how you can reap the benefits of each one in your carp fishing.

At the moment there are literally thousands of products on the market that carp anglers can buy to increase the attraction of their bait and it's likely that in the future there will be hundreds of others that will appear claiming to do the same. There are also hundreds of varieties of boilies all claiming to be 100 percent nutritional for the carp. Maybe some of them are, but I imagine that the vast majority are not.

Many of the baits available can supposedly be used in all conditions, at any time of the year, at any water temperature and to catch any size of fish. A bait like that is something that is even more difficult to produce

194

than one that is 'just' 100 percent nutritional and what is required is a selection of completely nutritional baits that cater for two or three ranges of water temperatures and for both smaller and specimen carp. With those, a company doesn't need to do much more apart from working on attraction of both fish and anglers to the bait.

A similar thing can be seen in the nutrition of other animals, for pets, for farm animals and wild animals. The range of diets available for these caters for at least young and old. However, since the majority of these are warm-blooded and are able to regulate their body temperature, no consideration is made for the effect of temperature on their metabolic rate or nutritional requirements. Something different occurs in aquaculture where, throughout the life cycle of the fish being farmed, the diet is changed and adjusted according to the size, age and environmental conditions, especially temperature, in which the fish is being reared. There are therefore diets for fry, for smolt (in salmonid farming), for on-growing and for broodstock. Each diet may have different secondary objectives in mind when it's formulated but what they all have in common is the main goal of assuring optimum development of the fish whatever the developmental stage.

The differences between the various baits on the market appear to be great. It's also clear that there's no relationship between bait quality and the size and prestige of the bait manufacturer. It's just as probable for a small company to create a successful bait as it is a bigger, better-known company. With time, it's likely that new companies appear on the market that are able to offer something different, making better use of experience and knowledge of the biological aspects of the fish in order that anglers increase their catch rate. You would think that the amount of research that goes into a bait before it's launched is greater for the bigger and more famous companies, but it isn't always the case. Where some are spending their extra cash on full page advertising in magazines, others are using it more wisely, to carry out standardised tank testing and validating their results against other baits and previous studies. This is the direction that modern bait design should take and for the more intelligent, forward thinking companies and executives, this is what will keep them in the market and allow them and the anglers that use their bait to be more successful.

It's in all our interests for great baits to exist. But how do we go about creating an original, successful bait? Firstly we have to consider the things that we've already been talking about; location, feeding and nutritional requirements. It's from these that we're able to obtain enough information to create something that's right up there with the most successful baits being manufactured today. Our novel bait should satisfy the nutritional requirements of the fish but at the same time these are different concerns from those of attraction. There are few things that these two concepts have in common. They are more or less mutually exclusive. This is to say that those nutrients that we have talked about already are in the bait for the reason of providing the fish with what it needs. That is their purpose. Additionally, ingredients may be added to the bait to increase the attraction of the bait, to increase the intensity of the feeding response and to get the fish to eat more of a particular bait. But this is a very different purpose and although we should talk about them separately, the goal is to combine the two in a bait as effectively as possible.

Let me give you an example. I recently discovered that a bait company whose bait I've used for a number of years has begun to include the ingredients of their bait on the packet. I've counted 31 ingredients in the bait that I use and therefore a very wide range of ingredients. Some are clearly nutritional ingredients and others are for attraction or binding, but among these are a number of ingredients with a less clear purpose. There are a range of flavours as well as sweeteners and flavour enhancers and colourings. It looks a lot like the ingredient list of a Christmas pudding in length and variety, but how many of the 31 ingredients could be omitted?

If we were to ask the bait manufacturer why each one is incorporated, they could probably give some kind of an explanation as to why but for some of the ingredients, even they might struggle. Many of the substances that have established themselves as 'carp-catchers' have done so by accident. There is no other evidence to their superiority over other ingredients other than the fact that they have been included in baits that have caught thousands of fish. But is this how we should carry on, by continuing to use a substance because we are basically frightened not to? Sure, an ingredient is in the bait that caught the fish but ask yourself if you're sure that its inclusion was the reason for catching the fish.

I firmly believe that ingredients should only be included if they do something positive to the bait and that difference has been demonstrated scientifically. If there's no evidence for it improving a bait then, we'd be better off leaving it out. As I've suggested, baits are often successful because of the extensive use. If 50 percent of anglers are using a particular bait, then it's more than likely that 50 percent of the big carp are caught on that bait. But does that mean it's superior? As we know, a carp can be a very easy fish to catch. You could catch one on a cigarette butt with a hook through it but does that mean we should all start using them as bait or adding tobacco to our base mix?

We should begin by trying to create dependency on the bait by including everything that a carp needs to live and grow normally. This can be achieved by using the values obtained from the studies that I've mentioned here. This is one part of making a successful bait since by reducing the probability that the fish needs to look elsewhere for some of the nutrients that it needs, we are effectively eliminating the competition presented by other anglers' baits and that of natural food.

Prebaiting is a common practice in modern carp angling where bait is put in a water over weeks or months before fishing sessions occur as a way of getting the fish accustomed to feeding on the particular bait. This strategy has been used for several decades and can be particularly effective when the bait that's being used is nutritionally adequate. Fish should then prefer the bait to others and this is a consequence of the adequacy of the bait compared with that being used by competitors and food items that are naturally present in a water.

If it were necessary to choose between attraction and nutrition, then which of these is more important? I would say that they are equally important but that attraction is more important in the short term, where the angler is short of time, where the fish are stocked in higher densities and they may be of a smaller size. However, if I'm targeting one fish and have the time to do a prebaiting campaign and the homework to find out where the fish can be found, then I'd definitely choose nutrition over attraction. This is because focusing on the nutritional aspects of the bait over simple attraction requires more time and dedication, and it may not be every angler's cup of tea. Nevertheless, the results have the potential to be especially worthwhile and rewarding.

The choice between attraction and nutrition is an interesting debate, but the truth is that it isn't necessary to choose one over the other. They can be effectively combined and both used to improve the performance of each other. This is called synergy, where the results of using both together are greater than the sum of the two used individually.

For us to be able to do this in a bait, it's important for us to understand what attraction is and how it's different from stimulation, palatability and the feeding response. We've spoken about these four concepts here but anglers often use one when they mean the other and we should clear it up before continuing.

Attraction in angling refers to bringing fish to the place you're fishing by adding something to the bait, in the mix or on the outside via a glug, dip or soak which has a positive effect on the fish. This serves as a stimulus and therefore results in stimulation of the chemosensory system of the fish. As we saw in chapter 2, the substances that have been shown to be cause this are relatively few and far between and are generally amino acids with positive stimulatory properties as opposed to those that cause rejection or indifference. We also know that of these few amino acids that have been shown to cause attraction, not all of these are sensed by olfaction (the fish's equivalent of our sense of smell) and we are therefore further restricted as far as substances that can be used to attract the fish over a considerable distance.

In the first chapter, we learned that the currents in lakes are in general weak and as a result the dispersion of attractive substances is not that effective. However, in both rivers and some parts of lakes such as inlets and outlets where greater current flow can be present, very different situations can occur. But in the majority of angling situations in lakes, the current flow is very low and therefore so is the distribution of an attractant.

Therefore, if we plan on attracting carp to the spots we are fishing then we can either 1) fish where we know that a favourable underwater current exists, 2) use an excessive amount of the stimulatory substance in order to create more probability of attraction, or 3) simply position baits in spots that are frequented by passing fish and hope that they stop to feed. An increased amount of attractant in the areas will increase the effectiveness of the third alternative.

I think that extended feeding time and greater intensity is a product in many cases not of attraction but of the fish stopping to eat and congregating instead of continuing on their way. The more I read and the more I fish, the less I'm convinced that what we throw into the water is bringing the fish from distances more than a few metres to the place we're baiting up. However, the possibility of keeping passing fish in those areas for a longer period of time and increasing the amount of bait ingested by the means at our disposal has to be beneficial to our fish in both the number of pick-ups and runs and as a result, an increased number of fish on the bank.

If we use a glug that includes the proven attractants then we are increasing the amount of attractant substance in the water of our fishing spots. If this is used in higher concentrations that those that have been shown to cause a positive stimulatory effect on carp (threshold levels), then we have the possibility to ensure attraction over a wider area according to the currents present, even if they are weak. However, it doesn't take dispersion over much distance to dilute the attractant to a level that is hardly perceivable by the carp. If you imagine a gram of glug, then dilution in ten grams of water reduces the concentration of whatever attractant it contains to a level that is ten times less than its original. Likewise, equal dilution in one litre of water would reduce the initial concentration by a thousand. And just a cubic metre of water would reduce the original concentration by a factor of a million.

So, stimulation over much distance is difficult if not impossible, although a highly potent substance over a short distance is very appealing to passing fish that have been encouraged to feed. Both feeding time and intensity can be increased. By increased feeding intensity, I'm referring to an increase in the total amount of bait ingested by one or more fish or an increase in the amount of bait consumed per unit time. However, this is only possible if, once the carp has discovered the bait by accident or through the use of attractants, the fish likes what it finds.

In order to make a choice regarding ingestion, the carp will try the bait or a part of it. Here I'm referring not to the hookbait since this is usually accompanied by loose feed and the probability of the hookbait being sucked up first is low. Upon testing the bait it will make a decision within a short period of time as to whether it will chew and swallow the food, chew and spit it out or simply spit it out. In a recent study that I am involved in I've timed the suck-spit alternative at a little over half a second. This is the worst case scenario for the angler. When he says that he's 'been done' then it's likely that it occurred in this time frame.

In that 0.5 to 0.6 second period a carp is capable of tasting the food item and either continuing to process it or spitting it out. It's not long, maybe not even enough time for a strike by even the sharpest angler. This shows just how important it is to present a bait that is palatable for the fish and to use the information that I've included here in order to improve the response of the fish to the bait. If we can increase the time that the bait is in the fish's mouth, then we increase our chance of hooking the fish, since many times the fish is not completely stationary when it's testing the bait and as a result we can observe movement of the rod tip, a bleep or two from the alarms or if the fish bolts, then a run. In chapter 3 we saw how the feeding mechanism works, how the food item, a bait or other is sucked in and dealt with in alternative ways. What increasing the palatability of the bait does is to increase the time that the bait is in the fish's mouth before rejection. We obviously don't want the fish to swallow the bait and hook but it never gets that far because the fish becomes aware that something is wrong before the bait gets further than the palatal organ.

Substances that make the bait more palatable include the classic taste substances, particularly sour and bitter which have been simulated using citric acid and calcium chloride respectively (Kasumyan & Morsi, 1996) and the amino acids that I've already mentioned and which I've included in order of palatability in the appendix. However, it's important to recognise that there's a big difference between attraction and palatability in terms of threshold level. Palatability requires much lower levels of the palatant in order to improve the time that the bait is kept in the fish's mouth before expulsion compared with the levels needed to attract or keep fish in the area. The latter refers to substances that are dissolved in the water column (e.g. from glugging) whereas those that affect the fish's taste are incorporated into the bait itself.

Although these may be the same substance, the levels are completely different. Threshold levels have been determined for both and here I'll describe some of the interesting research that's been carried out in this respect.

The other thing to remember is that palatants included in the bait have little effect on the exterior due to the effect that boiling or steaming has on a bait by sealing the contents in and preventing them being sensed by the carp directly. This can be increased by exposing the insides of the boilie by chopping the bait up. In that case, the contents of the boilie have the potential to increase the attractiveness of the bait as they will not only be available to be taste-tested by the fish on the surface of the chops but also pass into the water column to provide attraction in the same way as if they were part of the glug. Therefore, it's important to understand the different ways that stimulants work, whether they're included in the bait or in a liquid that the bait is dipped in before being cast out. The first is designed to appeal to the olfactory sense of the fish and the second to the gustatory sense as the fish comes close, comes in contact with the bait and begins to physically test it with its mouth. Palatability comes into play once the fish is orally testing the bait.

To summarise, attraction is the ability to draw fish into the spot using a substance that stimulates the fish (a positive stimulant or attractant) and once this has been achieved then we can observe an increase in the feeding response as long as the bait is palatable.

This means that there is a difference in the concentration between the amount of attractant that needs to be applied to a bait or a glug or soak. In the bait, low concentrations will suffice because the fish is in close contact with the bait and will usually try some of it to test its palatability. On the other hand, the glug needs to contain much higher concentrations because on entry into the water, it starts to be diluted and will quickly be reduced to much lower levels. Therefore, in the case of the glug, the higher the dose the better.

But what exactly are these levels? If we refer to the literature, there have been several studies that have looked at the threshold levels and ranges that carp are able to detect and in some cases those which the fish has been shown to prefer. For example, Marui *et al.* (1983) used an electrophysiology method to measure the response to different combinations of amino acids. They found that L-proline, the amino acid for which the carp showed the highest sensitivity, could be detected at levels of $10^{-8.5}$ M (molar), whereas other amino acid detection levels ranged from 10^{-4} to 10^{-8} M. In this study, the authors also defined the saturation level, which was a concentration above 10^{-3} M. This was the concentration at which no increase in the response to the amino acid was observed. They also showed that the taste system of the carp responded to neutral and acidic amino acids but not to basic ones and it was, as we have stated previously, the L-isomers of the amino acids that caused a greater level of stimulation. This study used amino acids added to water that flowed through the mouth and out of the gills of the fish. The top five amino acids as far as stimulatory effectiveness were L-proline, L-alanine, L-cysteine, L-glutamate and betaine. These are shown in the summary table (table 7) in the appendix and I've converted the concentrations from the less familiar M (molarity) to mg/L (milligrams per litre). I've also included the ranges of each amino acid over which they were detected in each study by the carp.

Goh & Tamura (1978) also determined the threshold level of

several amino acids including L-alanine to be in the range of 10^{-7} to 10^{-9} M in carp. Then, Saglio *et al.* (1990) used a similar technique (an olfactometer, which is basically a tube which you can put substances in one end and see the reaction of the fish as they flow past) to show the effect of different combinations of amino acids on attraction and exploration (searching for food) by the fish. In this case, basic amino acids (histidine, arginine and lysine) and polar, uncharged amino acids (glycine, serine, threonine, tyrosine, asparagine and glutamine) did not cause attraction but did increase exploration by the fish. Acidic amino acids (aspartic and glutamic) did not produce significant activity. However, non-polar amino acids (alanine, valine, leucine, isoleucine, phenylalanine and methionine) caused significant effects on both attraction and exploration. Also, different pairs (combinations) of acid groups were also mixed and tested and the most effective of these were shown to be a combination of non-polar and polar uncharged amino acids with the simplest combination being alanine, valine and glycine. Unfortunately, proline, cysteine and betaine, which have received attention in the majority of the other studies on attraction and taste preference in carp, were not included in this particular study. This is because proline is neutral and non-polar and cysteine is neutral and slightly polar. Betaine is not included because it's sometimes not considered an amino acid but rather as a derivative and is not found naturally in proteins.

We have already discussed the results of the study by Kasumyan & Morsi (1996) in the context of taste preference. In this study the top five aminos were cysteine, proline, glutamic acid, aspartic acid and alanine. The concentrations used for incorporation in pellets fed to the fish ranged from 10^{-1} M in the case of cysteine, proline and alanine to 10^{-2} M in the case of glutamic and aspartic acids. The threshold concentrations for cysteine were determined in a separate part of the study with levels of 10^{-1} to 10^{-2} causing improved attraction and consumption of pellets compared with a control pellet which did not contain any of the test substances. Some other substances were also tested in this study and threshold levels for the classical taste substances which showed high levels of palatability were determined. For citric acid (sour) this was 5 x 10-3 M and for calcium chloride (bitter) this was shown to be 0.9 M. This shows that carp are particularly sensitive to citric acid.

The previous study is one that I found particularly interesting and one that I've recently repeated in the laboratory. I did this using just cysteine and proline in varying concentrations in the same pellets used by the other researchers. Used together, I was expecting that the effect would be greater than either one used alone. This is not what I found, but I did find a positive correlation between the amount of cysteine incorporated in the pellet and the feeding response in terms of the amount of time that the pellet is maintained in the mouth and whether it's consumed or not. These findings have implications for the development of both bait and glug with formulation requiring application of what we know as far as threshold values and the ranges of substances that cause positive stimulation in the carp.

I would like to mention a final study on this subject before moving on. In Hara (2006), the author worked not with carp but with goldfish. Although the two fish are closely related, the same amino acid preferences were not found. In the case of the goldfish, L-arginine, L-glutamic acid, and L-proline were shown to be effective in inducing both movement (locomotion) and 'pecking' behaviour. Although betaine was used in this study, it was not found to be particularly stimulatory. However, cysteine was found to be the most potent amino acid for stimulating locomotor activity, but this was not found to have any effect on pecking behaviour in goldfish.

So to summarise, the amino acids of particular interest are those which have been named here as those found in each study as causing positive effects on locomotion, consumption or palatability. Mention is made of cysteine and proline regularly and betaine is included in some but not all of the studies.

It's somewhat surprising that betaine is used so extensively in carp fishing when comparatively little information exists regarding its effects on carp either in the water column or in the diet. It remains unclear whether betaine is as specifically attractive to carp as the other amino acids mentioned are. The majority of the information that I have read is related to other species with a large number of those being marine species rather than freshwater, such as sea bream and Dover sole. In freshwater it has been tried on rainbow trout and the specificity of betaine at 10-3 M was shown to be almost twice that of common carp. It has been used in feeding trials in two other carp species worthy of mention, in gibel carp (Xue *et al.*, 2004) and in rohu (Labeo rohita) (Shankar *et al.*, 2008). Both these studies have examined the effects of betaine incorporation in the diet and observed improved growth and increased consumption of feed as a result. It's therefore worth including betaine in a bait in the low levels that have been shown to increase feed consumption (0.1 percent squid extract or 0.25 to 0.75 percent betaine).

It has been suggested that a range of other substance are attractants for carp. Many of these have been included in baits but I would be reluctant to add anything to my bait that had not been proven to cause an effect. Some anglers think that it's better to include a bit of everything in their bait, but I don't agree. In the same way that I suggested that the use of minamino or fish protein concentrate could be counterproductive then I'd hesitate to adopt a 'try not to leave anything out' strategy. Whereas some of these additive or 'attractant' mixtures contain substances that on their own might be very attractive, using them with others can just be a waste of time and money. This is because, although they contain stimulants, they may also contain a similar amount of deterrents therefore having a net effect of zero. In the worst case, the deterrents might be more abundant than the attractants and then all you are doing is effectively urging the fish to go to the other chap's swim and eat his bait.

In *Carp Fishing Science* I did mention a number of additives that may have some properties as attractants but as time goes on I am more and more convinced that the carp is positively stimulated by a very narrow spectrum of taste substances. When all is said and done, the number of these that have been shown to increase palatability, consumption and the intensity of the feeding response can be counted on two hands. There are four or five amino acids that are very stimulatory and the rest are not. There are preferences for sour and bitter tastes and there is something to be said for betaine in a feeding stimulating context rather than attraction.

However, if we examine the current carp angling scene we see a never-ending range of flavours or bait and an infinite number of liquids, dips, soaks and glugs to add to it. This suggests that there are three possibilities for what's going on. That 1) the carp is not at all fussy with regards to what it eats, 2) the anglers are not at all fussy regarding what they buy, or 3) the bait boys know something that the aquaculture boys don't.

As someone who has spent a considerable part of his life in labs and around fish and who recognises the importance and relevance of standardised testing over trial and error, I find it very difficult to believe the third. If there was something in carp bait that made carp eat more of it and grow faster than carp in farms fed on a commercial diet then I'm sure that the carp farmers would be using pineapple flavouring or Robin Red or whatever was supposedly making the difference. And if the second answer were correct, then it has a lot to do with the first option.

I find it easier to believe that carp are not at all fussy about what they eat. But that can't be true or why do we blank? How can we go a session or a number of sessions for that reason without a bite and for me to say that carp aren't fussy? Well, as we saw with taste preference, the feeding response depends on many factors both inside the fish and caused by the environment. These factors vary from season to season, day to day and moment to moment and, as we have seen, fish don't feed all the time and they're also not found in the same place. By the same measure, sometimes they aren't where we expect them to be and they don't feed when we expect them to feed.

This is why we come to think of carp as being difficult to catch, but as we know, carp fishing can be any one of a wide range of levels of difficulty which depend on the stocking density of the lake, the amount of natural food, the age and experience of the fish and also our own ability to dominate a water and the fish in it. There are waters at one extreme where one run a season is a score and others where a fish every ten minutes is the status quo. But in any angling situation where the fish are feeding, or at least looking for food, our chances of capture can increase no end. Waters can transform from being apparently empty to an unending stream of carp.

So, carp can be very easy to catch when they're feeding. At those times they can be anything but fussy and will eat almost anything you throw at them. And if we go back to the statements about neither the anglers nor the carp being fussy, at those times when the fish are really having it, then it really makes much less difference what bait you buy. But depending where you fish and what you fish for, the red letter days may be few and far between and that's why we're covering these topics. It's not to be able to catch fish when things are easy. Anyone can do that. What we are trying to do here is provide you with information that will help you prepare for and get through any session but especially those that take you to the edge of reason and get you questioning why you have been sitting by a water for a couple of days or even a couple of weeks without a fish.

We've covered a great deal of ground here and have examined the two things that make a bait a successful one; attraction and nutrition. We have seen how applying certain substances to the outside of a bait can increase the amount of fish being drawn to the spot where you're fishing and others can be distracted from their normal movements around the lake and made to stop and feed where your bait is. We have also looked at the effects that incorporating some substances to the mix itself can have an effect on the palatability of the bait and the amount eaten by the fish. The substances we've discussed can have a very positive effect on your fishing and as a result boost your confidence and improve your results.

Unfortunately, I can only do so much and you still have to do a lot for yourself. But I expect that with time, more people will become interested in knowing more about the substances that I've mentioned and how they can be used to better catch results instead of doing what a great many do, which is using the same baits and glugs and believing every bit of angling hype and publicity without doing a bit of thinking for themselves.

I'm also only able to tell you the story so far at this point. There is still a lot of research ahead of us before it's possible to know all there is to about how everything works. By that I'm referring particularly to the carp's chemosensory system, how different substances affect the fish and its behaviour and how feeding intensity and frequency can change with time of the day and from season to season. And, I can only tell you what I know so far but I hope to keep adding to the information presented here as more things are discovered.

The area of attraction is one of those that interests carp anglers the most and where there are still a number of grey areas. Research in recreational fishing is restricted due to the low budgets of bait companies. This is understandable and I'm sure that most of them do what they can with the money that they have. With time, things should become clearer and hopefully there will be less use of unproven substances and marketing and more use of proven ones based on research rather than testing that isn't standardised.

Even so, there will always be differences between fishing in different waters for different fish. Other factors affect the feeding response such as the geographical location and the strain of carp and therefore it will never be exactly the same on two different waters and so it's unlikely that the same bait and attractant will ever be received by the fish in exactly the same way. The background smells and tastes that the carp experiences will change with the seasons and from water to water and an attractant in a water where that attractant is already present in a high concentration naturally will probably not be anywhere near as effective as where that attractant is absent from the carp's environment. This has not been looked at in any detail yet and it might not be for a while but that will keep us guessing. Anyway, finding out our own answers is part of the enjoyment of the sport is it not?

On a final note, and as I said at the start of this section, it should be remembered that attraction and nutrition are never enough independently. The ability for these two important parts of a bait to combine and be mutually beneficial is something that remains to be completely exploited in bait manufacture. If it were possible for a bait to be nutritionally optimised, then what that company or individual would have would be a 'nutritionally attractive' bait that even in the absence of additional attraction would be a benefit for the fish, the fishery owner, the bait manufacturer and of course the angler. Once that bait is optimised in the way of attraction then I think that bait will become truly great but for now it is nothing more than the golden fleece of carp fishing that every angler is searching for.'

c. Formulation

Bait formulation is not a recent technique with which to increase the attraction and nutrition of a base ingredient. In fact Isaak Walton in *The Compleat Angler*, first published in 1653, had this to say in chapter 9 on 'Observations on the Carp with Directions how to fish for him':

The Carp bites either at worms or at paste, and of worms I think the blewish Marsh or Meadow worm is best, but possibly another worm not too big may do as well, and so may a green Gentle; And as for pastes, there are almost as many sorts as there are Medicines for the Toothach, but doubtless sweet pastes are best; I mean, pastes made with honey or with sugar: which, that you may the better beguile this crafty Fish, should be thrown into the Pond or place in which you fish for him some hours before you undertake your tryal of skill with the Angle-rod: and doubtless if it be thrown into the water a day or two before, at several times and in small pellets, you are the likelier when you fish for the Carp to obtain your desired sport: or in a large Pond to draw them to any certain place, that they may the better and with more hope be fished for, you are to throw into it in some certain place, either Grains or Bloud mixt with Cow-dung, or with Bran; or any Garbage, as Chickens guts or the like, and then some of your small sweet pellets with which you purpose to angle: and these small pellets being a few of them also thrown in as you are Angling. And your paste must be thus made: Take the flesh of a Rabbet or Cat cut small, and Bean-flowre, and if that may not be easily got, get other flowre, and then mix these together, and put to them either Sugar, or Honey, which I think better, and then beat these together in a Mortar, or sometimes work them in your hands (your hands being very clean) and then make it into a Ball, or two, or three, as you like best for your use: but you must work or pound it so long in the Mortar, as to make it so tough as to hang upon your hook without washing from it, yet not too hard: or that you may the better keep it on your hook, you may knead with your paste a little (and not much) white or yellowish wool.

Fortunately we have made some progress since then and it's no longer necessary to add chicken guts to your groundbait or wool to your paste. However, it's easy to see how the anglers of yesteryear thought in a similar way to us regarding bait improvement. They clearly had an idea of the importance of the bait's taste to the fish but whether or not they possessed a similar understanding of nutrition is doubtful. In those days, although people ate all kinds of things, it's unlikely that a balanced diet was a concept that formed part of people's lives.

Nowadays we still think of fish in a similar sense to ourselves in many ways and when we think of smells and tastes then we imagine that fish perceive them in the same way. I hope that I've already addressed that subject well enough, but it still remains that boilie flavours often appeal to us because they mention what we like to eat ourselves. That explains to a certain extent why we buy flavours like tandoori and banana split. If you open the packet and take a whiff, the smell probably brings back some pleasant memories, but does the same thing happen with the carp? I don't think so. A carp has never had a takeaway. Even so, the supplier will say, "Aha, but that's why the fish like it so much, because it's something that they haven't tried before." And then he'll stand there with a big grin on his face while you put your hand in your pocket and pull out a ten pound note.

Under certain circumstances maybe the novelty aspect of a bait will score. But if we look at what this chap is saying in a biological sense, then we see that there's no real reason for the bait being exceptionally good. Carp, as with all fish, have evolved to recognise substances that are found in their own environment and not ours. This means that substances that are found there are associated with feeding, food and the search for it. In basic terms, this means that the carp are tuned to certain signals and it's unlikely that tandoori is one of them.

That's not to say that particular flavour won't be effective at catching carp, but it'll be because of substances in that flavour that appeal to the carp or because you have found the carp to be less fussy or simply hungrier that particular day. We interpret flavours as we want to as humans but this occurs in a very different way in fish. Whereas we enjoy trying new tastes and different foods, the same is not true for fish in the natural environment. They are tuned to locate what they know is related to food or a mate and also to avoid predators. They do not have the luxury of a health service or legislation that protects them from badly prepared or unhygienic foods. In their case, to make a wrong choice regarding a food item can result in sickness or death and maybe that's why carp are often cautious as far as accepting something new and it takes a long time for them to really accept it unconditionally.

We often have the opportunity to observe carp at close quarters and it's from that that we can learn a great deal about how fish react to our bait and we might be surprised that the response is not what we expect. There are times when they will eat anything that they find or that we throw at them but I would say that's the exception to the rule rather than the most common reaction. Even in the best stocked, easiest commercial water, carp are still wild animals. Although they may have become accustomed to a higher level of noise and movement they are still wary of danger, whether that comes in the form of an otter, a human or a baited rig. Getting carp to eat your bait is often like the opposite of weaning an infant off a bottle of milk. It's a gradual process that takes time and a certain amount of dedication. Even the most attractive bait requires thought regarding its use. Location is important but so are virtues such as patience and dedication.

The bait making process is just as important as the fishing. If we buy our bait from a manufacturer, we expect to be buying something that's nutritional and attractive and which allows us to concentrate on our fishing. Many people don't have time to create their own bait and prefer to use one made by a tried and trusted manufacturer. However, there are pros and cons of both buying or making a bait. A bought bait doesn't allow you to play with the levels of each ingredient or boost stimulation apart from dipping the bait in a soak or glug. On the other hand, homemade baits are generally cheaper to produce, you can put in them whatever you like and adjust them for different fishing situations, but this takes longer. And in the modern world, time is something that even the laziest among us seems to be short of.

Here I'm going to discuss bait formulation using some of the key points from the previous pages. I won't be talking about equipment, about what roller or mixer to get because quite simply there is nothing that I can tell you on the subject. My bait making experiences have been few and far between and it's only after talking to others whose job it is to mix, roll, boil and package and who in some cases do it impeccably that I've got to know more about the process. Also, there are better descriptions of this on the internet and in other people's books than I could possibly write.

What I'll concentrate on here are the following: 1) bait ingredients and quantities of the main food groups including energy, 2) incorporation of attractants and stimulants and 3) physical and chemical aspects of the bait. I will finish by mentioning something about glug formulation.

We saw that the important food groups to be incorporated in our bait are protein, lipid (fat) and carbohydrate as well as the micro-nutrients vitamins and minerals. Each of these should be added to the mix according to the requirement of the carp, which I've suggested is around 38 percent of the total dry weight of the bait in the case of protein. Another consideration for protein is the amino acid profile that should be ensured. For this it's necessary to consider the figures for each of the essential amino acids that I've included in table 2 of the appendix. These are the amounts of each amino that should be satisfied as percentages of the total protein provided. In order to avoid supplementation in excessive amounts, it's possible to mix more than one protein source together in order to complement a deficiency of one amino with an excess of another as described earlier (see table 1 of the appendix for some protein source examples).

A formulator should remember that amino acids added to the bait as supplements are free rather than bound to protein and able to influence the attractive properties of the bait. Therefore, if possible, supplementation should only occur with free amino acids that have been shown to cause either positive or indifferent stimulation of the fish and not those that have been shown to act as deterrents (see table 3 of the appendix for clarification).

In the context of protein sources, many of these are known to include anti-nutritional factors (ANFs) which negatively affect the digestibility of these. These often take the form of inhibitors of digestive enzymes such as proteases, lipases and amylases. Apart from inhibiting digestion, other ANFs such as phytic acid present in a range of cereals, seeds and nuts strongly bind to minerals making these unavailable to the fish. Therefore it's important to take care when selecting protein sources in order to avoid these kinds of counterproductive results. Often, the protein sources are exposed to some kind of treatment such as heating of solvent extraction, which destroy the ANFs. An example of this is soybean meal, which in its crude form contains a number of anti-nutritional factors, but following treatment of different types, these can be partially of completely destroyed. ANFs affect not just protein sources but sources of carbohydrate too.

Also, when we try to ensure that nutritional requirements are satisfied, it's important to calculate quantities based on the dry weight of the finished bait and not the total mix weight including the wet constituents such as binder and oil. For example if you are using eggs then they are about 80 percent water which means that if you use 200 grams of whole egg then this will only add about 40 grams to the finished bait, meaning that the dry components will make up relatively less of the total weight if you base that on the combined weight of wet and dry ingredients instead of the final dry weight. There are other binders that you can use including animal or vegetable gelatines which can be used with less water than the 80 percent that eggs add to the mix.

I try to ensure the lipid levels are over 10 percent, which is about the same as those used in carp farming. It's wise to ensure an important proportion of EFAs such as DHA and EPA with the best source of these being good quality fish oil, which will ensure that the lipid requirements described earlier are met. In the case of lipid alternatives, you should avoid saturated fats as these will reduce both digestibility and mixing problems. Try to find suitable alternatives to fish oil if you are more environmentally conscious but bear in mind the requirements for omega 3 and 6 described earlier.

Seasonal differences are another consideration when using lipids. The carp's requirement in terms of quantity and quality fluctuates during the year especially with respect to the build up to spawning. Repeating what I mentioned earlier, higher fat levels should be used in spring and summer where lipid requirements increase as a result of gonad development. As the temperature rises, the activity of the fish increases and therefore its energy demand and so to avoid the preferential use of amino acids as an energy source, it's important to increase lipid (protein sparing).

Carbohydrate sources are as varied in origin or even more so than protein and lipid sources. However, chemically and biologically there are fewer differences between them. Once processed, a carbohydrate source offers chains of sugar units that the organism can use. However, a preferred carbohydrate source would be one that is free of ANFs and includes shorter chains. This may be by hydrolysis of a crude carbohydrate or the use of a sugar. As a guideline, the baits I've formulated recently contain less than 25 percent carbohydrate and some as low as 10 percent.

Mineral and vitamin requirements can be satisfied by the premixes available for aquaculture use or bait production. Care must be taken using vitamin and mineral preparations designed for humans on fish for several reasons. First of all, the requirements are not the same for each because a fish and a human live in very different environments. Whereas fish can obtain minerals from the water column humans cannot extract minerals from the air. Both animals obtain a large proportion of their vitamins and minerals from the diet but the diets of each are very different. Some of the minerals required by fish are not even considered on the packet of the vitamin supplements that you can buy at the pharmacy, such as chlorine and sulphur and therefore a commercial aquaculture preparation is a wiser choice. The other thing to remember is that the vitamin levels of some human supplements are much higher than those required by fish and others are much lower. This means that one supplement tablet would be enough for some but not enough for others. Practically, this means that those that are deficient could in theory be obtained from another food item but those in high levels increase the chance of hypervitaminosis (an excess of a certain vitamin), which can be an equally serious situation for the fish as a lack of a vitamin can be. This is especially the case for fat soluble vitamins (A, D, E and K), which fish are unable to excrete as effectively as water soluble ones.

In the case of mineral supplements I've found that human mineral preparations are insufficient in some of the minerals that fish require. Particularly in the case of calcium and phosphorus, these are required in important amounts. Although the carp can obtain quantities from the diet and from the water itself, if our objective is to induce dependency on a bait due to its nutritional adequacy, then we have to consider putting these amounts in the bait. For this I've used calcium phosphate which provides both of these elements.

Energy levels need to be high enough to meet those provided by natural food. This was shown to be about 21 to 24 kJ per gram. Bait should fall within this range and can be calculated in two ways, either by sending a sample of the bait to a laboratory or by estimating the energy content from the individual ingredients that you have used either off each packet or using a nutrient database such as that of the USDA which includes values for energy content for the food included. You can check this either online, download the desktop application or if you are as geeky as me, install it on your phone.

Attractants and stimulants in bait can be added in the base mix or the liquid part before adding it to the dry ingredients. Single amino acids come in powder form or as crystals which, according to the amino and how it's been processed, may be quite large. I prefer to grind them in a mortar before adding them to avoid the appearance of the crystals in the finished bait and to ensure that the mix and the bait are homogenous. The same goes for betaine, which can be obtained as anhydrous betaine or betaine hydrochloride.

Here we're talking about attractants and stimulants that are included in the mix and which are most effective if you are chopping up the bait rather than thinking that important amounts are going to leach out and pull the fish into the swim. This is physically impossible unless your bait were made of sponge, which is not the case unless you're using a zig. The outer surface of the bait is relatively impermeable both to substances being absorbed from the water into the bait or substances from inside it leaching into the water. Higher attraction will always be achieved by using a glug.

However, the attractants and stimulants that you add to the mix can be released upon chopping or the carp sucking them in and chewing them up. At that moment the palatability of the bait is tested for the first time. The bait being broken up releases bits of whatever you've put in it and that includes the attractants and stimulants that will increase feeding intensity and duration.

Boiling or steaming a bait increase the bait's hardness, initially on the outside and finally spreading to the inside. Increased hardness allows the bait to last longer in the water but excessively tough baits are more difficult for the carp to deal with. Some people prefer boiling to steaming. The process is faster and is generally restricted to the surface of the bait rather than the inside and therefore what you are left with is a tough skin and a softer inside which prevents the boilie being pecked and gradually worn away by smaller non-target fish. Heating either by boiling or steaming reduces the amount of crude protein and carbohydrate to simpler peptides and sugars although this occurs mostly in the parts of the boilie exposed to higher temperatures. By that I mean the surface and you can often see this if you examine a bait closely and you can see that granules of your carbohydrate source take on a misshapen and melted appearance. Many people also prefer boiling because they're afraid of denaturing any enzymes that they might have included in the mix as a result of the longer times associated with bait steaming as opposed to boiling. This is a possibility if you decide to include enzymes in a bait.

I prefer steaming because I don't include any enzymes in my bait for the reasons that I stated earlier. Steaming is a practical alternative because ingredients that might be present in the surface of the bait with attractive properties are not washed out as can occur during boiling. Drying times are reduced by using steaming instead of boiling. However, for larger quantities of bait, steaming might not be as practical as boiling.

Bait texture varies from bait to bait. This is due to the coarseness of the ingredients. If you use flours instead of the coarser meals and ensure that the other ingredients are milled or ground before inclusion, then the mix takes on a smoother appearance. This will depend on the ingredients you use and of course whether you want them to be recognisable or not in the bait. For example, I noticed an important change in a recent rolling when I moved from maize meal to maize flour and due to the finer consistency and the time I took to grind some of the other ingredients, I ended up with a paste that was more homogenous and similar in appearance and texture to plasticine. I found this easier to roll but I only produce bait on a small scale for my own use and tank and field testing anyway. With more sophisticated machinery for larger scale production maybe this is not an important consideration. However, I also prefer to use finer ingredients because I'm interested in maximising the amount of the ingredient that can be digested by the fish, which is higher in the case of those with a higher surface area such as fine flours.

Density can also be adjusted in a bait by using different ingredients and quantities. Some of these are well-known for reducing the density of the mix and in excess result in the bait floating. An example of this is sodium caseinate, which if it's used in high enough levels can make baits float. If you're interested in making pop-ups then this is one of the ways to go. It's also possible to buy synthetic or cork granules for this purpose and to make the bait buoyant if you so wish. However, pop-ups are not the only reason for adjusting the density of the bait. In fact a low density bait which just about sinks gives the angler an advantage over one that is much denser than water. This is because although objects weigh much less in water than they do in air, they still respond differently when sucked at by a carp according to their density. Denser baits resist the same force of suction from a fish than a less dense bait of the same size. This means that a bait that just about sinks that's exposed to the force of the carp's suction has more probability of ending up in the fish's mouth than one that is denser. Therefore, reducing the density of your bait may make the difference between catching and going fishless in a session or in the long term increasing your bite and run rates.

The final aspect that we should consider is a chemical one. Palatants take the form of not just the stimulatory amino acids that we have mentioned but also a number of other substances that improve the reaction of the fish to the bait when tasted. There are two classical substances that I rate over the rest and these are acidic and bitter tastes, which in a number of studies in carp have been shown to be preferred over salty and sweet tastes. These can be used in the form of different acids to confer sourness to the bait or an alternative such as calcium chloride to provide bitterness. I have recently used anhydrous citric acid at an incorporation level of one percent. Due to the sensitivity of the carp's gustatory system to this substance I wouldn't use it in greater quantities. It should also be remembered that some of the amino acids and betaine are sold as hydrochlorides and if you are using those in a bait, then additional acidification may be unnecessary.

In the pages of this chapter I've made reference to the difference between the attraction that you can obtain by incorporating substances to the bait mix itself and others that can be used in a glug or soak. The former requires low levels of inclusion because they act when the fish comes in contact with the bait, particularly when it breaks the bait apart during processing and especially chewing. The latter requires high levels due to the fact that as soon as the bait hits the water it begins to dissolve. This is desirable in one respect but at the same time the ability to attract and hold fish in a spot is to do with the concentration. Therefore the higher the concentration the more chance it has of working effectively in a fishing situation. This will mean a difference of maybe a hundred times the concentration of that of the attractant used in the bait itself.

Liquids to dip your bait in are commonplace and every angler who is not a purist usually has a tub of something of other in his bag. I would very much like to know how many of those actually do what they say they do or are nothing more than confidence in a bottle. Unfortunately there isn't any way of knowing unless the manufacturers start including what it has in it on the label as some have begun to do with their bait. I'm sure that some are simply a bottle of the same flavour that's used in the bait itself.

Among the many there may be some that are particularly effective and contain the substances that I've mentioned or others. As time goes on these will probably be combined with effective delivery systems in order to increase the amount of the substance in the vicinity of the hookbait or reduce the rate of release to give the fish more of a chance to locate it before it's dispersed. Whatever happens, liquids that can optimise carp attraction are invaluable and have great potential for the future, especially when proven substances are used and the natural levels of those same substances are low and they're used in conjunction with a nutritionally adequate bait.

d. Costs

In the same way as my experience with bait manufacture is limited, to date my experience with selling bait is almost non-existent. However, if we look for a moment at the situation in feed production for fish farming, cost is probably the most important consideration of the operation if the economic activity is going to be successful. The fish farmers are only willing to pay a certain amount for the feed and therefore the cost of feed production must be low enough for a profit margin to exist for the feed producer. That profit is then used to finance feed production for the following year. When the supply of a feed is high, the price that the fish farmers are willing to pay drops and vice versa. Also, when production costs increase, for example when the price of fishmeal or fish oil rises, then the profit margin decreases. There are even times when production costs are higher than the market price and in that case the economic activity becomes unsustainable.

The bait industry may be a smaller market than that of feed production and it may involve a very different product but the same principles apply. In Europe there are a large number of bait producers from the lesser known to the more well-known. Each one is trying to survive. To do so, as in the feed production industry, it's important for a profit margin to exist. As time goes by, some bait ingredients increase in price and the bait company has two options in order to maintain their profit margin; they can either look for cheaper alternatives to ingredients or charge the customer more, with the possibility of the customer buying another company's bait or making his own. Those with greater integrity would more than likely not economise on ingredients and accept a reduction in profit in order to keep their customers.

I've been told that bait production is a tough game to be in. Recipes are still more or less secret and although still a relatively open market where a new bait company can appear and generate sales, there are still a few big companies that have a large share of it. There are literally hundreds of baits to choose from but a large number of anglers still stick by tried and trusted makes and kinds of boilie. From a bait production point of view, with so many alternatives out there companies should be taking the best care possible of their customers.

But production isn't easy. In order to mix, roll and market a bait that has a great texture, density and is both attractive and nutritionally complete, it costs money. After buying or renting a place to work and the various machines that you need to get production started, to ensure the levels of protein and amino acid profiles that we've been discussing then the bait is already costing several pounds sterling per kilo, even if you're buying your main ingredients in very large quantities. Then if you have to supplement with other aminos and add palatants, attractants and a stimulator, a binder and a decent quality lipid source, then the price continues to rise. And then you realise that you have to put it in some kind of a packet and any freezer bag just won't do. As well as 'tasting the part' it has to look the part as well. But if you don't do some marketing, then nobody knows about it and you won't sell any. So you have to pay a magazine for advertising which isn't cheap, and give out a few kilos to some well-known anglers in order for them to catch some fish on it so that some articles of anglers with big fish get written and people start placing orders. But hang on, the anglers need a place to buy it from so you need to get fishing shops and distributors stocking it. And they won't sell it for free so you'll have to give them a cut too.

So it's not surprising that profit margins on bait 'are low if the bait that you are producing is good quality. And the right know-how and experience isn't cheap in any field. So in order to stay in the market and keep producing a great bait, then you need to accept a small profit margin but be able to sell a lot of it and also cross your fingers for the right results. Some companies quite likely economise on ingredients 'by finding what they consider adequate replacements and preserve their profit margins that way, at the same time hoping that their customers don't find out what's in it.

As we've already seen, buying bait 'from a company or making your own can result in benefits and also disadvantages. It's certainly not as much fun buying bait online as it is making your own, but given the choice, most of us would rather be fishing than making bait. The drawbacks are that you are stuck with the 'sold as is' bait and there's no chance to modify it apart from getting your glug out, and the other is that you don't actually know what's in apart from any clues that the name gives you. If it says 'chocolate chip' on the packet then it might actually have some chocolate in it. But not only are the ingredients usually not declared but neither are the inclusion levels, which makes it difficult to compare them with the results that you get from the bait in terms of what you catch. This is something that will hopefully continue to change with time.

e. Field testing

Maybe the biggest difference between bait development for angling and feed development for the aquaculture industry is the testing procedure of the formulated feed or bait. In aquaculture, this involves standardised experiments in unbiased conditions using statistically verifiable numbers and groups of fish. In the angling situation this is not carried out. Its closest equivalent is field testing by anglers who are usually sponsored by the same bait company in a lake with a good head of fish. Here, there's no standardisation, often no measurable comparison and the results are consequentially subjective. Even so, they are often the deciding factor as to whether the bait is marketed or not.

This process of development without standardisation is not at all a criticism of how bait companies choose to validate their products. It merely confirms, that due to the very different natures of aquaculture and angling, comparison between baits in the wild as opposed to controlled conditions in a lab is much less feasible. And if companies were to carry out tank testing using a more scientific protocol than throwing a few baits into the office aquarium and seeing if the carp eat them or sending out a top rod to catch a 30 pounder with them, then even that wouldn't represent the real angling situation.

This is because a fish in a tank and a fish in a lake are as different as you can get, not least because a carp in a lake has a choice of any number of natural food items and is more cautious than a fish in captivity. They react differently and feed according to what they are accustomed to based on previous experience. If we consider all the differences (which are many), we might conclude that any kind of standardised scientific bait testing is impractical for baits. As a result of this, the conclusion might be something like, "To hell with it. If it catches fish, then it works."

I'm sure that something similar to that statement has been heard in more than one bait company head office at one time or another and that some of the baits on offer today have been presented to the angling community as the latest and greatest on nothing more than a whim. But that way of thinking is backwards. The simple fact is that a piece of sweetcorn is sometimes more effective than the latest boilie and that's a reminder that in order to continue progressing, the bait companies need to adjust their criteria.

And that is something that's already beginning to happen. In recent times we've seen a number of changes including some companies including the ingredient list on bait packets. And not just the list, but there's even a breakdown of protein, oil, fibre and ash. This is a great start because it shows that companies like the ones that are already publishing their ingredients lists are being honest, are not trying to hide anything and are proud enough of the product they're selling to provide you with the information you deserve to know. This breakthrough allows anglers to make an objective decision regarding the bait that they buy. Of course, there will always be anglers who prefer a name or a scent independently of what's in it, but for the more conscientious angler, the information that bait companies are beginning to provide allows comparison at the moment of forking out for bait and also comparability of results after the fishing has been done.

The other example of progress that I've noticed over the last couple of years is the occasional publishing of tank tests done by some companies. In these the comparison is between a single company's baits by the same. They don't do comparisons with the baits of different companies, or at least if they do they don't publish the results in magazines. From what I've seen these consist of observations regarding the response of the fish to the bait and a comparison of how much bait was eaten. Credit where credit's due, it's a promising start to hopefully even better things to come.

One of the other important differences between testing of aquafeeds and bait is with regards to impartiality. It's much easier for your results to be believed if you have no interest in the company whose product you're testing. This is one of the fundamentals of the scientific method where it's necessary to define a question, then formulate a hypothesis and then test the hypothesis by performing an experiment and carrying out observations. Following this, the data is analysed and interpreted and conclusions are drawn. If the diet or bait being tested is your own, then there is a tendency for the observations to be less than impartial and therefore the validity of the testing is affected.

Tank testing may not be the best alternative for bait testing and I'm sure many anglers would prefer a bait to be tested in specially designed lakes with glass sides on them so we can look in and see what's actually going on under the water and with some chap in a lab coat taking notes and counting how many boilies we're throwing in and how many are being eaten. But that's impractical because of the cost, which is something that affects even the smallest laboratories and of course space, which is another factor that affects how many times it's possible to replicate the experiment.

Tagged carp feeding on a test bait.

As anyone who works with live fish will tell you, groups of fish will never react completely the same way to a bait or feed. There will always be one group that eats more and another that eats less, one where the fish eat more slowly because they're more wary and another where the fish are much bolder and eat faster. It's therefore important that tanks are replicated in order to obtain an average between them. For example, in a recent test that I carried out to compare one bait with another, I used groups of eight carp per tank and had a total of three tanks per bait. This allowed me to feed three tanks with one bait and three with the other to the point of satiation where the fish are basically full and don't eat any more. Each tank had its own pot of food that I would weigh before and after feeding and as a result I was able to calculate how much bait was consumed by each group of fish during each feeding.

By having three tanks instead of one for each treatment (each bait type) this allowed me to take account of variation between the three groups of fish and obtain an average. If I had used just one tank per bait and they were nervous, shy, fussy eaters in one and bold, carefree, greedy carp in the other, then I wouldn't be testing differences between the two baits but instead differences between the two groups of fish. That's why, when I refer to standardised testing, the idea is to be able to objectively compare the factor that we're interested in. For example, in the study that I've just referred to, the question in my mind was regarding the total protein in the boilie and how much a boilie that I formulated with 38 percent protein would affect the growth of the fish. Therefore, the factor that interested me was growth and I had two experimental levels of protein and I replicated the experiment three times to give me a total of six tanks. And the greater the number of replicas then the easier it is to overcome errors due to natural differences between populations or groups of fish.

This is not a difficult thing to do and if I can do it on a restricted budget and limited space then why can't all the bait companies? Even if they didn't compare between the bait of different manufacturers, they could do what we are already starting to see and compare between their own baits, identify the differences between them as far as the fish's reaction to the bait and use the information to gradually improve their products in a better validated and standardised way.

Maybe I'm asking for too much but I feel that anglers' results would improve if we pooled information and were able to come up with baits that fulfilled both their potentials in both nutrition and attraction. But it seems that bait manufacturers prefer to keep their cards close their chests for fear of the recipe being copied and losing out on sales. That's why I take my hat off to those companies that are bold enough to print their ingredient list and begin to share information. And based on my own experience in fish farming, this may be the start of a real turnaround in the way that bait companies behave and could reap the same benefits that have been obtained in other industries.

I remember when I first started working in aquaculture and it seemed that everything in the salmon industry was a secret. None of the farms or companies would tell you what feed they were using or what their growth rates were, if the fish ever got sick or how they did certain things. But as the problems in the industry began to increase in the shape of disease or poor growth rates for example, then suddenly the companies got together and started to compare results and look for solutions together. And what was the outcome? This collaboration led to a number of breakthroughs, principally in the control of diseases and improved production figures.

Maybe the carp bait industry is smaller and less developed than aquaculture, but the two have several things in common. Not least, they are made up of a large number of private companies both big and small and despite being highly competitive in the marketplace, they are serving a common good. When all is said and done, there is something about making bait for the masses that is surely very pleasing, knowing that what a manufacturer is doing will bring pleasure to a great many people because of the fish that their bait enables them to catch. This is why I believe that something similar will happen among bait producers as happened to other industries as far as the sharing of information for the benefit of anglers. As a result, this sharing may help us to finally get to that cherished bait that hasn't yet been invented, one that combines nutrition and attraction in the best possible way.

Maybe we cannot scientifically test baits in a real situation in a lake cost effectively, but what we can do is scientifically develop baits in the lab which is the next best thing. Despite cost and space restrictions, the results of tank testing are valid if done correctly. However, one of the 'drawbacks' of lab testing is that the size of fish is usually much less than the fish we catch in lakes and rivers or at least those that we want to catch. So, instead of using 20 pound carp, most experiments are done with juvenile fish of less than a pound in weight. You might therefore say that there must be differences between, for example, the quantity and type of bait eaten by a small carp compared with that of a double figure carp or bigger. And there are, but this favours rather than disfavours tank testing with small fish, especially in the context of nutrition, since the best indicator of optimum nutrition is growth and since small fish grow relatively faster than big fish, it's therefore better to use juveniles. Also, compared with large carp, small carp consume a greater amount of food as a percentage of their body weight.

Tank testing can also be modified for different situations. The latest test that I've been involved in looks at the effect on palatability of different proportions of some of the amino acids that I have mentioned as causing positive gustatory stimuli in carp. For this I worked with five tanks with only three carp in each one. These were small fish of about eighty grams each but this size proved very practical for the test, which was more of a behavioural study than a feeding experiment. I added different quantities of each amino acid to agar pellets and counted the number of times during a period of a minute that the carp sucked in and spat out the pellets that I offered. These were provided randomly and individually to the fish in each tank and also the length of time that the pellet was kept in the mouth after being sucked in the first time was recorded, as was the total retention time during the minute. After more than a hundred observations with each amino acid combination and after analysing the result I was able to show which of these was preferred by the fish.

This is an example of how the number of treatments can be increased. I used a total of six different amino acid combinations but in theory, any number could be used and the same procedure applied to different concentrations of feeding stimulants or other attractants as long as the number of observations is high enough. By increasing the number of observations, this gives greater validity to the results since in a similar way to replicating the number of groups of fish in the other test, this increases the probability of determining the effect of the factor being studied rather than highlighting differences between individual fish or groups of fish.

By using techniques such as these, our ultimate goal should be the improvement of baits both nutritionally and regarding attraction and eventually combining the two optimally in a superior bait that will allow us to reap a number of rewards by using it. In my mind, that bait considers all of the carp's nutritional requirements, which I believe that even in the absence of additional attractants will be a bait that is an attractive alternative for natural food items and the baits of other anglers, which are the two biggest competitors of any bait used in angling. And after having reviewed the composition data of many baits produced by a range of companies it's clear that there's still some work to be done in order to get there. But get there they will. A bait of this type is one that would achieve both the status of a food bait, since a carp would be able to live exclusively off it because it would provide 100 percent of its nutritional needs, and at the same time occupy the position of an HNV bait. It would maybe result in the definitive HNV in the purest sense of the expression. HNV should not be about excesses, since excess, in the same way as in the aquaculture situation, is synonymous with waste, whether we are talking about a bait with an excess of protein or energy or anything else.

I have mentioned repeatedly several things since this book began. This has been done on purpose. One of these is the important and undeniable link between aquaculture and angling, which share a great number of aspects although the objectives of each are very different. The bad news is that what has been achieved in the field of aquaculture has to some extent been neglected by the angling community mainly because the bag of boilies in your local fishing shop is much more accessible to the average angler than any of the science that there might have been behind its development. The good news is that even though you might not find a label on the back of a bag of boilies comparing what the contents provide with the nutritional requirements of the carp in the same way as a container of human food and even pet food, the nutritional requirements for common carp and their variants, as you should realised if you have managed to get this far, have been more or less determined for the carp experimentally. Because of this, it's only a matter of time before someone comes up with the ultimate substitute for the rest of the baits on the market.

I hope to be involved in this revolution because I, like you, want to catch more carp. I am fortunate to be able to work on this problem and others that affect carp and other species. Among other things, I hope to be involved with what are commonly referred to as carp attractants but should at the moment be described as 'attractants for some fish species, many of which are not in the lake you're fishing in.' That's the plan anyway.

Maybe we don't need to know more or fill our heads with science mumbo-jumbo that prevents us relaxing by the lake or river. But that's why there are people to worry about what your bait contains for you. To some extent when we prefer a bait over another and pay good money for it, we place our trust in the bait companies. If it's said to be a 'wonderbait' we should be able to know why and the answer should be more extensive than, "Joe Bloggs caught a 50 pound common on it." Nutritional requirement comparison would enable anglers to make an informed decision and the use of actual proven attractants and stimulants in the bait or glug can only improve our enjoyment of the sport.

In the meantime, hopefully the information that I have presented here has provided you with food for thought, has helped to put the aspects that interest us most as carp anglers in a different perspective and that you can use any newly acquired knowledge to improve your catch results. I promise to keep you updated with any new information on the subjects of carp location, feeding and bait so please keep in touch.

Since this is the final chapter of the book, please let me wish you the very best for your carp fishing. It's a sport that continues to grow and as always with things that change and develop quickly it's easy to forget what it was that got us into it in the first place. So whether you prefer bread flake or boilies, a float in the margins or a bolt rig at two hundred yards, make sure that you always enjoy it.

Acknowledgements

The author would like to acknowledge the guidance and assistance of
David Griffiths, Simon Jeremiah, Mike Starkey
and Dr. Jurij Wacyk.

He would also like to thank Paola Arce for her continued support.

And to Dave Brindley and Ricky Hubbard for fishing banter and
enjoyable times on the bank so far from home.

References

The following is a list of publications that I've cited in the book. If you wish to read any and have any trouble getting hold of them, please send an email to the publisher and I'll be able to point you in the right direction:

Adámek, Z., Sukop, I., Moreno Rendón, P. & Kouril, J. (2003) Food competition between 2+ tench *(Tinca tinca L.)*, common carp *(Cyprinus carpio L.)* and bigmouth buffalo *(Ictiobus cyprinellus Val.)* in pond polyculture. *J. Appl. Ichthyol.*, 19: 165-169.

Arlinghaus, R., Niesar, M. (2005) Nutrient digestibility of angling baits for carp, *Cyprinus carpio*, with implications for groundbait formulation and eutrophication control. Fisheries Management and Ecology, 12, 91–97.

Barnard, P. (2006) Gustatory and olfactory feeding responses in Japanese koi carp *(Cyprinus carpio)*. Thesis MPhil Animal Sciences, Aquaculture, University of Stellenbosch, South Africa.

Brady, J. (1982) Introduction to biological timekeeping. In: Biological Timekeeping (ed. J. Brady), pp. 1–7. Cambridge University Press, Cambridge.

Bridcut, E.E., & Giller, P.S. (1995) Diet variability and foraging strategies in brown trout *(Salmo trutta)*: an analysis from subpopulations to individuals. *Canadian Journal of Fisheries and Aquatic Sciences*, 52, 2543–2552.

Broglio, C., Gómez, A., Durán, E., Salas, C. & Rodriguez, F. (2011) Brain and cognition in teleost fish. In: Fish Cognition and Behavior (Brown, C., Laland, K. & Krause, J. eds.) John Wiley & Sons, Ltd., Chichester. UK. 472pp.

Callan, T.W. & Sanderson, L.S. (2003). Feeding mechanisms in carp: crossflow filtration, palatal protrusions and flow reversals. *The Journal of Experimental Biology*, 206: 883-892.

Carr, W.E.S., Netherton, J.C., Gleeson, R.A. & Derby, C.D. (1996) Stimulants of feeding behavior in fish: Analyses of tissues of diverse marine organisms. *Biological Bulletin*, 190, 149.

Chow, K.W. & Halver, J.E. (1980) The minerals. FAO, Rome. pp. 104–108.

Crivelli, A.J. (1981) The biology of the common carp, Cyprinus carpio in the Camargue, Southern France. *Journal of Fish Biology,* 18, 271–290.

Degani, G., Yehuda, Y., Viola, S., & Degani, G. (1997a). The digestibility of nutrient sources for common carp, *Cyprinus carpio Linnaeus. Aquaculture Research,* 28(8): 575-580.

Degani, G., Viola, S. & Yehuda, Y. (1997b) Apparent digestibility coefficient of protein sources for carp, *Cyprinus carpio* L. *Aquaculture Research,* 28(1) 23-28.

Devitsina, G. (2006) Adaptive variability of the gustatory system receptor part of the carp *Cyprinus carpio* (cyprinidae, teleostei) after chronic anosmia. *Journal of Evolutionary Biochemistry and Physiology,* 42, 743–750.

Driver, E.A. (1981). Calorific values of pond invertebrates eaten by ducks. *Freshwater Biology,* 11: 579-581.

Driver, E.A., Sugden, L.G., & Kovach, R.J. (1974) Calorific, chemical and physical values of potential duck foods. *Freshwater Biology,* 4: 281-292.

Funakoshi, M., Kawakita, K. & Marui, T. (1981) Taste response in the facial nerve of the carp, *Cyprinus carpio. The Japanese Journal of Physiology,* 31, 381–390.

Giles, N., Street, M., & Wright, R.M. (1990) Diet composition and prey preference of tench, *Tinca tinca* (L.), common bream, *Abramis brama* (L.), perch, *Perca fluviatilis* L. and roach, *Rutilus rutilus* (L.), in two contrasting gravel pit lakes: potential trophic overlap with wildfowl. *Journal of Fish Biology,* 37: 945-957.

Goh, Y. & Tamura, T. (1978) The electrical responses of the olfactory tract to amino acids in carp. *Bull. Jap. Soc. Scient. Fish.* 44: 341-344.

Hara, T.J. (2006) Feeding behaviour in some teleosts is triggered by single amino acids primarily through olfaction. Journal of Fish Biology, 68, 810–825.

Hughes, R.N. (ed.) (1990) Behavioural Mechanisms of Food Selection. NATO ASI Series, Vol. G20. Springer-Verlag, Berlin, Heidelberg New York, 886pp.

Kasumyan, A.O. (1997). Gustatory reception and feeding behaviour in fish. *Journal of Ichthyology,* 37: 72-86.

Kasumyan, A.O. & Døving, K.B. (2003) Taste preferences in fishes. *Fish and Fisheries,* 4, 289–347.

Kasumyan, A.O. & Morsi, A.M.H. (1996) Taste sensitivity of common carp *Cyprinus carpio* to free amino acids and classical taste substances. *Journal of Ichthyology,* 36, 391–403.

Kasumyan, A.O. & Prokopova, O.M. (2001) Taste preferences and the dynamics of behavioral taste response in the tench, *Tinca tinca* (cyprinidae). *Journal of Ichthyology*, 41, 640–653.

Kasumyan, A.O. & Sidorov, S.S. (2005) Taste preferences of the brown trout *Salmo trutta* from three geographically isolated populations. *Journal of Ichthyology*, 45, 111–123.

Kmínková, M., Winterová, R. & Kucera, J. (2001) Fatty acids in lipids of carp *(Cyprinus carpio)* tissues. *Czech J. Food Sci.,* 19(5) 177-181.

Marui, T., Harada, S. & Kasahara, Y. (1983) Gustatory specificity for amino acids in the facial taste system of the carp, *Cyprinus carpio L. J. Comp. Physiol.* 153:299-308.

McLean, E. & Donaldson, E.M. (1990) The absorption of bioactive proteins by the fish gastrointestinal tract: a review. *J. Aquat. Anim. Health*, 2, 1–11.

Miller, S.A. (2004) Mechanisms of Resistance of Freshwater Macrophytes to the Direct and Indirect Effects of Common Carp. MS Thesis. Utah State University, Logan, UT, USA. 206pp.

Niesar, M., Arlinghaus, R., Rennert, B. & Mehner, T. (2004) Coupling insights from a carp *(Cyprinus carpio* L.) angler survey with feeding experiments to evaluate composition, quality, and phosphorus input of groundbaits in coarse fishing. *Fisheries Management and Ecology*, 11, 225–235.

Nilsson, J., Kristiansen, T.S., Fosseidengen, J.E., Ferno, A. & van den Bos, R. (2008) Learning in cod *(Gadus morhua):* long trace interval retention. *Animal Cognition*, 11, 215–222.

Nose, T. (1979) Summary report on the requirements of essential amino acids for carp. Berlin: Heenemann GmbH. pp. 145–156.

NRC (National Research Council) (1993) Nutrient Requirements of Fish, National Academy of Sciences, Washington, DC. 128pp.

Ogino, C. & Saito, K. (1970) Protein nutrition in fish. i. The utilization of dietary protein by carp. *Bull. Jpn. Soc. Sci. Fish.,* 36, 250–254.

Radunzneto, J., Corraze, G., Bergot, P. & Kaushik, S.J. (1996) Estimation of essential fatty acid requirements of common carp larvae using semipurified artificial diets. *Archiv fur Tierernahrung*, 49, 41–48.

Richman, S. & Slobodkin, L.B. (1960) A micro-bomb calorimeter for ecology. *Bulletin Ecological Society of America,* 41(3): 88-89.

Saglio, P., Fauconneau, B. & Blanc, J.M. (1990) Orientation of carp, *Cyprinus carpio*, to free amino acids from tubifex extract in an olfactometer. *Journal of Fish Biology*, 37, 887–898.

Schwarz, F.J. & Kirchgessner, M. (1984) Untersuchungen zum energetischen Erhaltungsbedarf des Karpfens (*Cyprinus carpio* L.). *Z. Tierphysiol. Tierernähr. Futtermittelkde.* 52: 46-55.

Shankar, R., Shivananda Murthy, H., Pavadi, P. & Thanuja, K. (2008) Effect of betaine as a feed attractant on growth, survival, and feed utilization in fingerlings of the Indian major carp, *Labeo rohita*. *The Israeli Journal of Aquaculture – Bamidgeh* 60(2), 2008, 95-99.

Sibbing, F.A. (1988) Specializations and limitations in the utilization of food resources by the carp, *Cyprinus carpio*: a study of oral food processing. *Environmental Biology of Fishes*, 22: 161–178.

Sibbing, F.A., Osse, J.W.M. & Terlouw, A. (1986) Food handling in the carp (*Cyprinus carpio*): its movement patterns, mechanisms and limitations. *J. Zool. Lond.*, A210, 161–203.

Stockner, J.G. (1971) Ecological energetics and natural history of *Heiiriodiscns turqiiu* (Diptera) in two thermal spring communities. *J. Fish. Research Bd. Can.*, 28: 73-94.

Stoner, A.W. (2004) Effects of environmental variables on fish feeding ecology: implications for the performance of baited fishing gear and stock assessment. *Journal of Fish Biology*, 65: 1445–1471.

Sukop, I. & Adámek, Z. (1995) Food biology of one-, two- and three-year-old tench in polycultures with carp and herbivorous fish. *Polskie Archiwum Hydrobiologii*, 42(1-2): 9-18.

Takeuchi, T. & Watanabe, T. (1977) Requirement of carp for essential fatty acids. *Bull. Jpn. Soc. Sci. Fish.*, 43, 541.

Uribe-Zamora, M. (1975) Selection des proies par le filter branchial de la carpe miroir (Cyprinus carpio L.). Doctoral Thesis, University of Lyon, Lyon. 127pp.

Varghese, T.J., Devaraj, K.V., Shantharam, B. & Shetty, H.P.C. (1976) Growth response of common carp *Cyprinus carpio* var. communis to protein rich pelleted feed. In: Proceedings of the Symposium on Development and Utilization of Inland Fishery Resources, Colombo, Sri Lanka, 1977, pp. 408–416.

Viola, S. & Arieli, Y. (1989) Changes in the lysine requirement of carp (*Cyprinus carpio*) as a function of growth and temperature. Isr. *J. Aquacult. Bamidgeh*, 41: 147-158.

Xue, M., Xie, S. & Cui Y. (2004) Effect of a feeding stimulant on feeding adaptation of gibel carp *Carassius auratus gibelio* (Bloch), fed diets with replacement of fish meal by meat and bone meal. *Aquaculture Research*, 35: 473-482.

Appendix

Here I'm including a selection of study data that has been discussed in the book and those which I think are particularly relevant for anglers and bait formulators. Where references are included, these can be found in the reference section:

Table 1: Essential amino acid content of some protein sources commonly used in bait formulation expressed as percentages (source: NRC, 1993).

Amino acid	Fishmeal	Meat meal	Poultry meal	Casein	Soybean meal
% of crude protein[1]	64.5	55.6	59.7	87.3	50.0
Arginine	3.82	3.60	4.06	3.40	3.67
Histidine	1.45	0.89	1.09	2.59	1.22
Isoleucine	2.66	1.64	2.30	5.00	2.14
Leucine	4.48	2.85	4.11	8.46	3.63
Lysine	4.72	2.93	3.06	6.92	3.08
Methionine + Cys[2]	2.31	1.25	1.94	2.98	1.43
Phenylalanine + Tyr[3]	4.35	2.99	3.97	9.12	4.20
Threonine	2.31	1.64	0.94	3.81	1.89
Tryptophan	0.57	0.34	0.46	1.21	0.69
Valine	2.77	2.52	2.86	6.71	2.55

[1] refers to total crude protein in feedstuff.
[2] cysteine can be synthesised from methionine.
[3] tyrosine can be synthesised from phenylalanine.

Table 2: Nutritional requirement of 10 amino acids for common carp from growth studies (Nose, 1979).

Amino acid	Requirement as % of protein
Arginine	4.3
Histidine	2.1
Isoleucine	2.5
Leucine	3.3
Lysine	5.7
Methionine	3.1
Phenylalanine	6.5
Threonine	3.9
Tryptophan	0.8
Valine	3.6

Table 3: Ranking of amino acids and classification into attractors, indifferent substances and deterrents (modified from Kasumyan & Morsi, 1996).

Ranking	Amino acid	Classification	Palatability index (%)
1	Cysteine	Attractant	74.1
2	Proline	Attractant	55.7
3	Glutamic acid	Attractant	42.4
4	Aspartic acid	Attractant	40.7
5	Alanine	Attractant	39.6
6	Glutamine	Attractant	39.3
7	Histidine	Indifferent	-14.0
8	Lysine	Indifferent	-21.0
9	Leucine	Indifferent	-23.0
10	Tyrosine	Indifferent	-24.6
11	Glycine	Indifferent	-26.7
12	Asparagine	Indifferent	-33.0
13	Isoleucine	Indifferent	-36.1
14	Norvaline	Indifferent	-38.7
15	Tryptophan	Deterrent	-53.1
16	Arginine	Deterrent	-59.8
17	Threonine	Deterrent	-61.5
18	Methionine	Deterrent	-84.9
19	Phenylalanine	Deterrent	-87.3
20	Serine	Deterrent	-87.3
21	Valine	Deterrent	-100.0

Table 4: A selection of lipid sources and the fatty acid types they contain expressed in grams per 100 grams (source: USDA).

Fatty acid	Sardine oil	Salmon oil	Sunflower oil	Palm oil	Peanut oil
Total saturated	29.9	19.9	13.0	49.3	16.9
Total monounsaturated	33.8	29.0	46.2	37.0	46.2
Total polyunsaturated	31.9	40.3	36.4	9.3	32.0
EPA	10.1	13.0	0	0	0
DHA	10.7	18.2	0	0	0

Table 5: Requirements for different vitamins in mg/kg dry weight of carp food (from Halver & Hardy, 2002).

Vitamin	Requirement as mg/kg of dry food
A	0.3-0.6
B1 (thiamine)	2-3
B2 (riboflavin)	7-10
B3 (niacin)	30-50
B5 (pantothenate)	30-40
B6 (pyroxidine)	5-10
B7 (biotin)	1-15
C (as ascorbate)	30-50
E	80-100
K	not defined
Myo-inositol	200-300
Choline	1500-2000

Table 6: A summary of information on mineral requirement of fish (Chow & Halver, 1980).

Mineral Element	Requirement per kg of dry weight food
Calcium	5 g
Phosphorus	7 g
Magnesium	500 mg
Sodium	1-3 g
Potassium	1-3 g
Sulphur	3.5 g
Chlorine	1-5 g
Iron	50-100 mg
Copper	1-4 g
Manganese	20-50 mg
Cobalt	5-10 mg
Zinc	30-100 mg
Iodine	100-300 mg
Molybdenum	trace
Chromium	trace
Fluorine	trace

Table 7: Threshold levels converted to mg/L for stimulatory amino acids and test ranges over which stimulation was observed showing the studies in which the values were obtained.

Study	Amino acid	Threshold) level (M)	Threshold level (mg/L)	Range
Goh & Tamura (1978)	L-alanine	$10^{-9.0}$	0.000089	10^{-7}-10^{-9}
Marui et al. (1983)	L-proline	$10^{-8.5}$	0.000364	10^{-4}-10^{-8}
	L-alanine	$10^{-8.0}$	0.000891	
	L-cysteine	$10^{-4.8}$	1.920256	
	L-glutamate-	$10^{-7.8}$	0.002332	
	Na Betaine	$10^{-5.6}$	0.294257	
Saglio et al. (1990)	Alanine +	$1.3 \times 10^{-7.0}$ +	0.011582	not
	valine +	$3.7 \times 10^{-8.0}$ +	0.004335	determined
	glycine	$5 \times 10^{-8.0}$	0.003754	
Kasumyan & Morsi (1996)	L-cysteine	$10^{-2.0}$	1212.000	10^{-1}-10^{-3}

Index

Lightning Source UK Ltd.
Milton Keynes UK
UKOW07f1857080215

245886UK00003B/120/P